TOPOLOGIES OF TRAUMA

TOPOLOGIES OF TRAUMA

Essays on the Limit of
Knowledge and Memory

Edited by
Linda Belau and Petar Ramadanovic

OTHER PRESS
New York

Library of Congress Cataloging-in-Publication Data

Topologies of trauma : essays on the limit of knowledge and memory /
    edited by Linda Belau and Petar Ramadanovic.
        p. cm.
    Includes index.
    ISBN 1-892746-97-2 (trade pbk.: alk paper)
    1. Psychic trauma—Treatment—Philosophy.   I. Belau, Linda.
II. Ramadanovic, Petar, 1964–.   III. Series.

RC552.T7 T67 2002
616.85'2106—dc21

                                                            2001036421

Contributors

Fadi Abou-Rihan is Assistant Professor of Philosophy at the University of Toronto and a candidate at the Toronto Institute for Contemporary Psychoanalysis. He is also coordinator of the Psychoanalytic Thought Program at Trinity College and the University of Toronto. His current research, clinical and theoretical, is on a book-length manuscript tentatively entitled *Hammering It Out: Between Nietzscheans and Psychoanalysts.*

Linda Belau is Assistant Professor of English at George Washington University. She is also Rockefeller Fellow at the Institute on Violence, Culture, and Survival for the Virginia Foundation for the Humanities and Public Policy. She is currently completing a manuscript entitled *Encountering Jouissance: Trauma, Psychosis, Psychoanalysis.*

Cathy Caruth, Professor of Comparative Literature and English, is director of the Program in Comparative Literature at Emory University. She is the author of *Unclaimed Experience: Trauma, Narrative, History* (Johns Hopkins University Press, 1996) and editor of *Trauma: Explorations in Memory* (Johns Hopkins University Press, 1995).

Thomas Elsaesser, Professor of Film and Television Studies at the University of Amsterdam, is the author of, among others, *Weimar Cinema and After* (Routledge, 2000) and *Fassbinder's Germany: History, Identity, Subject* (Amsterdam University Press, 1996). He has recently published on trauma in *Screen* (Summer 2001).

Bracha Lichtenberg Ettinger is a renowned artist, clinical psychologist, psychoanalyst, and feminist theorist, born in Tel Aviv and living in Paris and Tel Aviv. She is Research Professor of Psychoanalysis and Aesthetics in AHRB Center at Leeds University. Her paintings have been exhibited extensively internationally in major museums of contemporary art, such as Stedelijk Museum (Amsterdam) and Pompidou Center (Paris) and were recently exhibited at The Drawing Center, NY (Nov.-Dec. 2001). She is author of *Matrixial Gaze and Borderspace*, which is forthcoming from Minnesota University Press.

William Haver is Associate Professor of Comparative Literature at Binghamton University. He is the author of *The Body of This Death: Historicity and Sociality in the Time of AIDS* (Stanford University Press, 1996), *Imagine the Political* (Stanford, forthcoming), and *Pornographic Life: Art's Work and the Practical Constitution of Being* (Routledge, forthcoming).

David Farrell Krell is Professor of Philosophy and founder of the Humanities Center at DePaul University in Chicago. He is the author of numerous academic books, including *The Purest of Bastards* (Penn State, 2000) and *The Good European: Nietzsche's Work Sites in Word and Image* (University of Chicago, 1997).

Jean Laplanche teaches at the University of Paris VII, where he is Director of the Centre de Recherches en Psychanalyse et Psychopathologie. He is coauthor, with J.-B. Pontalis, of *The Language of Psychoanalysis* and the author of *Hölderlin et la question du père, Life and Death in Psychoanalysis, Problématiques I–V* and *New Foundations for Psychoanalysis*.

Brett Levinson is Associate Professor and Director of Graduate Studies in the Department of Comparative Literature at Binghamton University. He is the author of *Secondary Moderns* (Bucknell University Press, 1996) and *The Ends of Literature: The Latin American "Boom" in the Neoliberal Marketplace* (Stanford University Press, 2001).

Ellie Ragland, Professor of English at the University of Missouri at Columbia, is the author of *Essays on the Pleasures of Death* (Routledge, 1995) and of *Jacques Lacan and the Philosophy of Psychoanalysis* (University of Illinois Press, 1987). She is also the editor of *Lacan and the Subject of Language* (Routledge, 1991).

Petar Ramadanovic is Assistant Professor of English at The University of New Hampshire. In 1997–1998 he was a Fellow at the Society for the

Humanities, Cornell University. He is coeditor of a special issue of *Diacritics* on trauma and is author of *Forgetting/Futures* (Lexington Books, 2001).

Herman Rapaport is Chair Professor at the University of Southampton (U.K.) and has most recently published *The Theory Mess* (Columbia University Press). He is also the author of *Is There Truth in Art?* (Cornell University Press), and *Between the Sign and the Gaze* (Cornell University Press). "Fragments" recently appeared in a special issue on Blanchot in *Oxford Literary Review*.

Charles Shepherdson is Professor and Director of Graduate Studies in English at the University of Albany. He has published widely in contemporary continental philosophy and psychoanalysis, and is the author *Vital Signs: Nature, Culture, Psychoanalysis* (Routledge) and *The Epoch of the Body* (forthcoming, Stanford University Press). He has been a member in the School of Social Science in the Institute for Advanced Study at Princeton University and was the Joukowski Fellow at the Pembroke Center for Teaching and Research for Women at Brown University. He is currently completing another book tentatively entitled *Insinuations*.

Contents

Acknowledgments

We would like to thank the following publishers and journals for allowing reprint of some of the essays appearing in this collection. An earlier version of Thomas Elsaesser's "One Train May Be Hiding Another: History, Memory, Identity, and the Visual Image" was first published in Josef Deleu (ed.), *The Low Countries: Arts and Society in Flanders and the Netherlands* (Rekkem: Ons Erfdeel, 1996). Charles Shepherdson's "The Catastrophe of Narcissism: Telling Tales of Love" appeared in *Diacritics,* Volume 30, Number 1 (Spring 2001), pp. 89–105 as "Telling Tales of Love: Philosophy, Literature and Psychoanalysis." Another version of Brett Levinson's "Obstinate Forgetting in Chile: Radical Injustice and the Possibility of Community" appeared in *Revista de estudios hispánicos*, Number 34 (2000), pp. 289–307. And Petar Ramadanovic's "In the Future . . . : On Trauma and Literature" will be appearing in *Forgetting/Futures* by Lexington Books.

Introduction
Remembering, Repeating, and Working-Through: Trauma and the Limit of Knowledge

Linda Belau

Shortly after undergoing an illegal and traumatically successful abortion, Maria, the main character in Joan Didion's cinematic novel *Play It As It Lays*, visits a hypnotist in Silverlake hoping for help during the onset of a nervous illness. After failing to put Maria in a mesmeric trance (a trance, by the way, that would return her to her mother's womb, allowing her to recollect the most primal origin of her problems), the hypnotist, in an overt attempt to displace his inadequacy, insinuates that the very failure to induce the required trance is due to Maria's resistance. Although Didion's point may be that all modern healers—especially those in Los Angeles—are charlatans, there is some truth to the hypnotist's seemingly defensive diagnosis. Technically speaking, if hypnosis fails, there is a resistance. The patient has, in a sense, resisted giving his or her will entirely over to suggestion, and the recollection of certain events—traumatic events—remains out of reach. Freud, in fact, finds himself in a similar dilemma with the hysteric Miss Lucy R.[1] The

---

1. See Sigmund Freud, "Miss Lucy R.," *Standard Edition of the Complete Psychological Works of Sigmund Freud*, trans. James Strachey (London: Hogarth Press, 1955), Volume 2, pp. 144–164. (Hereafter abbreviated as *SE*.)

difference, of course, between Freud and the fraud from Silverlake is that the former is not satisfied with merely pointing out to the patient her resistance. Freud knows the analysand must experience her resistance more convincingly. This, at least, seems to be the fundamental point he makes in his essay "Remembering, Repeating, and Working-Through." In this meditation on the psychoanalytic technique, which, indirectly, at least, offers an early model of the structure and insistence of trauma, Freud makes an observation which might be read as anachronistic advice to our hypnotist:

> Now it seems that beginners in analytic practice are inclined to look on the introductory step as constituting the whole of their work. I have often been asked to advise upon cases in which the doctor complained that he had pointed out his resistance to the patient and that nevertheless no change had set in; indeed, the resistance had become all the stronger, and the whole situation was more obscure than ever. The treatment seemed to make no headway. This gloomy foreboding always proved mistaken. The analyst had merely forgotten that giving the resistance a name could not result in its immediate cessation.[2]

Here Freud seems to suggest that resistance is something that the signifier is not wholly adequate to. In other words, there appears to be a vital connection between repression and the emergence of the signifier, and Freud's essay demands to be read as a preoccupation with this connection.

As he structures his paper to fit with what it is enunciating, Freud basically analyzes the history of analytic technique itself. In the past, analytic technique was defined by Breuer's hypnotic catharsis. This eventually gave way to Freud's concern with acting out, with the manifestation, that is, of the forgotten past in the traumatic present. This technique, according to Freud, would focus on "discovering from the patient's free associations what he failed to remember," which, in turn, became the present practice of "studying whatever is present" in the analytic situation (147). Freud claims that the aim of these different techniques has always been the same, since recollection and repression are intimately connected. "Descriptively speaking," Freud writes, "[the aim of technique] is to fill in gaps in memory; dynamically speaking, it is

---

2. Sigmund Freud, "Remembering, Repeating, and Working-Through: Further Recommendations on the Technique of Psychoanalysis," *SE* 2, p. 155. Further references will appear in the text.

to overcome resistances due to repression" (148). In his account of psychoanalytic technique, Freud fully realizes the originary importance of hypnosis.

Even though it may now be a wholly outmoded technique, psychoanalysis could only have proceeded to the current analytic technique by dealing with hypnosis's limited view of memory's relation to the past. Under this limited view, the form of recollection that psychoanalysis attributed to the analysand took a very simple and direct form. Through hypnosis, the analysand returned to an earlier situation and gave an account of the mental processes belonging to it without ever confusing present thought processes with those of the earlier time. The point of hypnosis, of course, is to get the analysand to remember events, thoughts, and feelings pertaining to his past that were forgotten. In "Remembering, Repeating, and Working-Through," however, Freud's account of analytic technique is built on a much more complex model of hypnosis and its relation to recollection. Under the new technique, according to Freud, "very little, and often nothing, is left of this delightful smooth course of events" (149). What makes psychoanalysis less an idealism and more a praxis is that in an analytic situation—the current one Freud is outlining in his 1914 paper—the analysand "does not *remember* anything of what he has forgotten and repressed, but *acts* it out" (150). Memory—remembering something of the past—is always caught in a signifying chain. And something can only be remembered if and when it is articulated into a chain of knowledge. Simply giving the analysand's past over to the signifier does not deal with what is structurally repressed by this signifier. As the initial technique of psychoanalysis displays its insufficiency in its very quest for knowledge, Freud comes to realize that remembering is itself a peculiar form of resistance.

Turning toward this very insufficiency, analytic technique must now interpret how this resistance—a resistance that takes the form of a knowledge—is woven around that repressed trauma which eludes the signifier's grasp. As it comes to understand memory in terms of repression, psychoanalysis can no longer be satisfied with pointing out the analysand's resistance, especially when the memory in question happens to be a particularly traumatic one. Since this trauma cannot be remembered, since it is inconsistent with the field of knowledge pertaining to memory, since it is that which is structurally excluded from the field, it shows up in analysis less in a symbolic sphere than as a physical manifestation. This, Freud tells us, is the persistence of repetition in recollection. The analysand, according to Freud, acts out the traumatic, forgotten memory: "He reproduces it not as a memory but as an action; he *repeats* it, without, of course, knowing that he repeats it" (150). And he does not know he is repeating it precisely because it is repressed. The repressed returns (and of course it never precedes its return) in the form of resistance. Repetition thus is an act, and it shows itself in the symptom. More precisely, it is a particular acting out of the strategy for remembering trauma. This is what Freud comes to see as the analysand's symptoms are brought out during and because of the analytic situation. Repeating the forgotten of the past, the symptom forces Freud to recognize repetition as the remembering of that which, structurally inconsistent to the field of knowledge, is necessarily forgotten.

If we view fantasy as a privileging of knowledge over being and symptom as a privileging of being over knowledge, it is not, at this point, too difficult to see that remembering, caught up in the chain of knowledge as it is, is grounded in fantasy. Whereas repetition, as an attempt to deal with that which is structurally excluded from this field, should be aligned with being. Remembering is aimed at gaining knowledge and understanding of some object of the past. Repetition, however, shows how the very inconsistency of that knowledge toward being shows up on the body. Freud maintains that the compulsion to repeat forces the analytic process to deal with a traumatic past *as and in the form of a present scenario*. In other words, the trauma pertaining to an event is less an inherent aspect of the event itself than it is an effect pertaining to the impossibility of integrating the event into a knowledgeable network. Trauma is an affect that is always, in a sense, felt afterwards as the inconsistency of the field of knowledge itself.[3]

The third and as yet unspoken part of psychoanalytic technique, working-through is less viewed by Freud as an attempt to reintegrate resistance into a meaningful field, which would only cause it to continually return, than it is an attempt to mark in the field of knowledge itself the impossibility of integration. Since transference takes place because memory fails (the past is literally transferred to the present), the analysand can be brought to realize how knowledge and being are incompatible. By working-through his or her resistances, the analysand, the one traumatized, can begin to uncover how his or her resistance both exposes and covers what is most intimate. Where remembering attempts to reconstitute a traumatic event as an objective fact displaced into a field of knowledge, working-through forces one to realize that trauma is, as Slavoj Zizek suggests, "too horrible to be remembered, to be

---

3. See Slavoj Zizek, *For They Know Not What They Do: Enjoyment as a Political Factor* (London: Verso, 1991), p. 222.

integrated into our symbolic universe."[4] While repetition forces us to see that it is impossible to integrate trauma into remembrance, working-through forces us, in turn, to mark trauma as that which, in its devastating effect, is impossible to integrate.

In the end, all three components of the analytic technique—remembering, repeating, and working-through—are themselves three modes of conceiving trauma. Remembering illustrates how trauma is inconsistent to the field of knowledge; repetition, through return, makes manifest that inconsistency in a form foreign to knowledge; and working-through resists the integration of trauma by maintaining it as that which it is impossible to make into a "reality." All three are indispensable for any adequate understanding of trauma. Thus, we have decided, for the sake of explication, to follow Freud's formula for the psychoanalytic cure as we work through some topologies of trauma in this volume by separating the collection into three different, yet necessarily related concerns: the vicissitudes of traumatic recollection, the function of repetition in trauma, and the possibilities, beyond recollection and repetition, of working-through. Arranged in this manner, the essays offer a kind of progression without suggesting that this progression is necessarily linear. Pursuing an analysis of the nature of trauma, one simply is unable to consider the significance or function of recollection, repetition, or working-through without thinking through their intimate relation. While the vicissitudes of this relation insist that we think of these three categories together, we have imposed a kind of fictional separation for the purpose of organization though, given the structure and temporal nature of the psychoanalytic cure, this organizational strategy will not truly divide the essays into discrete, separate subjects.

Recollection

Pursuing the possibility that trauma studies might have something to learn from philosophy, David Farrell Krell begins the structural account of trauma through an examination of the ecstatic temporality of the past. In his essay entitled "*'Das Vergangene wird gewußt, das Gewußte aber wird erzählt'*: Trauma, Forgetting, and Narrative in F. W. J. Schelling's *Die Weltalter*," Krell considers the significance of trauma theory for an understanding of Schell-

---

4. Ibid., p. 272.

ing's notion of the absolute past. Unable to adequately complete his account of the past, Schelling grapples with a split in the origin—or a rift in the Creator—which makes the past radically out of reach, forgotten, lethic. According to Krell, Schelling's *The Ages of the World* circles around this question of the inaccessibility of the absolute past. And it is this same question, Krell maintains, that ultimately speaks to us about our own fundamentally split experience of the past, an experience that is both absolutely irrecuperable and (almost) absolutely inescapable. Arguing that the theory of trauma in the formation of consciousness and subjectivity is perhaps the only adequate approach to this inaccessible dimension of the past, Krell offers an account of Schelling's text as an implicit meditation on trauma and, more explicitly, on a traumatized divinity who suffers his own split in the form of the lost origin of the absolute past. Trauma, Krell argues, is the source of repression, which bars and distorts every possible memory of the past. It is the very nonorigin of origins that determines our relation to the absolute past and shapes every attempt to remember or memorialize that past. Through an account of Schelling's earliest notes on *Die Weltalter*, Krell approaches this question of trauma and its relation to the lost origin as he considers the significance of knowledge in Schelling's notion of the absolute past. What is the significance, Krell asks, of the inhibition in the past—a past, that is, which presupposes a time that came before the time of the world—and its subsequent contradiction in knowledge? Nothing other than the basic principle of repression, the very question of trauma and its forgetting, Krell maintains. By setting out in quest of the undiscovered source of primal repression, Krell considers the function of a traumatized divinity who witnesses the birthplace of the world as a site and situation of trauma and suffering in order to pursue the kind of narrative that might release the effects of the repression and give us back a rapport with the lost knowledge that constitutes the absolute past as our very future.

Offering another kind of meditation on the persistence of the traumatic past in our future, William Haver's essay offers a provocative analysis of the impossibility of memorialization and representation in the wake of the AIDS pandemic. Responding to a number of highly publicized attempts to convince us that the end of AIDS is in sight, Haver argues that any sort of historicizing or redemptive nostalgia in response to the AIDS crisis betrays an avoidance of the traumatic dimension of the AIDS pandemic. According to Haver, this avoidance is effected as we are asked to imagine that the pandemic is chronic rather than critical and, especially as we are lead to believe that the trauma of AIDS, and the exigencies with which it presents us, can be transcended, that

AIDS essentially belongs to the past. In "Interminable AIDS," Haver undertakes a reading of a number of thinkers—epidemiologists, virologist, activists, and poets among them—who have argued that we cannot reasonably hope for any relief whatsoever in the foreseeable future from the inexorable, interminable trauma of AIDS. We can no longer be nostalgic for a time before AIDS, Haver says. We can only think "that there was" a time before AIDS; we can only be nostalgic for the possibility of nostalgia, for the lost origin that the interminability of AIDS evokes. Pursuing AIDS as an originary ontological incompletion—always already wounded, always already contaminated—Haver insists that, in the interminability of AIDS, being is nothing but that abject wounding, that contamination. In this traumatic time of AIDS, we are haunted by the ghosts of that contamination which recalls to us not a lost paradise or homeland, but the very impossibility of such a recollection, to the abjection of being itself. As the figure of what we can never quite forget altogether, the ghost also figures that which memory can never satisfactorily recover. Constituting the very residue of memory, this figure marks an irrecuperable gap in knowledge: it points to the impossibility of forgetting what we have forgotten. Through a rigorous analysis of the status of this impossibility, Haver elaborates the consequent necessity of the indeterminate nature of trauma and recollection as he calls for a thought—undertaken neither with despair nor with hope, but as the nonpositive affirmation of finitude—of the persistence of the traumatic, interminable past of AIDS both in and as our future.

Trauma is described as a persistent interminable event that not only lacks in phenomenal character but also somehow translates into the very discourse attempting to reveal it, to the point that a discourse on trauma appears, in some aspects, as if it has itself undergone trauma. Thus, any attempt to approach the question of trauma discursively will necessarily intersect the fragility of the question of traumatic memory, effectively revealing the resistance that traumatic contexts offer to objectification or interpretation. While this affect, perhaps, can be seen in any of the essays written for this volume— each of which offers an analysis of the relation between trauma and its representation—it emerges most markedly in the next essay by Fadi Abou-Rihan. Offering a testimonial to the death of a friend, Abou-Rihan's "Demarcations: Pathetic, Unfinished Thoughts on a Life by Default" holds open the place of the traumatic in writing through the recollection of a radical inertia. Performing a different analysis of the relation between trauma and representation as the unbearable immediacy of his object, Abou-Rihan presents a meditation on the status of the pathetic, figured in and through a thought of the zero-degree of representation. Beyond pretense and reason, the pathetic, as a correlate of trauma, is neither depression nor melancholia. It is, rather, what Abou-Rihan calls the "untenable": a concrete limit. According to Abou-Rihan, his writing is not just about the pathetic, but is also, in spite of its explanatory posture, a tending toward and a desiring of the pathetic. Thus, Abou-Rihan's prose not only constitutes a phenomenological account of trauma, but it is also its manifestation. Traversing the gap that he comes to thematize as the pathetic, Abou-Rihan formulates the necessity of a rejection of the moralistic tropes of sympathy, innocence, and victimization, especially as these tropes have come to characterize much of the thought common to what he calls "AIDS writing." In this sense, his essay does further its argument—it does make some concessions toward the insistence of an intellectual history that supports it—but it is neither philosophy, history, literature, nor any kind of discrete disciplinary analysis. In its errant articulation, then, Abou-Rihan's prose suggests that the historical advent of trauma—an individual's response to a situation—has everything to do with the impossibility of demarcating the disciplines in an irretrievable past. And, as it evokes the pathetic—the traumatic origin of absolute knowledge—Abou-Rihan's writing reminds us that the various disciplines are themselves first and foremost characterized by the topology of trauma, that they have everything to learn from the exigencies of the traumatic.

While the vicissitudes of recollection project an irretrievable past into our future, betraying the persistent dimension of traumatic memory, nostalgic recollection evokes a perception of the past, which can function to conceal another traumatic past. This is the provocative insight of Thomas Elsaesser as he examines the contemporary scene of Dutch television and its relation to the traumatic image in "One Train May Be Hiding Another: History, Memory, Identity, and the Visual Image." Through his meditation on representation as a second-order reality in an inauthentic media history, Elsaesser offers a reading of some of the strategies that television production in the Netherlands has recently employed in the contemporary battle of identity politics. Maintaining that one of the foremost battlefields of the new identity politics is memory, Elsaesser suggests that contemporary media both exploits and exposes a lost relation to history and, especially, to our mastery of history. As it continually returns to traumatic stories and images of the past, television pursues its ongoing solicitation of what we might call our "cultural memory." Television performs for us the duty of building and maintaining our cultural memory as it accomplishes the placing of our collective self within the frame of the images and stories it offers us. While our media age strives to "remember the past," however, it effectively covers the traumatic past as it substitutes a more titillating version which relies on a certain innocence or unity of the image. But, as Elsaesser argues, it is precisely through this covering over that something of the traumatic past might be exposed, since television underscores our traumatized relation to our lost history through this very missed relation. Despite its compulsion to cover the traumatic past—to deny, in effect, the power of the uncanniness of the traumatic—television returns this uncanny sense of presence in its devotion to the titillating traumatic image. Unable to abandon the traumatic image, Elsaesser says, television begins to circle around another reality: that of obsession or trauma. Through his analysis of television's relation to this other reality, Elsaesser shows how our contemporary media, despite its more overt intentions, corresponds to a different kind of action and placing of the self. And in this correspondence, Elsaesser tells us, television constantly betrays its own most obvious feature: the compulsion to repeat.

Repetition

At the limit of recollection, the compulsion to repeat both inaugurates and exposes a gap in the field of knowledge: it indicates, that is, what representation can never accommodate. It bears the real; that something beyond-the-signified which, in the scope of the drives, is a repressed, forgotten correlate of being rather than a knowable object of representation. This limit, however, is certainly not the end of the story, for the forgotten, repressed real returns in a displaced form in the symbolic—as dreams, symptoms, acting out. According to Ellie Ragland, such displacements speak the unconscious Other at the surface of language. In her essay "The Psychical Nature of Trauma: Freud's Dora, the Young Homosexual Woman, and the *Fort! Da!* Paradigm," Ragland examines the link between the Lacanian real—the traumatic void that appears in language—and anxiety. Through her reading of Freud's Dora case and the case of the Young Homosexual Woman, Ragland shows how each woman's symptoms exemplify the catastrophe that bespeaks trauma. By working with catastrophe as revelatory of the limits of representation in memory, Ragland treats anxiety as an equivalence of trauma, arguing that representation and recollection end where the real cuts into imaginary consistencies. As Ragland links the relation of trauma to forgetting in terms of its speech, she offers a reading of the *Fort! Da!* paradigm in Freud's *Beyond the*

Pleasure Principle in order to unveil the nature of traumatic catastrophe as both a literal, historical event as well as a certain impasse or limit in representation. This limit, Ragland tells us, places the relationship between the real of trauma and the imaginary and symbolic constitution of identity as points of impasse and enigma. Through attention to this impasse, Ragland examines how the limits of representation, memory, and knowledge in trauma tell us something new about the affects of trauma, which Lacan tried to explain by his category of the real.

As Ragland's analysis of affect and anxiety offers us a way to begin to approach the impasse in knowledge that trauma evokes as the return of the repressed in repetition, Cathy Caruth's interview with Jean Laplanche pursues a similar ambition through an account of the interval that traumatic experience constitutes. Opening the question of trauma and its relation to latency, Caruth's interview concerns Laplanche's work on belatedness and the general seduction theory, focusing specifically on his expansion of Freud's early work on trauma. Since, according to Laplanche, a psychoanalytic analysis of trauma does not embrace a theory of knowledge as a whole, but rather concerns itself with the reality of the address of the Other, it is imperative that those who continue to explore the temporality of the question of trauma—as the return of the repressed—must take into consideration the logic of seduction, not necessarily as an act or a locatable experience, but rather as a fundamental structure of psychic reality. For Laplanche, the seduction theory does not provide a simple locating of external reality in relation to the psyche. Instead, his temporal reading of seduction suggests that there are always at least two scenes that constitute a traumatic experience, and knowledge of such experience necessarily bears on the possibility of a retroactive internalization after the fact of the initial experience of trauma. In the interview, Caruth and Laplanche discuss how trauma is never locatable in either scene alone but in what Laplanche calls "the play of deceit producing a kind of seesaw effect between the two events."[5] Thus, as Laplanche explains, the first trauma—which is not trauma but rather is described as seduction—is the way the ego builds itself so that later traumas—literal and historical events—are to be understood with the ego already in place. Trauma, that is, is intimately tied to the advent of seduction, of the implantation of the message of the Other into the subject. The fact and persistence of this implantation is precisely what

---

5. See Jean Laplanche, *Life and Death in Psychoanalysis*, trans. Jeffrey Mehlman (Baltimore, MD: Johns Hopkins University Press, 1970), p. 41.

organizes the temporality of trauma, Laplanche insists, a temporality that constitutes what he calls the destructive character of sexuality.

Although Laplanche suggests that Freud's introduction of narcissism in *Beyond the Pleasure Principle* begins a forgetting of the destructive character of sexuality, and, thus, the temporality of trauma, Charles Shepherdson asks if narcissism can be seen to possess such an origin and with it, a history. According to Laplanche, sexuality was enrolled under the banner of totality and love after Freud's introduction of narcissism. In narcissism, Laplanche tells us, Freud comes to see love as the totality of the object. The possibility for such a totality undermines the traumatic theory of sexuality insofar as it offers the possibility for an understanding of the subject beyond the fundamental split or difference which necessarily characterizes it. In "The Catastrophe of Narcissism: Telling Tales of Love," Shepherdson posits this very difference as the condition for narcissism as he describes the event that is the temporality of narcissism. Shepherdson pursues his different account of narcissism through a reading of Julia Kristeva's *Tales of Love,* which itself offers a history of narcissism from neo-Platonism to the present. According to Shepherdson, narcissism amounts to a constitutive, uniquely human disaster that cannot be confined to a particular historical moment, even if that disaster is figured differently at different times. Through his analysis of Kristeva's account of Plotinus and Ovid, Shepherdson shows that the history of narcissism cannot be maintained. This is not to say that Kristeva misses the point of narcissism or that a skeptical Shepherdson must direct his analysis beyond Kristeva's text, for, as Shepherdson himself indicates, to doubt the story that is being told by Kristeva would already be to enter the arena of narcissism—of representation, evidence, and suspended belief. Exploiting the logic of this double bind, Shepherdson argues, Kristeva's text does not simply amount to a history, but rather touches on the structural catastrophe of narcissism itself. Beyond its particular specificities, this structure of narcissism elicits a catastrophic origin whose nonhistorical character repeats itself compulsively, according to the temporal structure of trauma. The time of narcissism, Shepherdson tells us, is the time of an event whose traumatic character repeats itself at every moment, beyond the recovery of historical memory. In this sense, then, the event of narcissism resembles what Shepherdson calls an original trauma, an event that repeats itself compulsively because it was never experienced in the first place, never symbolized and made present as such to the subject.

While Laplanche and Caruth focus on the significance of seduction and belatedness in Freud's theory of trauma, the following essay by Linda Belau, entitled "Trauma, Repetition, and the Hermeneutics of Psychoanalysis," considers Freud's technique, including his seduction theory, in order to show how the narrative development of a psychoanalytic theory of trauma has always circled around a missing origin. Belau further considers how this very development calls for a hermeneutic practice that is grounded in the inadequacy of the signifier. Since something is always lost to memory, and to traumatic memory in particular, a straightforward interpretive approach must give way to a narrative practice that can account for the unaccountable. This is why psychoanalysis moves from early models of interpretation to the later and more nuanced strategy of construction as it attempts to translate the unconscious origin of the traumatic event into the analysand's understanding. Simply giving the analysand's past over to the signifier through interpretation does not deal with what is structurally repressed by this signifier. This is the fundamental insight that psychoanalysis will come to as the ethos of its technique. Through an analysis of the significance of the symptom in repetition, Belau examines the narrative dimension of repetition, especially as the analyst endeavors to "translate" the traumatic symptom. Through an open practice of narrating the impossible "content" of the trauma in the present scene of analysis, psychoanalysis imposes an investigative practice that incorporates a radical failure of translation. Following the work of Freud and Lacan, Belau argues that this failure of translation becomes the preeminent mode of understanding in psychoanalysis, offering the analysand a knowledge structured in repetition. As the analysis attempts—and subsequently fails—to translate the meaning or origin of the traumatic experience, the traumatic element emerges as something that, in the original experience, the analysand did not experience as such. In this sense, the traumatic element of the experience is retroactively posited by the analysis. This, Belau argues, exposes the true meaning of trauma in repetition, since it is within the vicissitudes of this movement that the unbearable limit of knowledge might be known, without return, as an impossible experience.

Working-Through

How is it that a knowledge without return might align itself with the true meaning of repetition? What would it mean to say that both recollection and its failure—repetition—are necessary to the task of working-through the trauma of the past? How does this necessity shatter the possibility for a utilitarian relation to our knowledge of trauma? In his essay "In the

Future . . . : On Trauma and Literature," Petar Ramadanovic explores the possibility that there is something beyond a utilitarian appropriation of knowledge, which might allow for the remembering or reinvention of trauma. In his reading of Toni Morrison's *Beloved*, Ramadanovic considers the literary repetition of trauma as constituting a history that is itself regarded as a testimony to the interminable process of working-through. According to Ramadanovic, one need only glance at any literary history to see that literature has played an important part in the mourning of catastrophic events. Yet, the question of trauma's presentation in the literary is not so obvious, he maintains. If trauma is constituted through repetitions, Ramadanovic asks, how does trauma become representable? How might one, for example, distinguish between the representation of trauma and compulsive repetition? Exploring the possibility for a different understanding of trauma, Ramadanovic shows how the repetition of trauma repeats something that is other than the compulsion to repeat. In this sense, then, Ramadanovic's question about the presence of trauma in literature—and particularly in *Beloved*—is asked as part of a general concern regarding the possibility for a future beyond trauma. Focusing on the juncture between *Beloved*'s haunting, *Beloved*'s literariness, and historical trauma, Ramadanovic examines how the past is related to the present and how a crime is related to its haunting effect. This conjuring of the ghost, Ramadanovic says, is both the condition of the possibility for the remembering of the past as well as a repetition or acting out of the past, which forces other repetitions. And it is precisely this conjuring that provokes a movement beyond repetition to the process of working-through as the ghost makes way for an understanding that is not based on interpretation. Here Ramadanovic introduces an approach to trauma that implicates the relation between what he calls the structural and historical forms of trauma. In this sense, Ramadanovic posits the work of mourning—the process of working-through, that is—between repetition and recollection, in the negotiation between the historical givens and the underlying and unconscious consequences of trauma.

In the process of working-through—between the historical advent and the structural topology of trauma—the possibility of community emerges in the wake of what Brett Levinson calls the "immeasurability of radical injustice." Working through the trauma of dictatorship in Latin America, Levinson's "Obstinate Forgetting in Chile: Radical Injustice and the Possibility of Community" examines the link between the injustices perpetrated by military regimes and the transition to democracy. Pursuing more optimistic prospects, Levinson argues that neither of the strategies for addressing military crimes—vengeance or forgetting (amnesty)—leads to any real justice. According to Levinson, both forgetting—in which the traumatic past is ignored—and vengeance—through which the traumatic past becomes an obsession—block the flow of history and the possibility of transition. Through an analysis of radical injustice and its relation to melancholia, Levinson considers how the process of mourning—of overcoming the stagnation of melancholia—might be undertaken in a political arena where every act of restitution is inadequate to the demand for justice. Without access to representation or memory, Levinson tells us, the survivor of dictatorship fails to mourn: the survivor, that is, does not confront the absence of the trauma, but rather its interminable, living presence. Because a transitional government cannot break with its past, but rather inherits it, the impossibility of justice persists in the structure of the new community. But this is nothing new, Levinson maintains, since an unfathomable abyss is necessarily located at the foundation of the democratic process. And it is precisely this limit of democracy that figures the trauma of injustice since, Levinson tells us, the national disaster materializes only after the dictatorship, when the failure of justice collapses into an unrealizable demand for vengeance.

Even in societies that are not in historical denial, Herman Rapaport tells us, the failure of justice persists, for the acknowledgment of traumatic sufferings is difficult to achieve. This, Rapaport maintains, is why works of art must carry the burden of remembering and working through the trauma of the past. If we are unable to adequately remember what has happened to the victims of historical trauma literally, then art makes a place for a more metaphorical memorialization. While cultural works can never take the place of legal justice, Rapaport tells us, he does consider how they might be enlisted as substitutes. In "Representation, History, and Trauma: Abstract Art after 1945," Rapaport argues that, far from being a simple refusal or inability to engage historical trauma, the postwar flight into abstractionism unveiled the fundamental logic of this traumatic time. Exposing a temporality in which the subject must recollect a past that is sealed off by a historical break characterized by a radical forgetting, the postwar artist's response to this break was itself representational, historical, and traumatic. One sees this very exposure, Rapaport suggests, in the practice of naming a painting "Untitled." Not only a mark of the namelessness, of the loss of painting's name, "untitled" indicates something that precedes all concepts, something that comes before the positing or stating of the work as a representation. According to Rapaport, the act of painting itself constitutes the repetition of something prior. Through an unconscious acting out, the artists repeat a break in the history of visual representation. And it is precisely this repetition, Rapaport says, that reflects a break in artistic consciousness that is analogous with trauma. Offering an analysis of the work of artists such as Jackson Pollock (who represents American Abstract Expressionism), Pierre Soulages (from the internationalist school of abstractionism), and Anslem Kiefer (working in the New German Expressionism), Rapaport explores the capacity for abstract art as a medium for both remembering and repeating—and, thus, working-through—the trauma of the past.

Exploring the aesthetic's faculty for confronting the trauma of the Holocaust, the final essay, by Bracha Lichtenberg Ettinger, offers an account of the redemptive capacities of artistic representation. In "Transcryptum," Lichtenberg Ettinger examines the role that art plays in working-through, understood here as both an overcoming of the particular, historic traumas of the past as well as an acknowledgment of the structural, psychic trauma of the Other. Arguing that any discussion of art is inseparable from the question of sexual difference, Lichtenberg Ettinger pursues a reading of the traumatic Thing, whose painful encapsulation is partly recognized in the subterfuge of artwork. The unseen object of originary repression, the Freudian/Lacanian Thing organizes Lichtenberg Ettinger's reading of the relation between beauty, repetition, and sexual difference as the locus of a non-place where the unexpected event—the work of art—might be born. Supplementing her analysis of the psychic trauma of the second generation of *Shoah* survivors with Nicolas Abraham and Maria Torok's notion of an intrapsychic crypt, Lichtenberg Ettinger considers the mechanisms that might account for the reappearance, rather than the secret burial, of traces of the trauma of the Other. Through this supplement, Lichtenberg Ettinger develops the relation of aesthetics to what she calls "wit(h)nessing" a trauma via artwork and the possibility of the passage of trauma between individuals. Such a passage, Lichtenberg Ettinger says, necessitates a joint unconscious process whereby partial-subjects and part-objects become witnesses without event. According to Lichtenberg Ettinger, it is precisely this act of transmission, of reflection, that grounds the possibility for working-through.

Part I

Recollection

1

"Das Vergangene wird gewußt, das Gewußte aber wird erzählt": Trauma, Forgetting, and Narrative in F. W. J. Schelling's *Die Weltalter*

David Farrell Krell

Here is the primal source of bitterness intrinsic in all life. Indeed, there must be bitterness. It must irrupt immediately, as soon as life is no longer sweetened. For love itself is compelled toward hate. There the tranquil, gentle spirit can achieve no effects, but is oppressed by the enmity into which the exigency of life transposes all our forces. From this comes the deep despondency that lies concealed in all life, without which there can be no actuality—life's poison, which wants to be overcome, yet without which life would drift off into endless slumber.

—F. W. J. Schelling, *The Ages of the World*

Is there reason to believe that trauma studies have anything to learn from philosophy? The happenstance that philosophy today, whether of the analytical or hermeneutical persuasions, is itself traumatized—having both run out of problems and bored even its most dedicated audiences to death—is no guarantee. It seems incredible that a never-completed work of romantic-idealist metaphysics, namely, Schelling's *The Ages of the World* (1811–1815) could have much to tell the contemporary student of trauma. What could the omnipotent divinity of ontotheology have to say to victims of violence? What would the God of traditional metaphysics and morals know about *ignomini-ous* suffering—about a *passio* deprived of the safety net of resurrection?

I am not sure. In the present paper I am operating on the (naive?) assumption that several aspects of Schelling's account of God's difficulties—those told in narratives about the distant past—are somehow related to the traumas that human beings have undergone in the recent past and are undergoing in our own time. While I am not prepared to say that Schelling's God is suffering from PTSD (post-traumatic stress disorder), there do seem to be grounds for saying that God's memories, like those of His or Her children, are "stored in a state-dependent fashion, which may render them inaccessible to verbal recall for prolonged periods of time."[1] As we shall see, that inability to recall over prolonged periods of time is precisely what Schelling understands to be the principal trait of time past and present. Further, if experiencing trauma is "an essential part of being human," and if human history "is written in blood," then being human is an essential part of divinity, and the blood spilled in human history is the blood of the lamb.[2] The memory of God is surely deep, but it is also anguished, humiliated, tainted, and unheroic.[3] If human memories are "highly condensed symbols of hidden preoccupations," and are thus very much like dreams, and if the memories that are "worth remembering"

---

1. Bessel A. Van der Kolk, A. C. McFarlane, and L. Weisaeth, ed., *Traumatic Stress: The Effects of Overwhelming Experience on Mind, Body, and Society* (New York: Guilford Press, 1996), pp. xix–xx.

2. Bessel A. Van der Kolk and A. C. McFarlane, "The Black Hole of Trauma," in *Traumatic Stress,* p. 3.

3. Lawrence L. Langer, *Holocaust Testimonies: The Ruins of Memory* (New Haven, CT: Yale University Press, 1991). It may be perverse to suggest that the Judaeo-Christian God of Schelling's philosophy has been traumatized; indeed, it may seem to be some sort of "revisionist" trick. Yet if the traumatic suffering of the Jewish people in the twentieth century bears no relation to the suffering of Yahweh, that very fact bodes ill for the chances of divinity. In this regard see Pierre Vidal-Naquet, *Assassins of Memory: Essays on the Denial of the Holocaust,* trans. Jeffrey Mehlman (New York: Columbia University Press, 1992). On the difficulty of remembering and memorial-izing what dare not be forgotten, see James E. Young, *The Texture of Memory: Holocaust Memorials and Meaning* (New Haven, CT: Yale University Press, 1993), esp. Part II, "The Ruins of Memory." It is unfortunate that Young's wonderful book was produced before Daniel Libeskind's "Between the Lines," his addition of a Jewish Museum to the Berlin Museum, the most remarkable of nonmemorializing monu-ments that I have seen.

are memories of trauma, then it is arguable that a memorious God could be nothing other than a suffering godhead.[4] Indeed, if psychic trauma involves not only intense personal suffering but also "recognition of realities that most of us have not begun to face," no God worthy of the *Logos* would want to be without it.[5] No Creator worthy of the name would be willing to forgo testing his or her creative powers against radical loss—the terrible test of survival.[6] Finally, such a suffering God would also have to become His or Her own historian, exercising a craft in which both memory and narrative are crucial—and disenchantment inevitable.[7] The suffering godhead would have to advance from trauma to melancholia, living a life "that is unlivable, heavy with daily sorrows, tears held back or shed, a total despair, scorching at times, then wan and empty," under the dismal light of a black sun.[8] In the light and dark of all these recent inquiries into traumatized memory, the question is not whether trauma studies have anything to learn from philosophy but whether philosophy is capable of thinking its traumas.

Having spoken of narrative, trauma, forgetting, the past, and time in general, let me begin with an effort to situate Schelling in some recent philosophical discussions about the possibility of recuperating the past. Is the past essentially available for our recuperation and inspection, or is it ruined by radical passage? Is the past so absolutely past that we must say it was never

---

4. Michael Lambek and Paul Antze, "Introduction: Forecasting Memory," Antze and Lambek, ed., *Tense Past: Cultural Essays in Trauma and Memory* (New York: Routledge, 1996), p. xii.

5. Cathy Caruth, in Caruth, ed., *Trauma: Explorations in Memory* (Baltimore, MD: Johns Hopkins University Press, 1995), p. vii.

6. David Aberbach, *Surviving Trauma: Loss, Literature and Psychoanalysis* (New Haven, CT: Yale University Press, 1989). See esp. chap. 6, "Loss and Philosophical Ideas," although there is little in Schelling's biography that would lend itself to a biographical reduction of his ideas concerning the difficulties of divinity.

7. Jacques Le Goff, *History and Memory,* trans. S. Rendall and E. Claman (New York: Columbia University Press, 1992). On the return of narrative to the historian's craft, see p. ix. On disenchantment, see p. 215: "The crisis in the world of historians results from the limits and uncertainties of the new history, from people's disenchantment when confronted by the painful character of lived history. Every effort to rationalize history, to make it offer a better purchase on its development, collides with the fragmentation and tragedy of events, situations, and apparent evolutions."

8. Julia Kristeva, *Black Sun: Depression and Melancholia,* trans. Leon S. Roudiez (New York: Columbia University Press, 1989), p. 4.

present? More pointedly, is trauma itself the source of repression—of all that bars or distorts every possible memory of the past? Would trauma then be the nonorigin of origins?

In Martin Heidegger's view, the temporal dimension of the past *(die Vergangenheit)* is the only dimension that needs to receive a new name for both the fundamental-ontological analysis of ecstatic temporality and the "other thinking" of the turning: from hence, according to Heidegger, we will think not the *past* but the *present perfect,* "what-has-been," *die Gewesenheit.* Yet, before Heidegger, Hegel too had preferred *das Ge-Wesene* to *das Vergangene,* as though the absolute finality of the past—which a number of contemporary French thinkers write and think as *le passé absolu*—would absolutely resist positive speculative dialectic. There appears to be a split between Hegel and Heidegger, on the one hand, and Merleau-Ponty, Levinas, and Derrida, on the other, a split between conceptions of the past as either essentially recoverable or absolutely bygone. (The case of Heidegger is, of course, much more intricate than I have made out here.) How old and how wide is this split?

I will approach the question only indirectly by offering an account of Schelling's earliest notes on *Die Weltalter,* notes not yet dated with certainty but probably from the year 1811. These notes focus on the words *Vergangenheit, gewußt,* and *erzählt,* and they culminate in the famous opening sentences and paragraphs of the introduction to all the printed versions of *The Ages of the World:* "*Das Vergangene wird gewußt, das Gegenwärtige wird erkannt, das Zukünftige wird geahndet. / Das Gewußte wird erzählt, das Erkannte wird dargestellt, das Geahndete wird geweissagt.*" In translation: "The past is known, the present is cognized, the future is intimated. / The known is narrated, the cognized is depicted, the intimated is foretold." Why the *known* must be *recounted* or *narrated* rather than depicted or presented dialectically is my question—it is also Schelling's question, and right from the start. My presupposition, not yet a thesis, is that Schelling speaks to *us* about *our own* fundamentally split experience of the past, which seems by turns to be both absolutely irrecuperable and absolutely inescapable.

In this paper I would like to do three things. First, I want to look closely at the oldest of Schelling's sketches toward *The Ages of the World,* trying to see how these first steps on Schelling's path determine the rest of the endless journey toward that book. Naturally, that will be too large an undertaking for a paper such as this one; I will therefore restrict my investigation to the first half of the 1811 printing of *The Ages of the World,* the first printing of the text. Second, I want to pay particular attention to the emergence of several figures of *woman* in Schelling's account of the past, woman as the night of Earth, as the wrath of God, and as the giver of life—inasmuch as she seems to be at the epicenter of trauma, repression, and forgetting in the divine life. Third, I would like to pose some more general questions about the nature of the trauma that Schelling seems to espy in the life of the divine, along with the mechanism of repression that he finds at work both in our own present and in the divine consciousness that began to stir in the remote past.

The Earliest Notes Toward *The Ages of the World*

Karl Schelling, serving as the editor of his father's never-completed magnum opus, identifies the first recorded plan of *The Ages of the World* as "The Thought of *The Ages of the World [Gedanke der Weltalter]*."[9] Of the three original *Bogen*, or fascicles, of the plan, that is, of the three folded sheets of foolscap, only two (A and C) are preserved. On the left side of the first page of Fascicle A we find a margin extending over a third of the width of the page. In it are nine numbered notes and two unnumbered ones; these notes consist of key words, many of them abbreviated and therefore difficult to decipher. Across from these notes, covering two-thirds of the page, appears the exposition of the plan itself.

Why bother with such a problematic sheet of notes, especially before the Schelling-Kommission has prepared it in its historical-critical form? The answer must lie in Schelling's own preoccupation with the art of beginning and with all beginnings. Virtually all the *Weltalter* sketches, plans, and drafts thematize in a reflexive and reflective way the problem of beginning.[10] More strictly, they deal with the impossibility of beginning at the beginning, since

---

9. Friedrich Wilhelm Joseph Schelling, *Die Weltalter Fragmente in den Urfassungen von 1811 und 1813,* ed. Manfred Schröter (Munich: Biederstein Verlag and Leibniz Verlag, 1946), p. 187, cited henceforth by page number in the body of my text. Schröter's volume appeared as a *Nachlaßband* of *Schellings Werke Münchner Jubiläumsdruck.* The new historical-critical edition of Schelling's works has not yet released the volume on *The Ages of the World* and the unpublished notes related to it.

10. Slavoj Žižek, *The Indivisible Remainder: An Essay on Schelling and Related Matters* (London: Verso, 1996), p. 13. Žižek rightly recognizes the force of the unconscious in Schelling's *The Ages of the World,* yet in his desire to develop a political philosophy based on the idea of freedom, he does not grant "the unconscious act" that occurs "before the beginning" its full power. That said, Žižek's is a stimulating interpretation, one that deserves a more careful reading than I can give here.

the beginning is in some radical sense *bygone*. Not only is the beginning past, it also pertains to a time before time, a time that in the current age of the world (namely, the present) never was present. Schelling will eventually say that the beginning is an *eternal beginning*—that in a sense the beginning has neither end nor beginning (p. 78). We therefore cannot simply assume that our own present and future flow from this distant or "elevated" past—Schelling always calls it *die hohe Vergangenheit*—for which we are searching. True, he is driven by the belief that we must stand in some sort of *rapport* with the elevated past; yet he is hounded by the suspicion that the past is closed off to us, encapsulated, isolated, cut off from us. Sometimes it seems to him that the past is all by itself, *solus ipse,* absolutely solitary, well-nigh *un passé absolu.* If we do experience some sort of *rapport* with it, all the critical apparatus of science and philosophy must be brought to bear on this presumed relation, and from the very beginning. Yet something more than science and philosophy will have to be brought to bear from the outset—something like a *fable* or a *narrative*. Let us therefore begin with the very beginning of the *Früheste Conzeptblatt,* reprinting its text as it stands, in all its enigmatic form, and introducing some necessarily conjectural comments on it as we proceed—with trepidation—to translate it.[11]

1. *Ich beginne.*
2. *alles an Verg.*
3. *Die wahre Vergang. d. Urzust. d. Welt . . . vorhand. unentfaltet eine Zeit.*
4. *Philos.-Wiss. Verg.*
5. *Was gewußt wird, wird erzählt.*

"Number one. I begin." Or, in the progressive form, "I am beginning." One might wish to use this progressive form in order to avoid the sense "I *always* begin," which would mean as much as "This is the way I *have* always *begun.*" Finally, there is nothing that prevents us from reading the present tense as an elliptical future tense, "I shall begin." Perhaps the first thing that is odd about

---

11. Our commentary should not be confused with Schelling's exposition, which does not always seem to be in tandem with these notes in the left-hand margin. Although I will reprint the whole of Schelling's left-hand margin, I will take up his exposition only in part. Whether or not such intense focus on the margin of this earliest sketch will help us with a more general reading of *Die Weltalter* remains to be seen. At this point, that is merely my hope.

the beginning of this earliest sketch is that its apparently straightforward, candid, self-referential, self-indexing "I begin" (look at me start, can you see me getting underway at this very instant?) can yield a number of different tenses—simple and continuous present, present perfect, and future.

It is perhaps important to notice that the simple past is *not* among the tenses into which we can translate *Ich beginne*. The past seems to resist both Schelling's beginning and our own. And yet everything hangs on the question of a possible access to the elevated past.

"Number two. everything in the past [or: everything *concerning* the past]." Is the sense here that all that is, all being, reverts and pertains to the past? Or is Schelling making a distinction, as he is wont to do, between *things* past—in the mundane sense of the history of our present world—and the past in itself, the past in some more lofty sense?

"Number three. The true past. The primal state of the world . . . at hand, undeveloped, a time [or: an age] . . . " The past properly speaking is a time or an age unto itself. In that former time the world was at hand in its undeveloped state, whereas now, in the present time (the Age of the Present), the worlds of both nature and history are constantly unfolding. Yet could the elevated past—with which we stand in some sort of *rapport*—be truly undeveloped? When and how could its developmental dynamism have been introduced? This is the very conundrum that had stymied Schelling's philosophy of nature: his *First Projection toward a System of Nature Philosophy* (1799) was unable to imagine what might have initiated movement and life into a static universe. If dynamism and dualism pervade nature now, they must always have done so, and right from the start. For omnipresent life and ubiquitous animation are *contagion*.[12]

"Number four. Philosophical-scientific past." The past is the proper object of dialectic, which is the method best suited to speculative knowledge. However,

"Number five. Whatever is known is narrated." If knowledge is the goal of philosophy as science, it is difficult to understand why the known must be recounted, narrated, told as a story. The suggestion is that even though the past, considered philosophically-scientifically, is the proper object of knowl-

---

12. For a discussion of Schelling's *First Projection toward a System of Nature Philosophy* and a listing of the sources, see my *Contagion: Sexuality, Disease, and Death in German Idealism and Romanticism* (Bloomington, IN: Indiana University Press, 1998), Part Two.

edge, the proper medium of knowledge concerning the past is not presentation, depiction, or portrayal, all of which pertain to the present, but some other
form of communication. Schelling will often call it "the fable." Perhaps he is
thinking of the astonishing figure of *Fabel* in the Klingsohr fairy tale of
Novalis's *Heinrich von Ofterdingen.* In any case, a hidden reference to Novalis
seems to lie in the opening of Schelling's exposition.

Let me return now to the top of the front side of Fascicle A, back to the
beginning, or to the *second* beginning, in order to take up Schelling's exposition—which I will here, for simplicity's sake, translate without reference to
the many corrections in Schelling's text: "I am what then was, what is, and
what shall be; no mortal has lifted my veil." Thus, once upon a time, according
to some old narratives *[nach einiger Erzählung],* from under the veil of the
image of Isis, spoke the intimated primal essence in the temple at Saïs to the
wanderer.

It is unclear why this traditional narrative—a fable in Novalis's if not in
Aesop's sense—begins the exposition. Nor is the import of the fable un-
equivocal. One recalls that for Schiller's poem, Novalis's prose text, and
Hegel's account of the myth in his philosophy of nature, the goddess's words
are sometimes heard as a warning, sometimes taken as an invitation. Lifting
the veil sometimes grants immortality, sometimes mortality. If Schiller's
wanderer is struck dead because he dares to lift the veil, Hegel has the written
inscription on the hem of the goddess's dress dissolve under the penetrating
gaze of spirit, while the far more gentle Novalis declares that only those who
dare to lift the veil—with respect, but without remorse—deserve to be called
apprentices at Saïs. Schelling's exposition offers us no clue as to how the old
fable is to be heard. Yet it does assert the importance of the tripartite division
of the ages for philosophical science: Past, Present, and Future are not dimensions of the present time but independent times of the world.

If reams of questions begin to pile up for readers of the exposition, the
numbered remarks on the left seem to anticipate the difficulty. Let me return
again to the left-hand margin:

6. *Warum unmöglich*
7. *da ich mir nur vorges. in dem ersten Buch d . . . dieser Verg. zu behandeln,
   so wird es nicht ohne Dial.*
8. *D. Vergang. folgt die Gegenwart. Was alles zu ihr gehört—Natur Gesch.
   Geisterwelt, Erkentn.-Darstellung—Nothw. wenn wir die ganze Gesch.
   d. Gegenwart schreib. wollten, so d. univ. unter aber nur d. Wesentl.
   denn . . . nur d. Syst. d. Zeiten kein Ganzes d. Nat.n.*

"Number six. Why [it—the narrative—is] impossible." The exposition tells us that it is not enough to know the One. We must also know the three divisions of the One, namely, what was, what is, and what will be. And after we *know* these three, we must *narrate* them, even if something about such narrated knowledge is "impossible." Yet the nature of this impossibility— which has to do with both the supremacy of narrative over dialectic and the repression of narrative in our time—is not clear to us.

"Number seven. because I have proposed [reading *vorges.* as *vorgesehen* or *vorgestellt*] to treat only what pertains to this past, it will not be without dialectic [*Dial.*]." It is not yet clear why dialectic is called for at all in our scientific-philosophical pursuit of the past; indeed, we can be rather more assured of Schelling's troubled relation to dialectic. In the various plans and drafts of *Die Weltalter* Schelling employs dialectic—and yet almost always he expresses his worry that dialectic may be no more than manipulation of concepts without the requisite seriousness of purpose or thoughtfulness. Schelling often seems to trust images and fables more than he does dialectic, which he faults for being a kind of intellectual sleight of hand, a conceptual legerdemain. "The past" will be about that time before (the present) time when the intellect was unclear about all that was, when dialectic was more strife and suffering than controlled negation and confident synthesis. Perhaps the very fact that the first book of *The Ages of the World* will need dialectic is the mark of a flaw or an impossibility? That is an interesting (im)possibility, if only because the editor of these early drafts, Manfred Schröter, himself consistently degrades the first half of the 1811 draft as being too "naive," too suggestive, too full of images—in a word, as being insufficiently dialectical. We will have to come back to the question of dialectic, because the narrative or recounting that Schelling has in mind can be understood only in (nondialectical) opposition to dialectic—only in some sort of distance and releasement with regard to dialectic.

"Number eight. The present follows the past. All that belongs to it— nature, history, the world of spirits, knowledge-presentation—Necessary if we wished to write the entire history of the present, thus of the universe [reading *so des universums*], but only in its essential aspects; for [this is] only the system of the times, not the entirety of all their natures." Here the decoding is particularly hazardous. It is clear that Schelling intends to provide no more than a "system of the times," not a detailed inventory of everything in nature and history. What is entirely unclear is why and how the present can be said to follow the past. For what has been emphasized so far is that the past is not only essentially prior to or earlier than but also cut off from the present time of the world. If past, present, and future are not to be taken as measures of the current time (namely, the Present), but as "three times that are actually different from one another," as the exposition says (p. 188), then it is not clear at all that the present should follow upon the past. The problem is blurred when one translates the plural of *Zeit,* namely, *die Zeiten,* as "ages" or "eras"; when one translates them and tries to think of them as three distinct *times,* the problem becomes rebarbative. Indeed, that *rapport* on which Schelling stakes everything, the relation that ostensibly links the present to the past, remains entirely problematic: everything that Schelling does to elevate the past to its "true" and "genuine" status vitiates the *rapport* that those of us who live in the present (that is, all human beings, past, present, and to come) might have with it; everything that Schelling does to expose the efficacy of the present in repressing the true past debilitates our faith in his or anyone's ability to accede to it.

Let us now turn to the ninth of Schelling's marginal notes on the left-hand side of the page:

9. *Die Zukunft so d. Besch. d. Welt nur . . . D. hier bg. Werk wird in 3 Bücher abgeth. seyn, nach Verg. Gegenw. u. Zuk. welche hier . . . in d. hier beg. Werk nicht als bloße Abm. d. Z. sond. als wirkl. Zeiten vers. wäre d. — Welt — allein.*
   Ein Altes Buch.

"Number nine. The future. It is thus [usually taken to mean] the way the world turns out [reading *Besch.,* very uncertainly, as *Bescheidung*] . . . The work presented here will be divided into 3 books, according to Past, Present, and Future, which here in the work that we have begun are not mere dimensions *[Abm. = Abmessungen]* of time, but are to be understood as actual times — the world — alone. [¶] An Old Book —." Much in these final lines resists our reading — especially the relation of "—the world—alone" to the three "actual times." Why does Schelling insist that there are three distinct ages or times? He does so, he says, because of "an Old Book." The book is *Ecclesiastes,* and to its question "What is it that has been?" Schelling replies, "Precisely what will come to be afterwards." And to the further question, "What is it that will come to be afterwards?" he replies, "Precisely what also has been before." Because it is not speaking of the essence, says Schelling, and because it evades the problem of the *past* by speaking in the *perfect,* the Old Book can equate past, present, and future and declare that there is nothing new under the sun. Yet the sun of that Old Book shines on the things of *this* world alone, the *present* world, says Schelling, so that *Ecclesiastes* is actually pointing in the direction of something else. "The time of this world is but one vast time, which in itself possesses neither true past nor genuine future; because the time of this world does not possess them, it must presuppose that these times belonging to the whole of time are outside itself" (p. 188).

In Schelling's view, the true or genuine past is clearly privileged. At least he will say throughout his work on *The Ages of the World*—which never gets *out of* the past precisely because it never *gets into* it—that as much soothsaying skill is needed to discern the past as to augur the future. Two final unnumbered notes on the left-hand margin now try to distinguish past from present:

> *Wenn es die Abs. ist dieß Syst. d. Zeit. zu entw. s. steht d . . . doch Verg. u. Gegenw. nicht gleichs . . . D. Verg. gewußt.*
> *Woher nun Wiss. d. Verg. in jenem hohen, [sic] Sinn philos. verstanden? Wenn aber warum nicht erzählt?*

"If the intention [of this work] is to develop this system of the times, then past and present are not posited as identical . . . The past is known. [¶] Now, whence our knowledge of the past, understood in that elevated philosophical sense? But if [it is known], why [is it] not narrated?"

Here the left-hand margin comes to an end, but the exposition continues to elaborate the questions posed. And the principal question seems to revolve about the apparent contradiction that what is known is narrated, but that the past, while indeed known, is not narrated—but then *why* not? Schelling argues that "the true past time is the one that came to be before the time of the world; the true future is the one that will be after the time of the world," and the present time—with its own epiphenomenal past, present, and future—is but one "member" of time. Yet no one has as yet lifted the veil: what was, is, and will be—considered as three distinct times—remains concealed.

Schelling's exposition now finds the statement that will serve as the opening for the introduction to *The Ages of the World* in all its drafts: "The past is known, the present is cognized, the future is intimated. The known is narrated, the cognized is depicted, the intimated is foretold" (p. 189). Yet this refrain—both more and less than an assertion—only underscores the severity of the double question posed in the margin. If the past is known, where does that knowledge come from? How can we in the present time of the world know anything of the past? The second question is more confusing, and Schelling's marginal formulation of it is quite condensed: "But if [the past is known], why [is it] not narrated?" Up to now Schelling has made use of an ancient myth—the myth of Saïs, reported to his contemporaries by Herder and recapitulated by Schiller and Novalis—and an Old Book that is part of the Good Book; apparently, therefore, *something* of the past has indeed been recounted. Yet Schelling wants to know why is it recounted in such cryptic, Sibylline forms:

> Science would thus be the content of our first part [on the past]; its form would have to be narrative *[erzählend]*, because it has the past as its object. The first part, namely, a science of the preworldly time, would speak to everyone who philosophizes, i.e., everyone who strives to cognize *[erkennen]* the provenance and the first causes of things; but why is that which we know not narrated with the candor and simplicity with which everything else we know is narrated; what holds back the Golden Age, when science will be story [or history: *Geschichte*] and the fable will be truth? (p. 189)

We cannot read Schelling's words without thinking ahead to Nietzsche's account, in *Twilight of the Idols,* of "how the true world finally became a fable." Schelling's account would only alter slightly the sense of the *endlich,* "finally." For what Schelling envisages is a recurrence of that time, that Golden Age, in which truth and fable were coextensive, the time when inquiry was—and will be—indistinguishable from story. The gold of that Golden Age will prove to be the densest of metals, the metal that feels as though it has an oily skin, a skin that exudes balsam, a balsam that heals flesh, the flesh that is of organs and that wishes to adorn itself with gold.

After two false starts ("There still slumbers in human beings a consciousness of the past time . . . ," and "It is undeniable that human beings are capable of cognizing only that with which they stand in living relation . . ."), Schelling avers that human beings today still retain a "principle" from the primordial time, or pre-time, of the world. The past serves as a kind of matrix or foundation of the present, *die Grundlage*. Yet that matrix or foundation has been "repressed" or at least "covered over" *(verdrungen oder doch zugedeckt),* somehow "relegated" to or "set back" into the dark *(ins Dunkel zurückgesetzt)* (pp. 189–190). Schelling calls this principle of the proto-time the human "heart of hearts," *das Gemüth.*

We would need to trace the history—or the story—of this word *Gemüth* from Kant's third *Critique* to Heidegger's *Being and Time* in order to feel the full weight (past and future) of Schelling's asseveration. For Schelling, the *rapport* we sustain with this earlier time, the time before our own worldly time, arises within the human *Gemüth,* which is not a *faculty* but a *principle* ruling from the beginning. His genealogy of time(s), carried out in the second half of the 1811 printing,[13] will be a genealogy of *Gemüth*—and here it is almost as though Schelling were quoting *Being and Time,* if one can quote from a future that can only be intimated. At all events, it will be a genealogy designed to sustain a *rapport* in the face of the most powerful repression. For even when the past is repressed or covered over in the present, there is something in the human heart of hearts that has the experience of *déjà vu;* even when the past is "set back" into the dark, it preserves treasures. One is reminded—if one may take yet another leap into the future—of the way in which Husserl insists that even at the zero-point of internal time consciousness, where retention fades away into absolute nothingness, *something of the past is preserved.* For Husserl, such preservation will constitute the secret font of *Evidenz.* It is perhaps not out of place for us to note here that Husserl is also involved in Schelling's more dialectical deduction of the three times of the world, inasmuch as that deduction has to do with the problem of what Husserl calls *die lebendige Gegenwart,* the living present. Yet Schelling's problem, as we shall see, is the obverse of Husserl's: whereas Husserl needs the living present in order to explain our retention of the past, Schelling fears that the living present will expand excessively and thus block all passage to the genuine past.

Those who live in the present age time are all like the Greeks—as the sages of ancient Neith (at the temple of Saïs) saw them, according the story in Plato's *Timaeus:* we are like children who have no memory, especially no memory for the beginnings of things. And if we have a vague premonition of an ancient memory, we cannot find the words to tell it. Thus Plato's Socrates will always

---

13. See the *Urfassungen,* pp. 74–88. Schelling's genealogy of time from eternity lies outside the purview of this paper, if only because of the complexity of the topic. The birth of each moment of time occurs in the "polar holding-apart" of the entire mass of past and future (p. 75). These births are separations *(Scheidungen)* compelled by love as longing or languor *(die Sehnsucht).* They are always a matter of the father's contractive force and the son's expansive force; they are also a matter of suppressing the past on behalf of a present perfect, "as absolute having-been" (p. 79), "that gentle constancy" (p. 80), which tends toward the *future* as toward the promise of love. On its way to the future, love creates time, space, and the natural world. However, as we shall see, such creations alter the creator. On *die Sehnsucht,* "languor," see Krell, "The Crisis of Reason in the Nineteenth Century: Schelling's Treatise on Human Freedom (1809)," *The Collegium Phaenomenologicum: The First Ten Years,* ed. John Sallis et al. (The Hague, Netherlands: M. Nijhoff, 1989), pp. 13–32.

call upon some higher power represented in a myth, so that by collection and division, by dissection and analysis of the old stories, he can struggle to remember what we all have forgotten. We are all like Faust: two souls dwell in our breast, and it is the art of interior discourse—the dialogue of self and soul—that enables philosophy first of all to search for what it has forgotten and then to give birth to dialectic. If candor and simplicity *(Geradheit und Einfalt)* are the virtues of philosophical reasoning and dialectic, it is nevertheless the case that something prevents our heart of hearts from hearing and understanding the stories of the remote past. The present seems to have repressed the past, condemned it to the inner darkness of *un for intérieur.* What could have been the motive of such repression? Why are the treasures of the past locked away in an interior vault? What accident or contingency or shock could have induced such a repression? And what kind of narrative will release the effects of the repression and give us back our *rapport* with our own provenance, give us back our future?

One recognizes the astonishing parallel with, or anticipation of, psychoanalysis. One could understand the parallel as a straightforward historical inheritance—from Schelling to Schopenhauer to Freud to Lacan—or one could problematize (or at least leave open) the very meaning of "inheritance" and historical succession. One would thereby show greater respect for both psychoanalysis and Schelling—precisely by setting out in quest of the undiscovered source of primal repression. That source lies hidden in a time so remote that it appears—to both Schelling and Freud—as timeless.[14]

Niobe's Children

Schelling saw the 1811 text of *The Ages of the World* into print, then retracted it. He did this twice, first in 1811, then once again in 1813. Different commentators highlight different parts of these drafts—some 200 pages of text. In my view, it is again the earliest part of the 1811 text that seems most remarkable, most memorable, and most repressed. For it is the first half of the 1811 printing of "The Past" that presses back to the most recalcitrant materials—including the material of matter itself. Whereas the second half of the text finds familiar comfort and solace in the Christological story, the story of a

---

14. For more on repression *(Verdrängung),* see the second half of the 1811 printing, pp. 99–100.

loving solar Father and his mirror image Son, the first half finds itself forced to introduce the themes of darkness, wrath, and the mother. Whereas the second half expresses confidence in the divine will of expansive love, the first half cannot escape the lineage of love that is longing, languor, and languishing *(die Sehnsucht),* as well as craving and tumult *(Begierde, Taumel).* Whereas the second half of the 1811 printing is happy to fall back on the reiterated story of the spiritualization of all matter, the first half tarries with the matter and the materials—gold, oil, balsam, and flesh—that seem themselves to invite divinity.[15]

The posthumously published text of the 1811 printing is marked by many revisions and corrections, and is therefore difficult to read and cite. The narrative always seems to be fighting against a strong current, or against two strong currents, one of which wants to sweep it up and away into the remote past, the other threatening shipwreck on the familiar shores of Christological consolation and salvationist delights. These crosscurrents make the going rough, both for the reader and (presumably) for the writer; the waters are choppy, the interruptions irregular but quite frequent. The text is filled with what the trained logician will gleefully expose as blatant contradictions: the first words of "The Past" tell us "how sweet is the tone of the narratives that come from the holy dawn of the world," whereas seven lines later we hear, "No saying reverberates to us from that time" (p. 10). Among the many topics pursued by Schelling in the first half of the 1811 printing (pp. 10–53), let me single out three: first, the problem of the living present and the negative deduction of the times of the world; second, the problem of the basis or birthplace of the world; third, the wrath, strength, and tenderness of God. All three topics should contribute to the overriding methodological question that haunts *The Ages of the World* and reappears in every draft in virtually the same words, words we have already heard from the "earliest conception," but here taken from the introduction to the 1811 printing: "Why cannot what is known to supreme science also be narrated like everything else that is *known,* namely with candor [or straightforwardly, *mit der Geradheit*] and simplicity *[Einfalt]*? What holds back the Golden Age that we anticipate *[Was hält sie zurück die geahndete goldne Zeit],* in which truth again becomes fable, and fable truth?" (p. 4).

---

15. Oddly, it is in the second half of the 1811 printing that *Sehnsucht*—the languor and languishing of God—is most discussed (see pp. 57, 77, and 85), even though the mother seems to have disappeared altogether from the Father-Son axis.

Clearly, the Golden Age is as much of the future as of the past; it is intimated or anticipated more than known, and yet it is the proper object of our scientific-philosophical pursuit of the elevated past. The fabled past, anticipated as the hallowed future, poses problems for the truth of the present. Science, which is to say, dialectical philosophy, will have to tell stories as well as deduce, will have to listen to narratives as well as to arguments. Not only its enemies but also its friends will ridicule it for its fascination with that night in which all cows are black. Yet if the ridicule will not banish Schelling's fear, it will not quell the disquiet in all who mock, will not dispel the suspicion that something *is holding back* the recurrence of the Golden Age. Some as yet nameless trauma or suffering is still causing the past to be *repressed* or covered over and buried. Freud will use Schelling's word *Verdrängung,* perhaps not knowing that it is Schelling's word, although he will quite consciously use Schelling's definition of the "uncanny." The methodological question—the question as to whether and how we can ever resist the force of repression—is what invites us to ask about (1) the negative deduction of the times of the world from the enigma of the living present, (2) the birthplace of the world, which is a site and situation of trauma and suffering, and (3) the sundry qualities and contradictions of divinity. As we shall see, all three of these topics (but most notably the second and third) have to do with figures of the female and the feminine in Schelling's text.

1. If the past is a time of silence and stillness, so that no saying comes to us from it—no matter how sweet the tone of its narratives may be—how will we approach it as an object of silence rather than science? Nothing is more difficult. For we live in a living present, a present that seems to dilate and stretch its envelope forward into the infinite future and backward into the infinite past, such that these two dimensions are never truly released by the present. "Most human beings seem to know nothing at all of the past, except for the one which expands in every flowing instant *[in jedem verfließenden Augenblick],* precisely through that instant, and which itself is manifestly not yet past, that is, separated from the present" (p. 11). Schelling's problem is the opposite of Husserl's and is perhaps closer to Aristotle's. Whereas Husserl will deploy the antennae of retentions and protentions in order to prevent past and future from vanishing beyond the zero-point, a prevention that is necessary if internal time-consciousness is to provide the matrix for all evidence, Schelling, like Aristotle, sees the contiguity of the dimensions of time as a problem. Access to the past is closed if the past is still (of the) present, so that Husserl's solution is but a restatement of the problem of continuum. What Schelling seems to yearn for is passage back beyond the zero-point into the territory that

both he and Husserl will populate with figures of Night and Death, the funereal figures of the spirit world.[16] Schelling has recourse to that Old Book, *Ecclesiastes,* which he reads in an admittedly bizarre way: if, as the Old Book avers, there is nothing new under the sun, then we must ascend beyond the solar system, or at least beyond the system of the present world, in order to encounter something new—a system of times or ages of an expanded world. Within such a system, "the genuine past, the past without qualification, is the pre-worldly past *[die vorweltliche]*" (ibid.). Schelling realizes that he is trying to sound the seas of time, and that abyss may bottom out upon abyss, in such a way that the appropriate response is horror (p. 13). Only the discovery of a "basis" or "true ground" of the past that sustains the present world will banish the sense of horror.

2. Schelling realizes that he is speaking in an all-too-human or anthropocentric way when he asks about the basis. "Who can describe with precision the stirrings of a nature in its primal beginnings, who can unveil this secret birthplace of essence *[diese geheime Geburtsstätte des Wesens]?*" (p. 17). Schelling has already called *The Ages of the World* the companion science to Creation *(Mitwissenschaft der Schöpfung)* (p. 4), and the search for pristine beginnings can be nothing less that that. If the essence of all essence is divine, if divinity is purest love and love infinite outflow and communicability *(unendliche Ausfließlichkeit und Mittheilsamkeit)* (p. 19), we can expect the essence of essence to be the expansive force. Yet if divinity exists, if it *is,* then it must be *on* its own and *as* its own; to be is to be a precipitate that resists total outflow. Divinity must be what Walt Whitman in "Crossing Brooklyn Ferry" calls the human being, namely, "a float forever held in solution." Divinity must have a ground *(einen Grund);* otherwise it would dissolve, disintegrate, evaporate. However, such a ground would be "what eternally closes itself off, the occluded *[das ewig sich Verschließende und Verschlossene]*" (ibid). Such occlusion would be unfriendly to outsiders; it would spell the death—death by fire—of any creature that sought love from it. Self-closing would be the very figure of a wrathful God, the figure of eternal fury *(ewiger Zorn),* which, as we shall see, is an unexpected figure of *woman.*

---

16. For Husserl's figures and metaphors, see Edmund Husserl, *Analysen zur passiven Synthesis,* Husserliana, vol. XI, edited by Margot Fleischer from lecture and research manuscripts dating from 1918 to 1926 (The Hague, Netherlands: M. Nijhoff, 1966), esp. pp. 172–222 and 364–385; see also my discussion in *The Purest of Bastards: Works of Mourning, Art, and Affirmation in the Thought of Jacques Derrida* (University Park, PA: Pennsylvania State University Press, 2000), chap. 7.

3. Schelling begins to deduce the two opposed forces that constitute the divine essence—the expansive, dilating force of the will of love, and the contractive, centripetal force of the will of ground. For Schelling, these two forces constitute what one might call the ontological difference: in God one finds both a to-be *(Seyn)* as the basis and a being *(das Seyende),* both contraction and expansion. Presumably, the birthplace of the world would host both the to-be and being, both ground and love, inasmuch as lovemaking—and prior to it, desire, longing, and craving—leads to the conception that in turn leads to birth, the birth that is itself to serve as the birth*place* of the natural world. As Schelling pushes back into the past that belongs to love and ground, dilation and contraction, he confronts his first two images of the lordly mother—first, the image of proud Niobe, whose children are being slaughtered by Apollo and Artemis, and second, an image of the Amazons. The strength of God, the very pith of his essence *(die Stärke Gottes),* is what makes Him Himself alone, sole, "cut off" from everything else *(von allem abgeschnitten).* Yet if there is something *living* in divinity, it must be superior to God's mere to-be *(über seinem Seyn),* or beneath it as the deeper ground of its ground. Schelling elaborates, apparently thinking of a painting by Raphael and a Hellenistic statue of Zeus:

> Heaven is his throne and the earth is his footstool *[sein Fußschemel].* Yet even that which in relation to his supreme essence must be called not-in-being is so full of force that it irrupts into a life of its own. Thus in the vision of the prophet, as Raphael has depicted it, the eternal appears to be borne not upon the nothing but by figures of living animals. Not one whit less grand is the depiction by the Hellenistic artist of the very extremity of human fate: carved on the foot of the throne of his Olympian Zeus is a relief of the death of Niobe's children; and even the god's pedestal *[Schemel des Gottes]* is decorated with forceful life, for it represents the battles of the Amazons. [pp. 20–21]

All three images—living animals, Niobe's children, and the Amazons—are meant to evoke that great force of *life* that subtends the being of God. Yet at least two of the three evoke violence and death. The Amazons are devoted to Artemis and Ares, and are remembered for the bloody battles they fought against Herakles and Theseus. Niobe's seven sons and seven daughters were killed by the Olympian twins, Artemis and Apollo, after Niobe had mocked the twins' mother, Leto. According to ancient interpreters, the slaughter of

Niobe's children may in fact be a cryptic retelling of the battle of the Olympian gods against the seven Titans and Titanesses. In any case, Niobe's children are images of anger and the night—joining an image of animated animality— which is precisely where Schelling himself will locate the birthplace of the natural world.[17]

To be sure, Schelling devotes himself to "the tender godhead, which in God himself is above God" (p. 21), and not to the God of wrath. This tender divinity he clearly associates with the expansive will of love, and he counter- poses it to the God of wrath who closes in on herself. I say "herself" because the age of wrath, the time of the night, will be identified with womankind and even with the mother. If God "herself" is shut off in such a night, closing in on "herself" and furious toward everything that might be external to her, wrath- ful toward every creature, she is also *abgeschnitten,* "cut off." She hovers in the selfsame relation to herself that obtains between us and our own elevated past, which has been cut off from us.

Matters of the divine birthplace are more complicated than castration and emasculation, however. Schelling refers to an "active occlusion, an engaged stepping back into the depths and into concealment," a description that is reminiscent of the earth in Heidegger's *Origin of the Work of Art.* For Schelling such an occlusive force is also a force that suffers *(Leiden).* The folding in upon itself or contraction of the essence is prelude to the expansiveness of love, yet it is unclear to Schelling whether love—the tender will—can ever leave behind its capacity for passion and passivity, pain and suffering. Everything about this "beginning" is obscure: "Darkness and occlusion make out the character of primal time. All life at first is night; it gives itself shape in the night. Therefore the ancients called night the fecund mother of things; indeed, alongside Chaos, she was called the most ancient of essences" (p. 24). If light is taken to be superior to darkness, it is nonetheless true that the superior presupposes the inferior, rests on it and is upheld by it *(trage und emporhalte)* (p. 25). Zeus's pedestal, God's footstool, on which Niobe and the Amazons

---

17. One should note here the importance of phrygian Niobe also for Friedrich Hölderlin's understanding of tragedy: in the *Anmerkungen zur Antigonä,* Hölderlin identifies her as the "more aorgic realm," the realm of savage, untamed nature, which (in the figure of Danaë in the fifth choral song of *Antigone*) counts or tic(k)s off the hours for the father of time, Zeus. Niobe, Melville would have said, stands where Una joins hands with Dua on the clock of "The Bell-Tower," or, rather, where their loving clasp is severed. On Hölderlin's Niobe, see Friedrich Hölderlin, *Sämtliche Werke und Briefe,* ed. Michael Knaupp (Munich: Carl Hanser Verlag, 1992), vol. 2, p. 372.

hold sway, is and remains the ground—a ground so nocturnal and so abyssal that in the 1809 *Treatise on Human Freedom* Schelling had called it the *Ungrund,* the "nonground." In his address to the Bavarian Academy of Sciences on October 12, 1815, entitled "The Divinities of Samothrace," which Schelling hoped would provide the very ground (footstool? pedestal?) of his *The Ages of the World,* which was so difficult of birth, he explicitly related the rigors of wrathful, primal fire to the magic of Persephone.[18] In *The Ages of the World* he writes: "Thus too wrath must be earlier than love, rigor earlier than mildness, strength earlier than gentleness *[Sanftmuth].* Priority stands in inverse relation to superiority" (pp. 25–26).

For a project that seeks the beginning, the *a priori* prior, and seeks it in the *elevated* past, it is surely odd to say that its object is *not* superior. Indeed, one of the crosscurrents that I referred to earlier is the force of "the early" as such: Schelling will always feel swept away by the phantasm of the earlier, and he will release himself to its attractive force because he is convinced that there can be no superior goal for science. He can never be certain whether he is being drawn upward to the expansive will of love or being displaced from the center to the periphery—which was Franz von Baader's and his own description of *evil* in the 1809 *Treatise.* Schelling's essential indecision about these forces induces a call for their *existentielle Gleichheit,* "existential equality." He notes that although the South Pole exerts a weaker magnetic pull than the North Pole, and although the female sex is reputedly "weaker than the male," even so, the one must for a time bow to the other. What is odd, however, is that in the beginning for which he is searching, nothing can be less certain than the putative weakness of the female—an imputation that sounds more like a prejudice of our present age, which has no sense of the true, elevated, superior past.

In the elevated, superior past, the first existent is in fact a double essence *(ein Doppelwesen)* (p. 29). When it comes to the primal images of the world, which our tradition calls *ideas,* the principle of existential equality and of doubling prevails: such ideas cannot be thought "in the absence of everything

---

18. F. W. J. Schelling, "Über die Gottheiten von Samothrake," in *Sämmatliche Werke* (Stuttgart and Augsburg: J. G. Cotta Verlag, 1861), I/8, p. 356. See also the long endnote 64. Perhaps this relatively brief and compact text—voluntarily documented, however—offers the best testing ground for the theses contained in the present paper. Note that Schelling also refers to the abyss or nonground *(Ungrund)* in the second half of the 1811 printing, at p. 93.

physical" (p. 31). The spiritual cannot be thought without its being bound up with "the first, most tender corporeality *[mit der ersten, zartesten Leiblichkeit verbunden]"*; the highest form of purity *[Lauterkeit]* takes on "the first qualities of suffering *[die ersten leidenden Eigenschaften]"* (ibid.). "The spiritual and the corporeal find themselves to be the two sides of the same existence so early on that we may say that the present moment of their supreme intimacy *[Innigkeit]* is the communal birthplace of what later come to stand in decisive opposition to one another as matter and spirit" (p. 32). If these opposites were not twins, they could never partake of one another: "If there were no such point where the spiritual and the physical entirely interpenetrated, matter would not be capable of being elevated once again back into the spiritual, which is undeniably the case" (ibid.). Schelling begins to look for this "point of transfiguration" in which spirit and matter are one, and he believes he sees it in the very place where Novalis too, in his very last notes, saw it: spirit looms in the most dense and compact metals—gold, for example. For the density of gold is soft to the touch: gold seems to have a skin, and its skin seems to have a smooth, almost oily texture. Gold has the softness, viscosity, and tenderness that is similar to flesh *[die Weichheit und fleischähnliche Zartheit]*, which it combines with the greatest possible density and malleability *[Gediegenheit]* (p. 33). Not only Novalis but also Hegel praised the *Gediegenheit* of gold. Hegel too found it in the skin—specifically, in the skin of the black African.[19]

The Golden Age is therefore an age in which matter and spirit—and presumably also female and male—are in perfect harmony. Schelling finds the principle at work in organic nature in particular. The ethereal oil that nourishes the green in plants, "the balsam of life, in which health has its origin," makes the flesh and the eye of animals and human beings transparently healthy. Health is a physical emanation (Schelling again uses the word *Ausfluß,* which earlier described the expansive force of love) that irradiates everything pure, liberating, beneficent, and lovely. The most spiritual form of this radiance is what Schiller had identified as *Anmuth,* the grace, gracefulness, and graciousness that transcend the merely charming. Yet no matter how transfigured or spiritualized the physical may seem to be in *Anmuth,* which may be related more than etymologically to *Gemüth,* the physical and corporeal is undeniably palpable in it: *Anmuth* astonishes us precisely because

---

19. See Krell, "The Bodies of Black Folk: Kant, Hegel, Du Bois, and Baldwin," in Kevin Thomas Miles, ed., *The Academy and Race: Toward a Philosophy of Political Action.*

it "brings matter before our very eyes in its divine state, its primal state, as it were" (ibid.). Perhaps that is why artists who sculpt or paint the divine are drawn to Amazons and Niobes and other living beings.

Trauma, Repression, and the Absolute Past

Yet beautiful, gracious, and graceful life is not without its fatality, its passion, and its suffering. As Schelling is swept back to the beginnings, to the distant and elevated past, suffering and fatality become ever more central to his narrative. It is as though the way up were the way down. For centripetal being *(Seyn)* feels the centrifugal, affirmative force of love only as suffering, and even as a kind of dying. If contraction is embodiment, and expansion spiritualization, pain and suffering are bound up with both: contraction cramps, expansion distends. There is a principle of gloom that does not cease to strive against spirit, light, and love—indeed, light and love themselves participate in that gloom. The farthest reaches of the past are reaches of strife and supreme enmity or revulsion *(Streit, höchste Widerwärtigkeit)* (p. 37). Schelling finds himself propelled back to the era of Chaos, the yawning abyss in which matter is fragmented into the smallest particles, only to be unified in sundry mixed births. For the inner life of the essence, such Chaos can be experienced only as suffering and pain. Which essence? The essence of all essence, where *Wesen* can mean—and perhaps must mean—both creature and Creator. "Suffering is universal, not only with a view to human beings, but also with a view to the Creator—it is the path to glory *[der Weg zur Herrlichkeit]*" (p. 40).

The age of the Titans is the age of "monstrous births." During this preworldly, protocosmic time, wild visions and phantasms beset the essence. "In this period of conflict, the existent essence broods as though on oppressive dreams looming out of the past: soon in the waxing strife wild fantasies pass through its inner life, fantasies in which it experiences all the terrors of its own essence. . . . Its corresponding sensation is the feeling of anxiety" (p. 41). Even the primal time of Chaos—out of which, according to the myth of Plato's *Statesman,* both the Titanic time (dominated by Ouranos and Cronos) and the Olympian time (of Zeus) arise—is haunted by a still more primal past. So many crises and separations (both words translate the word *Scheidung,* which was the key word of Schelling's 1809 *Treatise)* are experienced, that the centripetal force fears it will be pulled apart; being trembles *(zittert)* like a dog before the storm or a bomb before it explodes.[20] The essence is anything but free. The lightning bolt of freedom, wielded by Zeus (or was it wielded by Prometheus the Titan? or by some essence earlier than both the Olympian and Titanic?), cannot be grasped. Spirit and consciousness suffer "a kind of madness," and even if it is the divine *maniva* described in Plato's *Phaedrus*, the essence that suffers it does not *feel* divine. Even if its tumult proves to be the origin of music and dance, the essence that suffers it feels like the helpless prey of voracious animals—perhaps the very animals Raphael painted as the sustaining ground of eternity. Among the most remarkable lines of the 1811 printing, reminiscent here of Hegel's remarks on "Bacchic tumult" in his analysis of "the religion of art" in the *Phenomenology of Spirit*,[21] are the following:

> Not for nothing is it said that the chariot of Dionysos is drawn by lions, panthers, and tigers. For it was this wild tumult of inspiration, into which nature was plunged by the inner view into its essence, that was celebrated in the primeval cult of nature among intuitive peoples, with their drunken festivals of Bacchic orgies—as though thereby to lament the demise of the old and pure things of nature. Working against this tumult was the terrific pressure of the contractive force, that wheel turning crazily on itself in incipient birth, with the frightful forces of circular motion working from within, symbolized in that other terrifying display of primitive ritual custom, to wit, insensate, frenzied dancing, which accompanied the terrifying procession of the mother of all things, seated on the chariot whose

---

20. In the second half of the 1811 printing (p. 61) Schelling concedes that *Scheidung* is never complete: there can never be an absolute rupture with the effects of the past. What the 1809 *Treatise on Human Freedom* had called *die ewige gänzliche Scheidung* is therefore still eternal but never total. Heidegger, of course, read the *Treatise* with considerable attention. What he apparently never read—even though Manfred Schröter was an admired colleague and friend—was *The Ages of the World*. (I am grateful to Otto Pöggeler for this last observation. In a personal communication, Pöggeler asked me to speculate as to *why* Heidegger might have avoided *Die Weltalter*. Neither he nor I came up with a telling answer, yet we suspected that there is something *subversive* about the latter text, subversive perhaps also of Heidegger's own confidence in a *Gewesenheit*—a present perfect—that putatively enables him to appropriate the past for an "other" beginning.)

21. G. W. F. Hegel, *Phänomenologie des Geistes*, ed. Johannes Hoffmeister, 6th ed. (Hamburg: F. Meiner Verlag, 1952), p. 504.

brazen wheels resounded with the deafening noise of an unrefined music, in part hypnotic, in part devastating.

Schelling is no doubt thinking of the Korybantic dancers, which he had written about in the 1809 *Treatise on Human Freedom.* Whereas their rites of self-emasculation served Schelling in 1809 as a parallel for modern Cartesian philosophy, which with its mind-body split mutilates science and philosophy, here the allusion occurs in the context of a discussion of essence itself. The Korybants, of which the Whirling Dervishes are distant descendants, dance the inner strife of essence. Their terrifying rites, which require them to throw their severed organs against the statue of the Great Mother as her brazen car clatters by, suggest something quite specific about the divine father's suffering and pain, to which Schelling was referring earlier. If later, for Nietzsche, music will give birth to Greek *tragedy,* the most savage of Greek (or oriental) cults will, prior to that, give birth to music: "For sound and tone appear to originate solely in that struggle between spirituality and corporeality. Thus the art of music alone can provide an image of that primeval nature and its motion. For its entire essence consists of a cycle, taking its departure from a founding tone and returning to that beginning-point after an incredible number of extravagant sallies" (p. 43). No one assists at the birth of essence. Human beings help one another at birth, and so do gods. "Yet nothing can assist the primal essence in its terrifying loneliness; it must fight its way through this chaotic state alone, all by itself" (ibid.). "The spinning wheel of birth," discussed also in the second half of the 1811 printing (pp. 68–69), represents the overwhelming force of nature; as it turns, both Schelling and his readers are confused about whether the force it represents is centripetal or centrifugal, or both. What is certain is that this spinning wheel of fortune—as the opening song of *Carmina Burana* emphatically tells us—points sometimes up, sometimes down.

From Schelling's concluding discussion, let me extract only two points. The second has to do with the greatest of the Titans, namely, Prometheus— the Titan without whose craftiness and foresight Zeus would never have defeated the other Titans in order to institute the reign of the Olympians. The first has to do with that transfigurative point in the beginning of the beginning when spirit and matter interpenetrated with grace—the grace of gracefulness or beauty in motion. Schelling knows that many of his readers will be shocked by this apparent elevation of matter to equiprimordiality with spirit, and so he tries to absorb some of the shock:

By the bye, what is it about matter that most people consider an insult, such that they would grant it an inferior provenance? In the end it is only the humility *[Demuth]* of matter that so repels them. Yet precisely this releasement *[Gelassenheit]* in the essence of matter shows that something of the primeval essence dwells in it, something that inwardly is purest spirituality and yet outwardly is complete passionateness *[Leidenheit]*. As highly as we honor the capacity for action *[Aktuosität]*, we nevertheless doubt that in itself it is supreme. For even though the essence out of which God himself emerges glistens with purity, such glistening can only stream outward, can achieve no effects. On all sides, gentle suffering and conceiving seem to be prior to the achieving and the active. For many reasons, I do not doubt that in organic nature the female sex is there before the male, and that in part at least this accounts for the presumed sexlessness of the lowest levels of plant and animal life. (pp. 46–47)

Many will find Schelling's association of women with suffering, passivity, and the lowest levels of life as troubling as they find women's association with wrath reassuring—or at least refreshing. Yet I may be at fault for translating *Leiden* too quickly as "suffering": it is the root of *Leidenschaft,* "passion," so that the "passivity" of releasement *(Gelassenheit)* may be something quite animated and vital. Indeed, as we shall now see, Schelling wishes to upset the usual ways we think of activity and passivity. Let us not underestimate the impact of Schelling's words: here the traditional metaphysical priority of activity over passivity falls away. For Schelling, Meister Eckhart's releasement prevails over the "actuosity" that our tradition has always preferred— and which it has always identified with the logos and with the masculine.[22] Schelling coins a new word or two here, the most telling one being *Leidenheit,* the quality of suffering, or the capacity to undergo passion. True, he celebrates *passio* and identifies it with the principle of matter. He does not break with the traditional association of *materia* with the mother, or the mother with woman, or woman with sensuality and sexuality, but he does break with the long-

---

22. It is important to note, however, that *Gelassenheit* in Schelling's text sometimes has consequences that would perhaps have surprised Eckhart, or at least driven him to his own most radical conclusions. For one of the things that Schelling eventually feels compelled to let go and release is God. Schelling concludes the second of two "preliminary projections" of the *Weltalter* by asserting that "to leave God is also *Gelassenheit*" (p. 200).

standing tradition of Plato's *Timaeus* when he suggests that the female sex comes first—in the beginning, at the beginning, as the beginning of the beginning.[23] Even a sparkling God, radiant and unalloyed, is a flash in the pan until he can achieve effects. And "he" can achieve effects only when "he" achieves for "himself" a gentle passivity, a passionate nature, a releasement by virtue of which alone he may become pregnant with a future. In the second half of the 1811 printing, Schelling describes God's past and future as bound up with nature: "Nature is nothing other than divine egoism softened and gently broken by love *[der durch Liebe gemilderte, sanftgebrochne göttliche Egoismus]*" (p. 85). Perhaps that gentle breaking, that loving acceptance of humble yet passionate passivity, will also make her a better storyteller?

One final passage, the Promethean, which seems as ungentle as any passage might be. For Prometheus is surely titanic strength, light, and power. Yet the Prometheus that Schelling has in mind is the Prometheus of Aeschylus, Prometheus *bound*. Bound by what, to what, for what? Schelling's answer is surprising:

> There is something irrational in the first actuality, something that resists confrontation. Thus there is also a principle that repels the creaturely, the principle that is the proper strength in God: in the high seriousness of tragedy, Force and Violence, the servants of Zeus, are depicted as those who fetter Prometheus, who loves human beings, to the cliffs above the surging sea. It is thus necessary to acknowledge that this principle [i.e., the principle that repels creatures] is the personality of God. In the language of traditional philosophy that personality is explained as the ultimate act or the final potency by which an intelligent essence immediately subsists. It is the principle by which God, instead of mixing with creatures, which surely was the intention—separates himself from creatures eternally. Everything can be communicated to the creature except one thing, namely, its possess-

---

23. In a personal communication, John Sallis reminded me that in *Timaeus* woman "comes second" only in the final lines of the dialogue, lines that can only appear as *comic* in the light of the dialogue's earlier insistence on the eminence of the *chora,* "the mother and nurse of becoming." See the first chapter of my *Architecture: Ecstasies of Space, Time, and the Human Body* (Albany, NY: SUNY Press, 1997); see also John Sallis, *Chronology: On Beginning in Plato's Timaeus* (Bloomington, IN: Indiana University Press, 1999). Finally, or in the first place, see Jacques Derrida, *Khôra* (Paris: Galilée, 1993).

ing in itself the immortal ground of life, that is, its being itself, that is, its being by and on the basis of itself. [p. 52]

Would such incommunicability and lack of generosity be unworthy of God? Not at all, says Schelling, if it were essential to his being. Yet both Zeus and Yahweh turn to violence in order to repress that past in which they *were* the very woman they *loved,* or in which they were unable to make the distinction between themselves and Demeter. Whether the Christological story—which is always the story of fathers and sons—can help us to confront the mother and mortality is to be doubted. The only rescue for us groundless, orphaned mortals, Schelling suggests, is pantheism—beyond both idealism and realism, and also beyond dualism. For pantheism, which is the oldest of the old stories, embraces every form of life, whether divine or creaturely. The problem is that the narratives of pantheism have been banished by more recent history, so that the all-encompassing unity of life that pantheism celebrates lies beyond our reach. Precisely this system of the primal time, writes Schelling (and here the first half of the 1811 printing ends), "comes to be increasingly repressed by subsequent ages *[durch die folgende Zeit immer mehr verdrungen]* and posited as past *[und als Vergangenheit gesetzt werden soll]*" (p. 53).

Why pursue the repressed past? In order to discover a living divinity who will not keep her distance from mortals, who will not accept violence, and who will embrace the mortals as the children to whom she gave birth. What would it take for such a God to embrace her children? She would have to overcome the trauma, the shock, and the suffering that initially caused her to cut herself off from her children. She would have to accept the full implications of what Schelling in the second half of the 1811 printing calls *Zeugungslust,* the desire to procreate, as the only possible form of Creation and the only possible form of divine life. The castration and emasculation suffered by her male worshipers is therefore not an *imitatio matris,* inasmuch as her sex is not elaborated by a cut. It is elaborated as an unfolding and infolding— *Entwicklung* and *Einwicklung* being two of Schelling's favorite words for the expansive and contractive forces at work in her. Yet neither will it do to cry *Veni, veni creator spiritus* and then dream endlessly of *das ewige Weibliche*— recapitulating from beginning to end and back again Mahler's glorious Eighth Symphony, the "Symphony of a Thousand." For the sobering fate of the Amazons and of Niobe's children—seven males, seven females—is portrayed on the pedestal of divinity. When God learns of his femininity as well as her masculinity, when God learns longing, he and she alike will learn that languishing is a part of passion. When God learns what love entails, she and he will discover that they are dying, and that their death is coming to meet them out of a past so distant that it seemed it would never arrive.

It will.

Such a death could only be announced in a story, a narrative, which is itself an *arrêt de mort.*

Not enough—indeed, nothing at all—has been said here about the question this paper set out to discuss, namely, the necessity that makes the known past an object of narrative or recounting, of saga or fable. It is a necessity that prevails beyond all dialectics—and my own dialectical foray does not seem to be up to the tale. Yet what can be said about that necessity affirmatively rather than negatively? Narrative recounts creation, is itself creation. Creation is procreative, centripetal and centrifugal at once. Creation recounts the itinerary taken by the gods to mortals—to mortal women and men.

Schelling, along with his friend Hölderlin, had been attuned to such tales since the days of their youth. For his part, Hölderlin knew why Zeus could not keep his distance from Niobe, Io, Rhea, Semele, Europa, Danaë, and the countless other mortals for whom he longed and languished. Hölderlin told the story in many different places, as far back as *Hyperion,* but the most famous of his recountings is in *Der Rhein.* It is a story he would have whispered to his friend Schelling as they walked through the thick woods that border the Neckar, the woods and the riverbank that smacked sweetly of pantheism:

> A riddle wells up pure. Even
> Song can scarcely veil it. For
> As you begin, so you shall remain.
> Much is achieved by necessity
> And also by discipline, but most
> Can be achieved by birth. . . .
> Who was it that first
> Ruined the cincture of love,
> Tearing it to shreds?
> After that they made their own law
> And surely the spiteful ones
> Mocked the fire of heaven, only then
> Despising mortal paths,
> Choosing overbold
> And striving to be equal to the gods.

But they have enough of their own
Immortality, the gods, and if they need
One thing, the celestial ones,
Then it is heroes and human beings
And whatever else is mortal. For if
The most blessed ones of themselves feel nothing,
Then it must be, if to say such a thing
Is allowed, that in the name of the gods
Another feels for them, takes their part;
They need him.[24]

One should remember, however, that the last words of this poem recall the feverish days and nights of the present time, to which our lives seem to be fettered. We are chained to a hectic and forgetful time. Trauma and forgetting seem to accompany us every step of the way, and are the troubling themes of our very best narratives. The present in which we tell these stories to one another is itself a Chaos, linked by both its repressed memories of suffering and its longing for a caress to the remote past and a distant future. Ours is thus an inevitably traumatized present:

. . . when everything is mixed,
Is without order, and all that recurs is
Primeval confusion.

---

24. Hölderlin, *Sämtliche Werke und Briefe,* vol. 1, pp. 342–348, lines 46–51, 96–114, and, for the lines appearing below, 219–221.

2

Interminable AIDS

William Haver

> *For the blinding sight of the deep flash when the living goes to dead—the very transformation of Sodom and Gomorrah into the past tense of total annihilation—was precisely "history," now; her history-now; exactly her memory, and, as such, it set the boundary over which she could not possibly leap.*
>
> —Sue Golding, "The Address Book"

Undoubtedly there are innumerable forms the aspiration to "transcendence" can assume when it is a question of AIDS. Who among all those who are HIV positive or living with AIDS would be nothing but the fact of his or her seropositivity? Who would willingly *be* AIDS, nothing but AIDS? Who would not for an afternoon, an evening, a week, for all eternity, willingly be also something other than a victim or patient, something other than affliction? Who does not resist the reduction to being nothing but AIDS? This resistance to a reductive identification as and with AIDS might be construed to manifest an aspiration to transcend the matter of AIDS. Yet this aspiration to transcendence, if "transcendence" it be, should not be conflated with other, more problematic, claims to having (nearly) overcome or (almost) passed beyond all that is precipitated in this acronym, "AIDS." It is with these other, more problematic, claims that this essay is concerned. The claim that we have (nearly) overcome or (almost) surpassed what is called AIDS, the claim that ours is soon to be no longer the time of AIDS (not only that the era of AIDS is drawing to a close, but that time itself is no longer "of AIDS," that temporality and finitude no longer belong to AIDS as its "ownmost"), has taken two principal forms in recent years. We are first of all asked to imagine the imminent possibility of a cure; second, we are invited to surrender to the seduction of believing that the pandemic has been, or is shortly to be, effectively contained. Both seductions offer the relief of a virtually soteriological transcendence; both depend upon the resolute conviction that AIDS is nothing but the virological object the terms "HIV" and "AIDS" are said to denominate.

The apparent provisionally successful but nonetheless dramatic and encouraging reduction in viral load in the bloodstream in some cases within certain protocols of combination antiretroviral therapies (including nucleoside reverse transcriptase inhibitors [nucleoside analogues], protease inhibitors, and nonnucleoside reverse transcriptase inhibitors) have recently led some, less cautious than most scientists and medical practitioners, to speak in terms of a "cure"; indeed, of the "end of AIDS."[1] Certainly there is little doubt that combination antiretroviral therapies hold out more promise than did AZT treatments, and may in fact herald something of what is called a breakthrough. But it is nonetheless precipitous, even scientifically irresponsible, to speak of a cure. Nevertheless, this talk of a cure has had a number of proximate effects, effects that only serve to reinforce and legitimate the exercise of what Catherine Waldby (following Michel Foucault, Donna Haraway, Linda Singer, and others) is among the most recent thinkers to analyze

---

1. See, for example, Andrew Sullivan, "When Plagues End: Notes on the Twilight of an Epidemic," *New York Times Magazine,* (10 November 1996), pp. 52–62, 76–77, 84; rpt. in *The Independent,* 16 February 1997. For more or less immediate responses to the positions Sullivan represents, see, for example, Dan Savage's sarcastic reply, "The AIDS Crisis Is Over—for Me: Why I Think It's Time for New Attitudes About Risk, Charity, and Letting Go," *The Village Voice* 42, no. 8 (25 February 1997): pp. 34–39; Edward King, "A Cure for Over-Optimism," *Positive Nation* 16 (March 1997): pp. 6–7. For an example of the far more cautious and circumspect position of medical scientific researchers, see Jon Cohen's brief report on the fourth "Conference on Retroviruses and Opportunistic Infections," held 22–26 January 1997 in Washington, D.C., in "Advances Painted in Shades of Gray at a D.C. Conference," *Science* 275 (31 January 1997): pp. 615–616. The most pertinent consideration of discourses of the "cure," although it dates from the period when AZT was the great white biochemical hope, is undoubtedly still John Nguyet Erni, *Unstable Frontiers: Technomedicine and the Cultural Politics of "Curing" AIDS* (Minneapolis, MN: University of Minnesota Press, 1994).

as "biopower" in the pandemic.[2] Even at this early date, there is considerable anecdotal evidence to suggest that increasing numbers of physicians, formally or informally, willingly or regretfully, are excluding a certain number of potential candidates for combination antiretroviral therapies from the protocols. Because HIV is among the genetically volatile viruses,[3] the medications for the protocols must be administered according to a strict schedule in order to prevent HIV from mutating to a strain resistant to the medications, and consequently to prevent the resistant strain from being transmitted to a new host; the danger is thus that the "cure" would in fact refire yet one more of multiple AIDS pandemics. The physician must decide who among various candidates is sufficiently "responsible" to sustain the medication timetable and sufficiently disciplined to prevent further transmission. Clearly, like it or not, we—physicians, candidates for treatment, and bystanders alike—are caught up in the exercise of biopower. What is important here is that all this renders the notion of a "cure," even in the instances of the most efficacious treatment, essentially ambiguous. One might point to other, no less problematic, proximate effects of this talk of a cure—for example the Labour proposal in the United Kingdom to cut off government support from people living with AIDS whose viral load drops below a certain point; or the fear, expressed in the popular gay press and elsewhere, that the prospect of a cure will lull those at risk for HIV infection into a false sense of security, a fear that leads in some instances to a thoroughly authoritarian moralism.[4] My point in offering these disparate, even contradictory, examples of responses to the prospect of an imminent "cure," is that whatever is being said to be (almost) cured here, it most assuredly is not "AIDS."

Were we not careful or suspicious, we might alternatively give in to the seduction of imagining the "end of AIDS" as an effective containment of the

---

2. Catherine Waldby, *AIDS and the Body Politic: Biomedicine and Sexual Difference* (London: Routledge, 1996).

3. John Holland, "Replication Error, Quasispecies Populations, and Extreme Evolution Rates of RNA Viruses," in Stephen S. Morse, ed., *Emerging Viruses* (New York: Oxford University Press, 1993), pp. 203–218.

4. A recent cover story in *The Advocate* entitled "The return of bad habits" warns on the front cover that "Sex, drugs, and bathhouses are back . . . A new bio of gay icon Brad Davis reminds us of the dead end we face—Bad Brad." See David Heitz, "Men Behaving Badly," John Gallagher, "Slipping Up," and Robert L. Pela, "Our Man Brad," in *The Advocate* 737 (8 July 1997), pp. 26–29, 33–35, and 34–38, respectively.

pandemic. Perhaps because AIDS has not made incursions into the (straight, white) so-called "general population" as rapidly as had once been predicted, recent reports that the incidence of AIDS among some groups (or at least the number of reported new seroconversions in North America) is declining have been greeted with something like relief that the "war on AIDS" is being won, or at least as an indication that what is involved here is a war that can be won. Even when this relief is not couched in entirely misleading military meta-phors, it depends upon an ignorance, in some cases undoubtedly willful, of centrally important facts, probabilities, and considerations.

First, responsible virologists, epidemiologists, and others have noted the essential heterogeneity of the Human Immunodeficiency Virus, the fact that "the virus" is in fact many different strains of the virus that differ significantly in virulence and pathogenicity (for example, and perhaps most obviously, the difference between the globally dominant strain, HIV-1, and the far less virulent and pathogenic strain, HIV-2, found predominantly in parts of West Africa).[5] Furthermore, it is predicted that viral evolution will be, contrary to many conventional analyses of viral epidemics, not toward symbiosis (a sus-tainable, even benign, relation between virus and host), but toward increased virulence and pathogenicity.[6] This viral heterogeneity not only complicates efforts to develop a universally effective vaccine (perhaps essentially), but also means that the AIDS pandemic is in fact "composite," that we are faced with what Bruce G. Weniger and Seth Berkley call "side by side" pandemics.[7] If "HIV," and hence "AIDS," designates a phenomenon that is in at least these essential aspects multiple rather than unitary, then no part can be said to stand for, or express the essence of the whole; what may look like a decreased incidence in one "population" need not be true of everything designated by the acronym "AIDS."

Second, it is in part for these reasons that a number of epidemiologists have argued that the pandemic is manifested in recurring (and increasingly viru-lent) distinct waves. Roy M. Anderson, for example, has argued that what

---

5. See Jay A. Levy, "HIV Heterogeneity in Transmission and Pathogenesis," in Jonathan M. Mann and Daniel J. M. Tarantola, eds., *AIDS in the World II: Global Dimensions, Social Roots and Responses* (New York: Oxford University Press, 1996), pp. 177–185.

6. Roy M. Anderson, "The Spread of HIV and Sexual Mixing Patterns," in Mann and Tarantola, eds., *AIDS in the World II*, p. 85.

7. Bruce G. Weniger and Seth Berkley, "The Evolving HIV/AIDS Pandemic," in Mann and Tarantola, eds., *AIDS in the World II,* pp. 57–70.

now looks like the declining phase of a classically conceived epidemic (such as bubonic plague or influenza) is not the "beginning of the end," but a "trough" between successive "waves," and that we must expect the overall duration of the epidemic (before it recedes into merely endemic status) to be "many decades."[8] Thus, the Global AIDS Policy Coalition notes that we are in a brief respite between the first wave and a larger second wave. They estimate that by 1990 some 10 million people were infected worldwide; by January 1996, some 30.6 million were infected (of whom 28 million live in the "developing world"), and estimate that by 2000, between 60 and 70 million people will be infected (of whom fully half of all infected adults will be in Southeast Asia). And this, they argue, is but "the lull before the storm"[9] They note, as have many other observers, that the pandemic will continue to exact its heaviest toll among the world's dispossessed, becoming increasingly focused, as Ronald Bayer argues, on "socially marginalized groups."[10] It is only by regarding the dispossessed or the "socially marginalized" as utterly expendable that it is at all possible to imagine an imminent end of AIDS.

Were we to ignore the empirical evidence that there is neither a cure nor an end to the pandemic and imagine that at some definite but unspecified point we shall have gotten beyond all that of which the heterogeneous strains of HIV and its multiple epidemics are the occasion, we would not have pre-sumed that nothing has changed, perhaps, but we would not yet have thought seriously and rigorously that everything has changed; we would have thought "AIDS" as a past, but not as our future, least of all as our present, not even as a past present in our future and in our present. But insofar as "AIDS" signifies, and has always signified, far more than an empirically determinable "virus" and its effects, we can no more imagine a world after the end of AIDS than we can any longer recall a world before the advent of AIDS (for we can only imagine the fact that there was a world before AIDS, not that world "itself"). This is not merely to say that AIDS might be construed as what is called an "event," but that even as such it opens upon radically altered material condi-tions of possibility for the existence of our species. For "AIDS" is, among

8. Roy M. Anderson, "The Spread of HIV and Sexual Mixing Patterns," in Mann and Tarantola, eds., *AIDS in the World II*, pp. 71–86.

9. The Global AIDS Policy Coalition, "Global Overview: A Powerful HIV/AIDS Pandemic," in Mann and Tarantola, eds., *AIDS in the World II*, pp. 5–40.

10. Ronald Bayer, "Societal and Political Impact of HIV/AIDS," in Mann and Tarantola, eds., *AIDS in the World II*, pp. 117–128.

much else certainly, a metonymy for what are collectively called "emerging viruses." This is to say neither that HIV is the first of the emerging viruses, nor that HIV is a virologically unprecedented phenomenon. Least of all is it to say it is the last. John Holland, for example, speculates that it is probable (but unpredictable) that others among the emerging viruses will be the occasion of equally or more devastating pandemics in the future.[11] "AIDS" says that probability; "AIDS" is the future in the sense that we can no longer pretend, as was briefly our wont, that the future could be a decontaminated, or at least perfectly symbiotic, utopia. Indeed, as Joshua Lederberg says (and an entire genre of what is called "science fiction" has proliferated around this possibility), "[t]he survival of the human species is not a preordained evolutionary program. Abundant sources of genetic variation exist for viruses to learn new tricks, not necessarily confined to what happens routinely or even frequently."[12]

This possibility depends upon two prior recognitions. First, as Lederberg maintains (and any number of virologists would agree), "the very essence of [a] virus is its fundamental entanglement with the genetic and metabolic machinery of [a] host."[13] Viruses do not exist, least of all replicate and evolve, in some kind of viral ontological purity (a laboratory, for example), only subsequently (and accidentally) to become caught up in the lives of their hosts; they "are" in fact that entanglement itself. We do not merely "share" the biosphere with viruses; viruses are in part our "sharing" of the biosphere; the term "virus" names not so much (or at least not only) a "thing" as it does a relation: better, "virus" says that the thing is first of all a relation before it attains its objectivity. The virus as such is alien only after the fact, in its attenuation from its being-with, its co-belonging (and therefore its coevolution and ultimately endemic symbiosis with its hosts; the problem, as the famous example of the Australian rabbits and myxoma virus makes clear, is that a host species can become extinct, or nearly so, before symbiosis is accomplished).

Second, and consequently, any alteration in the ecosystem creates the

---

11. John Holland, "Replication Error . . ." in Morse, ed., *Emerging Viruses,* p. 212; in the same volume, see also Howard M. Temin, "The High Rate of Retrovirus Variation Results in Rapid Evolution," pp. 219–225.

12. Joshua Lederberg, "Viruses and Humankind: Intracellular Symbiosis and Evolutionary Competition," in Morse, ed., *Emerging Viruses*, p. 8.

13. Ibid., p. 4.

possibility for the emergence of an apparently "new" virus.[14] Speaking of hemorrhagic fevers rather than AIDS, Karl M. Johnson puts it succinctly: "[M]ost of the 'new' hemorrhagic fevers emerged only because of large and often still accelerating ecologic changes made by a burgeoning *Homo sapiens*. . . . [T]hese hemorrhagic fevers foretold that our earth is, in fact, a progressively immunocompromised ecosystem."[15] So this, too, is what "AIDS" says: that what we had taken to be a more or less stable ecosystem, biosphere, or even a "world," is henceforth essentially—that is, irreparably—damaged; that we cannot anticipate a world after "AIDS," a world restored perhaps not to a pristine luminescence, but at least to a sustainable, albeit negotiable, ontoecological coherence. Just as we cannot responsibly look forward to anything like a cure for AIDS or a vaccine against HIV, so too, having failed to vaccinate the world in an ecological prophylaxis against the emerging viruses, we cannot cure the world of its consequent viral instability. From this perspective, if we could still talk of perspective from within the disruption of perspective altogether, we might conceive the advent of AIDS and the other emerging viruses to be an event, *epochal* in the strong sense of the term, that exposes our ontoecological extremity. Yet at the same time we would have to think this extremity as also something other than a historical, or even epochal event. In a meditation as remarkable for its modesty as for its insight, Jan Zita Grover demonstrates, first, that it would be but nostalgic fantasy to suppose that a time "before AIDS" was one of ontoecological coherence and stability, that there was once upon a time an ecosystem not always already immunocompromised, an undamaged biosphere; second, and concomitantly, that being is, precisely, damage as such.[16] Being does not—somehow—precede the wounding that it in fact is. It is not that there are

---

14. Thomas E. Lovejoy discusses various ecological factors in the emergence of "new" viruses in "Global Change and Epidemiology: Nasty Synergies," in Morse, ed., *Emerging Viruses,* pp. 261–268. There exists a considerable literature, rather less sober in its considerations than Lovejoy's in that it tends to conceive outbreaks of hemorrhagic fevers (such as Ebola River virus) and AIDS as nature's revenge on the human species for ecological insults. See, for example, Frank Ryan, M.D., *Virus X: Tracking the New Killer Plagues—Out of the Present and into the Future* (Boston, MA: Little, Brown, 1997).

15. Karl M. Johnson, "Emerging Viruses in Context: An Overview of Viral Hemorrhagic Fevers," in Morse, ed., *Emerging Viruses,* p. 55.

16. Jan Zita Grover, *North Enough: AIDS and Other Clear-Cuts* (Minneapolis, MN: Graywolf Press, 1997).

uncontaminated bodies, or worlds, essentially healthy, that subsequently suffer the vicissitudes of illness or ecological insult, but that bodies and worlds, always already bound to illness, death, and damage, are the material fact that being, always already wounded, is wounding or damage as such. In this sense, the epochal event of AIDS and the emerging viruses cannot be construed as a fall from ontoecological grace; the AIDS pandemic is essentially without origin, essentially that being-without-origin that wounding *is*.

We must thus think AIDS to be interminable in at least four respects. First, and a massive literature bears witness to the fact, we cannot responsibly identify an origin, or even a beginning, of the pandemic;[17] second, we cannot anticipate a cure in whatever might count as a future the thought of which would orient and direct a praxis; third, we cannot forecast a conclusion to the pandemic as such (that is, we cannot count on the pandemic burning itself out among the "socially marginalized" dispossessed); and, fourth, we cannot look forward to a time when AIDS is merely endemic, merely chronic, merely one more predicate of being (because AIDS is, in fact, the fact of existential extremity: "AIDS" is not "diabetes").

That AIDS is without term, that AIDS is interminable; that, once upon a time, infinitely long ago (nearly twenty years ago our historians are agreed, but what might be the sense of that chronology?), AIDS emerged and, having emerged, is forever after without beginning; that being endless, what is called AIDS has long since evacuated the very concept of futurity of whatever consolations, in the guise of either hope or despair, it might once have borne; that AIDS consecrates us to a world that is the very absence of redemption or salvation (not even a god can save us now); that AIDS always denotes not only an epistemological object, but also an unobjectifiable terror to which the concept as such is essentially inadequate; that AIDS, therefore, can never become nothing-but the history that it nevertheless also is; that being must henceforth be thought as the extremity of an irremediable exposure: all of this means that we are of AIDS, with the full force of the partitive; that we belong to AIDS; that we belong to what of AIDS is its ownmost. AIDS thus constitutes a surround: not merely a border or edging, nor even merely a horizon (hermeneutic or otherwise), but absolute saturation, the fact that

---

17. A note of overwhelming dimensions would be possible here. Let me simply note that I have learned most from Michael Bresalier, "Problems of Response: AIDS and the Question of Origins in Medical Scientific Practice," Masters thesis in Environmental Studies. Toronto: York University, 1996.

"AIDS" is always also something more than what we can possibly say or know it is. It is in this sense of the surround that Aaron Shurin's *Unbound*, more than a series of meditations "about" AIDS, is, as his subtitle indicates, *A Book of AIDS*.[18] It is insofar as *Unbound* is a book *of* AIDS that it provokes us to think the surround, the very interminability of interminable AIDS.

It is not by what is called choice that Shurin writes of AIDS, even when he is not writing about AIDS. Yet, necessarily, to write of AIDS is to write about AIDS. In an essay from 1995, Shurin recalls that "[b]y the time, early 80s, AIDS began to claim unavoidably my most attention, the poem was emerging as explorative maneuver, and the idea of thematized writing had become problematic. . . . A poetics of inquiry and ellipsis was being privileged over one of declaration and intent" (pp. 71–72). Here we might think we are in a space of artistic and intellectual freedom, where topics, methodologies, theories, poetic practices are arranged, displayed, rearranged, invented, and destroyed promiscuously, if not at random at least wilfully—a volume or space furnished according to the particular genius of a poet. "But the rupturing emergence of the epidemic ready to impale one looked monolithic from any view" (p. 72); thus, "in the holistic dimension of AIDS each seemingly independent or oblique avenue leads inevitably to the viral core" (p. 73). And: "For a writer, this is experienced as a demand. How to write AIDS named me" (p. 72); "AIDS reality has enacted my imagination" (p. 74). It is impossible not to write of AIDS. More than a simple contextual or historical determination (in which case "AIDS" would be nothing more than a catastrophe visited upon being), the surround is not a more or less distant horizon (at least at arm's length), but that of which being derives its being. AIDS saturates being, and thus cannot be said simply to be situated "within" space and time; AIDS is not temporal, but temporality; not spatial situation or location, but an absence of space altogether, the inescapability of being saturated with AIDS.

AIDS, therefore, is always something more than its objectification, something more than the concept it nevertheless also is; AIDS is always something more, something other, than what we can possibly say or think it is. Shurin notes in an essay from 1988 that he is "infected by a vocabulary, a prisoner of its overspecialized agenda," a vocabulary that expresses the knowledge of HIV and AIDS—macrophages, lymphadenopathy, hairy leukoplakia, for

---

18. Aaron Shurin, *Unbound: A Book of AIDS* (Los Angeles: Sun & Moon Press, 1997); further citations will be made parenthetically in the text.

example—that collectively constitute an object, a concept, called AIDS. These terms are deployed as "markers" that describe and delineate an object, a concept, markers that at once express and produce knowledge. Yet in, and as, that very expression and production of knowledge, this vocabulary marks what of AIDS exceeds that knowledge, "the distance between my body and absolute fear" (p. 16). It is this distance of which everything we know, or can possibly know, is the index that is the amorphous terror, the saturating surround, that AIDS also is. It is with this surplus, the interminability of what remains after we have learned all we can possibly know, that Shurin is concerned; this unavoidable supplementary terror is that which in writing about AIDS, Shurin writes of: AIDS writes Shurin as Shurin writes of AIDS. And it is this that constitutes a demand: "Who could have moved me to this end but the men whose names are mentioned here, who were my informants and guides, and whose natural affectional alliances made an epidemic based on love and desire possible?" (p. 8).

This is an extreme, nonnegotiable demand that, first of all, articulates itself simultaneously as a certain haunting, an interpellation, a command, even an accusation; what is demanded, commanded, here is an attention to what can never become nothing-but history. It is the immaterial matter of haunting and ghosts. Like the ghosts who populate the contemporary simulacrum of a folklore, Shurin's ghosts are the transgression, or the figure of the transgression, of the infinitesimal but absolute difference between life and death; the ghosts belong neither to death nor to life, both to death and to life. Always not yet quite visible, but not entirely invisible; not yet quite audible, but not entirely inaudible; not yet quite palpable, but not entirely insubstantial; always almost recognizable, but not quite anonymous, ghosts are uncanny because they are always the figure, at one remove, of being the objects of a sensible intuition, the figure of appearance. Just as it figures appearance, the ghost disappears; always just gone—just now—the ghost is the very figure of that moment "when life goes to death," as Golding says: the uncanny is what we have always just missed, in which sense the apparition is traumatic, "homage to a missed reality," as Lacan says somewhere. The ghost is always insatiably hungry—for revenge, transcendence (peace), resolution, whatever, but in any case, always the figure of a lack. The ghost either figures a wanting-to-be that can never quite be, or a craving for nonbeing that can never quite not be. In its insatiability, the ghost belongs to that which can never quite become nothing-but history. The ghost is the figure of what we can never quite forget altogether, but also of that which memory can never satisfactorily recover: the figure of the impossibility of forgetting what we have forgotten.

The ghost is the figure of what disrupts every attempt at historiographical pacification. If we are fascinated with the uncanny, with the ghost's essential transgression of the infinitesimal, absolute boundary between life and death, it is that very fascination, that haunting, that makes historians of us all, for, as Jacques Ranciere has noted, it is the historian who claims "to cross and recross the river of the dead":[19]

> The difference proper to history is death; it is the power of death that attaches itself solely to the properties of the speaker, it is the disturbance that this power introduces into all positive knowledge. The historian can't stop effacing the line of death, but also can't stop tracing it anew. History has its own life in this alternative throbbing of death and knowledge. It is the science that becomes singular only by playing on its own condition of impossibility, by ceaselessly transforming it into a condition of possibility, but also by marking anew, as furtively, as discreetly as can be, the line of the impossible.[20]

We must therefore acknowledge that AIDS is interminable in the sense that we never have done with the dead, that the dead never become nothing-but history; the work of mourning is never fully accomplished. Moreover, the work of mourning, a historiographical operation, enacts its own impossibility of accomplishment, the incompletion that it most essentially is, in the very work that would pacify the ghost and render the uncanny intelligible; the work of mourning wakens the dead in the very movement that would lay them to rest.[21] And so Shurin is haunted by both the fear of forgetting and the desire to forget (p. 16). Inexorably, AIDS is for Shurin that unavoidable, unthinkable, unsublatable contradiction, that nontranscendence—the interminable as the surround:

---

19. Jacques Ranciere, *The Names of History: On the Poetics of Knowledge,* trans. Hassan Melehy (Minneapolis, MN: University of Minnesota Press, 1994), p. 63.

20. Ibid., pp. 74–75.

21. Commenting on my earlier consideration of the work of mourning, Deborah P. Britzman has argued that even in Freud, the work of mourning always bespeaks its essential incompletion, and that melancholia is therefore no simple "failure" of historiographical pacification; this current consideration owes much to her arguments.

Hell is round, the motif, revealed to me at the reservoir point after being awakened from a weeping dream-cry, may bear Dante's centripetal impasse, but also dimensionalizes AIDS from the personal to the historical: the curve one rounds is also around one, surrounding, a world. For the gay community, this circumnavigate descent can be read as the procession of history itself disappearing. "Che e costui che senza morte/ va per lo regno de la morta gente?" "Who is this that without death goes through the kingdom of the dead?" [p. 74]

The historiographical practice that Shurin's poetics in part is, is as much a disruption as it is a pacification; the very work that would pacify, disrupts. Such is the essential peril of survival, among the effects of a certain determinate but undetermined history.

All of this is among what Shurin's ghosts have in common with even the least uncanny ghosts who populate the imagination of contemporary "popular culture." But in several essential aspects, Shurin's ghosts differ from the consumer-friendly denizens of that imaginary. First, harbingers of "a terror more truculent than fear of the Impossible," these ghosts "pursue. They know my name, and my whole shaken body responds to their address" (p. 66). Far more uncanny and disturbing than Althusser's infamous cop, these ghosts interpellate "Aaron Shurin!" and command Aaron Shurin's attention. There is something accusatory here, something that might almost call for a confession of guilt (perhaps, simply, the guilt of living on). Second, and perhaps consequently, this call (ghost to something-other-than-a-subject, collect, and with the terrible force, if not the meaning, of the Heideggerian *Ruf*) is at some level psychologically and phenomenologically inexplicable. Why one ghost among so many, Shurin wonders, only to realize that "you *don't* choose. The ghost chooses *you!*" (p. 68). If Shurin writes of AIDS, it is because it is impossible not to write of AIDS; if Shurin is called, it is not merely to Althusserian subjectivity. Third, Shurin's ghosts are not site-bound:

The ghosts who walk in my city (my ghostly city) are cast as vividly as any childhood stored in a dipped *madeleine*—with that fleeting precision memory affords, and the rubbed-out edges it requires. And they rise just as suddenly. But their appearances are oddly interdependent, communal. They haunt *bodies* rather than places. Born as adults in affectional mutuality—exchanged caresses and comradely struggles—my reappeared friends remain so framed, and show their faces by traversing planes of living faces: faces overlaying faces. Their anxious, drifting outlines cross and merge with passing strangers—strangers filled with similar resonating passions, and hungers large enough to invite in, whole, another's presence. They flash and seize. (pp. 66–67)

Let us extract from the complexity of this meditation three interrelated points. Shurin's ghosts are "oddly interdependent, communal"; and they are so insofar as they bespeak the essentially anonymous being-in-common of a shared affectivity, a literally polymorphous carnality, the pleasures of material bodies (rather than "the body" as the image of the ego); and, finally, there is an essential determinate indeterminacy (an "overlay"), an essential confusion of the categories of friend and stranger. Shurin's ghosts command an attention to the presence of their present absence, charging Shurin with both a nonforgetting and a desire to forget. As survivor, guilty of his own survival, Shurin becomes, both willingly and unwillingly, a historian; as such, he accounts his first task, and his constant preoccupation, to be that of the witness who, like Lot's wife, testifies to "what I have seen that you must now know" (p. 14).

What is at stake in this testimony? To what is Shurin to testify? What has he seen that we must now know? What is not to be forgotten; what is to be disclosed or exposed; of what *aletheia* would this testimony constitute surety? Is it merely a matter of the secrecy of the past guarded in its very revelation by the custodial historian? Or, a more interesting possibility, is the testimony with which Shurin is charged precisely an exposure of and to the essential indeterminacy of an essentially anonymous, essentially erotic-affective, essentially unobjectifiable being-in-common within which the confusion of friend and stranger, dead and living, is essential? Is this exposure not the exposure of/to a certain extremity? On this reading, the necrological pleasures of the obituary (p. 15); the gossip surrounding HIV status with its attendant histories and attention to the progression of AIDS (pp. 17–18); the "repeatable, unrepeatable necrology" of the Baron de Charlus or of Aaron Shurin (p. 84); and, indeed, the litany of the Names Project Quilt (p. 18) are not (or at least are only intermittently) stagings of scenes of intersubjective recognition. Insofar as obituary, necrology, gossip, and litany are all organized around the singularity of the proper names borne by Shurin's ghosts, they name what absolutely refuses subsumption or sublation (that is, transcendence). They name the essential anonymity of the erotic-affective being-in-common of singularities. What, after all, is so moving in the recitation of names at displays of the Quilt, or on the anniversary of *Kristalnacht,* or inscribed on the Vietnam memorial—or in Shurin's *Unbound*? For any of us, such lists can only intermittently stage an intersubjective recognition scene; how is it, then, that we mourn for, and as, strangers? Is it perhaps that the very anonymity of such nominations, such testimony, is the index of a sociality that might have undone the very structures (more, the very structurality) of what passes for "society"? What if Shurin's ghosts bespeak a being-in-common that would not depend upon the possession of acceptable credentials, the display of which excludes those whom by virtue of that very exclusion we thereby call "strangers"? Why do we insist upon advertising our pedigrees to each other? Are we not, with Shurin, haunted by other possibilities of being-in-common? Is it not perhaps also, and essentially, for those other possibilities—lost—that we mourn when we grieve the stranger? Is it perhaps for an endangered erotics, even the obscene, the "chaotic force of eros," a "depth charge for *change*," that we mourn? (pp. 12–13).

Is this nostalgia for a "time before AIDS" that would—magically—escape the interminability of AIDS? Well, yes, albeit with complications that are not merely symptoms of ironic reserve, complications that distance Shurin's from innumerable other memoirs of the 1970s in queer urban North America.[22] Shurin names his nostalgia as such. In an essay of 1995 in which he contemplates a photograph taken twenty years—an epochal infinity—previously, of "a paradise of pure loss" (p. 78), "[t]he spontaneous fraternal beatitude, renegade eros and radical hilarity of *that* San Francisco hover, like elements of [Chaucer's] celestial Jerusalem, at the apex of memory; no maturity, no fine mellowness, no deepened work dissolves them" (p. 77). This is a "depiction," a *"retention,"* of "life before AIDS" (p. 79). But if so, this is no naive claim to the transparency, or even necessarily the verisimilitude, of representation, for "one no longer knows the actual from the iconic—the icon becomes the actual!" (p. 78). Insofar as we are dealing with an icon, a figure, it is not simply a question of a relation of adequation between representation and represen-

---

22. For a recent example of an *essentially* nostalgic memory of a "time before AIDS," see Allan Gurganus, *Plays Well With Others* (New York: Alfred A. Knopf, 1997); far more naive in all respects is Katie Roiphe's cultural journalism, *Last Night in Paradise: Sex and Morals at the Century's End* (New York: Vintage Books, 1997), remarkable in that it expresses a nostalgia for a time the writer on her own account never knew—historiographical nostalgia as voyeurism. The academic social science literature is hardly immune to this nostalgia. For an example of a nostalgia for the early guts and glory days of AIDS activism (ACT UP, in particular), see Benjamin Heim Shepard, *White Nights and Ascending Shadows: An Oral History of the San Francisco AIDS Epidemic* (London: Cassell, 1997).

tamen; rather, it is a figure of loss as such. The present actuality of this past, its present pastness, and hence the past's presence in the present, resides entirely in its iconicity, its figurality. Furthermore, "something *has* shifted: . . . the very nature of paradise has changed. Even while—eyes dewy—focused back on primal beauty, the unforeseen—HIV—transfigures sight, beholder *and* beheld . . . what did *not* hold—infected—returns to alter the image of origin." Here Shurin then cites Gertrude Stein parenthetically: "Let me recite what history teaches. History teaches" (p. 78). In Ranciere's more general theoretical terms:

> There is history because there is a past and a specific passion for the past. And there is history because there is an absence of things in words, of the denominated in names. The status of history depends on the treatment of this twofold absence of the "thing itself" that is *no longer there*—that is in the past; and that never was—because it never was *such as it was told*. Historical affect is bound to the personal absence of what the names name.[23]

A time before AIDS can only be remembered *as* "a time before AIDS," and as such belongs to AIDS; the time before AIDS is *of* AIDS. Had the past had a different future—as if we were not the past's future—it would not be the past we remember. And the past exists nowhere outside of this remembering ("history" is possessed of no "in itself," the past is irremediably altered by its future). Insofar as the very memory of "a time before AIDS" is itself *of* "AIDS," there is not, nor ever has been, a "time before AIDS." The AIDS pandemic is interminable; it devours past and future in its present.

Between Dante ("Who is this that without death goes through the kingdom of the dead?") and Stein ("Let me recite what history teaches. History teaches."), Shurin recognizes that it is at a remove, as icon or figure of pastness as such ("pure loss"), that the past insists in the present; in this singular loss is figured loss as such. The figure of *this* past figures the past as such, and it is only as such a figure that it insists in the present; history teaches only that history teaches. Here, then, the memorial—whether physical monument, museum, historiography, or historical memory "itself"—is frequently taken to stand as guarantor of transcendence, bulwark against the ravages of time and the erosion of memory, prophylaxis against a certain forgetfulness; on the

---

23. Jacques Ranciere, *The Names of History,* p. 63.

contrary, as we have seen, the memorial is always a double operation, at once a fixing and pacification of the past, but at the same time, and in that very movement, an essential disturbance or insistence of the past, as figure or icon, in the present. Then, "[w]hat constitutes a memorial, a legacy? Where do the bodies I don't see go—no graves, no burning ghats—and how do they reseed a city lost to loss?" (p. 88). What memorial could constitute an appropriate acknowledgment of an essentially anonymous sociality, an essentially transitory being-in-common? What honor, what homage, is it possible to render all that escapes every attempt to fix, stabilize, and objectify it? What trace might honestly mark this passage, this movement that refuses all the seductions of transcendence? What saying could be of, rather than merely about, this passing, this disappearance? What saying might figure the immemorial interminability of this pandemic that renders vain not only every future project but futurity as project, that reduces every past to secrecy? What writing might also be something other than a relation established in representation between an active, knowing subject (the epistemological top) and an inert, passive (dead) object (the ontological bottom)? Is it possible to write history *historically*?

Shurin's writing of AIDS, I suggest, is not, or at least not merely and certainly not essentially, a representation of all that provokes it. True, this writing is testimony to "what I have seen that you must now know" (p. 14); and "the virus has made us talk about it" (p. 15). But this testimony, this talking about HIV and AIDS, does not (or, does not merely) make of us cognitive subjects, epistemological tops ("philosophers," "historians," et al.). And let us take it as true that "I'm a reporter, I see now, rereading this tale. Ten years of AIDS has altered my poetic gift, narrowed my eye, humbled my language"; but, "[d]eath's literalness is what I've been given, and *the poetics of struggle have forged from it not transcendence but enactment*" (p. 35; emphasis added). Shurin's poetics, then, are neither simply representations of struggle, nor a poetics that emerges out of struggle, but a struggle's ownmost poetics, a poetics, *this* poetics, *as* struggle. Writing does not release Shurin from AIDS (into knowledge or wisdom, for example), but is the fact of the impossibility of such release; it is not that Aaron Shurin writes about AIDS, but that a certain thinking engagement with AIDS, the practice of a certain attention to an irreducible erotic-affective being-in-common—a "writing"—*is* that engagement and attention of which "Aaron Shurin" designates a congeries of effects: "AIDS reality has enacted my imagination" (p. 74): "To characterize this visceral struggle as esthetic is to recognize an ecology of paradigms, a

streaming mutuality of influences artistic and social, and to pay attention—
poetics—as if one's life depended on it" (p. 75).

As indeed it does. A visceral struggle, an aesthetics, an engagement with
and attention to its provocation, this poetics is not essentially concerned with
the production of what are called works of art, nor with judgments on or
appreciation of a "work of art" that is but the strangely immaterial remainder
or residue of art's work.[24] That a work of art exists is simply one effect, not
necessarily the most important, of the happening that is art's work. "Here, the
procedures and vocabulary of art fuse with those of daily life . . . to demonstrate the impermissibility of such a separation under these aggressive
circumstances" (p. 73). Art's work becomes a fundamental existential comportment, the micrological negotiation of being-in-the-world, a form of life.
But to say that art's work is existential comportment is neither in the normative sense to aestheticize suffering and death (the interior decoration of death's
beautiful souls), nor does art's work substitute for an erotic-affective negotiation of the damage that being entirely is; art's work is no transcendence, but
the work of nontranscendence; no achievement of the beautiful, neither as
sublation or sublimation. The one who in the performative practice of such a
poetics is figured as a "poet" neither practices a profession in which he and/or
she has faith, nor professes a faith actualized in art's work. One might as well
call oneself a professional breather as a professional "poet." (Critical reviews
would be possible: "X's inhalations possess all the finesse and subtlety we have
come to expect of this most accomplished breather, but in his recent pneumatic
oeuvre a certain too ready sophistication has crept into his exhalations . . .")
The point is this: that art's work, the performative aesthetic practice that *is*
existential comportment, is not a surface that conceals the depth of being's
being, but the surface that is being's most profound depth. As such, it is a
matter of life and death, the disjunct simultaneity of life and death, the
existential comportment of a sovereign being-alongside-death.

Is it then a question of a Heideggerian resoluteness of dasein's ownmost
being-toward-death? Perhaps: I leave the question to others. But an affirma-

---

24. Pertinent to any larger discussion of what of art's work would constitute its
happening (or performance) and to which the work of art thereby produced is largely
incidental would be Jean-Francois Lyotard, *Postmodern Fables,* trans. Georges Van
Den Abbeele (Minneapolis, MN: University of Minnesota Press, 1997), pp. 217–249;
Jean-Luc Nancy, *The Muses,* trans. Peggy Kamuf (Stanford, CA: Stanford University
Press, 1996), pp. 1–39; John Greyson, *Zero Patience* (Cinevista Video, 1994); and an
entire tradition of Zen-inflected "aesthetics" in classical Japan.

tive answer would depend at the least upon a reading of *Being and Time* that did not conflate dasein with subject, ego, or even the individual; and that did not interpret being-toward-death as a relation of temporal extension to a telos or terminus; and that therefore did not confuse resoluteness with an attribute or quality that would be the psycho-phenomenological manifestation of a heroic will. Whatever may be the case in Heidegger, here it is first of all a matter of the body (indeed, of the body that matters); second, of being-alongside-death as an interminable disjunct simultaneity, the relation of nonrelation; and, third, of a certain astonishment, a sovereign astonishment at being not dead that being, as wound, most essentially is.

First, then, the body is nothing other than its difference from the essential indifference of the corpse. This difference is an ultimately unsayable, uncanny difference, an almost negligible difference that is nevertheless absolute, an untraversible, untranslatable yet infinitesimal difference. The material body has no place in fantasy or the imaginary; the body is not an image of the ego. The "body" designates a primordial exposure, the extremity of the material density, the heavy animality, that it in fact is; the "body" designates what of being can never be an object for itself. As such, the body is the fact of place, rather than a point in space; concomitantly, the body in the singularity of its self-identity is not a volume to be filled either by self or by identity. The body therefore knows nothing of lack or insufficiency; the body as such is always, and in all cases, utterly sufficient. What we most often call illness or disability are merely judgments of a relation to the abstractions of so-called "cultural" norms: your feet always reach the ground. The body always gets by. The difficulties of illness and disability, of which the body as such knows nothing, belong to the world. That is to say, strictly speaking, that the body of itself never knows pain; in pain, the body becomes—*is*—pain. It is only on the basis of this fact that the body bears what is unbearable; the body that matters never experiences itself as degeneration, but only as it is—not as the history of which it is the material effect, neither as it was or will be. The body knows suffering, pain, and death only in the extremity of an absolute intimacy: insofar as "I" am body, "I" am not embodied, but the fact of embodiment. It is in this sense that the body is bound to death. This bondage is not interpretable, least of all as fate or destiny (which would situate "death" in the infinite postponement of futurity). The body is bound *to*, not *for*, death: the body is nothing other than its inescapability. The body is bound to the nontranscendence that it in fact *is*. Death and bondage, pain and suffering, bring any I, however psychological, however phenomenological, to the here, now that escapes every psychology, every phenomenology. Here, now, the body is the extremity of being bound to death.

Thus, for the material body as such in the extremity of its exposure, death is not a *terminus ad quem* or a telos, which would abstract the body both into its image and into the abstractions of temporal extension. The body, always *in extremis* (be it the extremity of pain or the extremity of pleasure), is the fact of being always already alongside death. This being-alongside-death is first of all a nonrelation, the absolute but infinitesimal difference between body and the corpse that it nevertheless always also is. This difference, this nonrelation, is absolute. What is called "life" is not a volume or space to be filled or not; one is never half-alive or half-dead. The living body never lacks: it is—absolutely—a plenum, with no "relation" whatsoever to the corpse (that it nevertheless always already also is). Being-alongside-death, however, is the relation of that nonrelation (a relation of nonrelation) we might call "consciousness." The relation of nonrelation is a disjunct simultaneity, therefore the interminable exposure of its extremity.

Now this being-alongside-death, the absolute contingency of the body's interminable difference from the corpse, is inescapable for the person living with AIDS. (Perhaps it will be said that this is the "human condition"; true enough, but I would hurry to counter such abstractions, which are not without a certain political convenience, by suggesting that in that case only the PLWA has become human.) But in any case, this being-alongside-death is not a state of being or of mind, a condition, or a ground. It is simply a—the— matter of fact: it is what is the case. As such, it is not merely an object of cognition, of recognition, or of enlightenment. Being-alongside-death is engaged not in the operatic tragedies of a work of art (do shut up, Tristan: go home and clean the toilet), but in the perversity of art's work, in the performative existential comportments, the micrological negotiations by which we learn and unlearn, make and unmake a proliferation of worlds.

The ghosts who populate *Unbound*—Jackson Allen, Charles Solomon, John Davis, Leland Moss—in their being-alongside-death were not in life half-dead, or merely undead; they did not merely subsist in some crepuscular limbo, with neither affect nor effect, between life and death (all of which are simply ways of reducing the living body of the PLWA to being nothing-but a victim, a proleptic corpse, a ghost). Rather, they engage their dying ("death's proximity," or "death's daily life" [p. 63]) in a nonpositive affirmative poetics as the affirmation of their living. Thus Shurin writes of PLWAs that "if anything besides rage is clear in these drowning surroundings [AIDS as surround], it's the clarity of those few who seem to quicken in their sickness and dying" (p. 31).[25] Here, the PLWA is not reduced to the status of victim, but is encountered as one of those who "live out their evictions in full tenancy" (p. 19). This is not the thought of a half-death, but of the body's vital plenitude alongside—an infinite yet infinitesimal distance from—death: AIDS is not, either in its denomination or in its material effects, a lack of being. Thus, for example, Shurin writes of Eric *"living of* AIDS" (p. 20); of Jackson who dies creatively, actively, engaging "the material world in luscious objectivist presence" (p. 23); of Leland *"trying to die well"* (p. 32); indeed, of young John's *"joie de mourir"* (p. 37); in general, then, of "the meticulous dimensions of life lived thoroughly by those in the process of losing it" (ibid.). And engagement with the interminable being-alongside-death is art's work. (N.B.: This statement is convertible, and it is precisely this convertibility that makes of Shurin's poetics something other than a set of protocols for the production of works of art.) This constitutes a death-bound, fatal, aesthetic practice. This is life lived in the disjunct simultaneity of extremity, *in* (rather than in spite of) suffering and pain, with no future that would redeem that pain, with no salvation or the consolations of eschatology. Art's work, entirely other than a therapeutic practice, produces no work of art, no aesthetic artifact; rather, it is the art of disappearance, a lesson in how to disappear, a lesson in sovereign nontranscendence:

> *My friends reading these drops on paper, of this, now I am sure: We can die with our hats on, we can die with our boots on, we can call ourselves by name as we enter the rolls, we can pierce the ground and draw in the dust—in the dust of ourselves!—on dissolving knees—the complex design of our presence and release.* [p. 24][26]

---

25. Many other citations would be possible, but here is Gillian Rose who, having rehearsed the symptoms of the cancer that would claim her life, wrote, "For what people now seem to find most daunting with me, I discover, is not my illness or possible death, but my accentuated being; not my morbidity, but my renewed vitality" (Gillian Rose, *Love's Work* [London: Chatto & Windus, 1995], p. 72).

26. I have learned much of the "arts of disappearing" from dissertations in progress by John Paul Ricco in art history at the University of Chicago and Taze Yanick in philosophy at Binghamton University; I am grateful to John and Taze for the provocations their work continues to be for me.

3

Demarcations:
Pathetic, Unfinished Thoughts
on a Life by Default

Fadi Abou-Rihan

It was not that I feared to look upon things horrible, but I grew aghast lest there should be nothing to see.

—E. A. Poe

Pain is impossible to describe
Pain is the impossibility of describing
Describing what is impossible to describe
Which must be a thing beyond description
Beyond description not to be known
Beyond knowing but not mystery
Not mystery but pain not plain but pain
But pain beyond but here beyond
—*Laura (Riding) Jackson*

This essay was written in the months following Michael's death. It bears witness to my Identification with his gradual dis-investments, to the descent into inertia that was becoming mine. Its words are not only a phenomenological account of the trauma—if one can still speak of trauma in such instances—but also its manifestation. They are the words of an emotional numbing secure in its over-intellectualising retreat. Implicit in them is a rejection of the moralistic tropes of sympathy, innocence, and victimisation common to what I knew of the AIDS writing at the time. They are dedicated to Michael W. R. Davey, in memoriam, and to she who sometimes goes by the name of Max.

I

One might construe the pathetic as inherently contradictory, a passivity evoking an other's reaction, a passivity provoking at least an attempt at an action, even if it be pitying. But, in its extreme, the pathetic blocks action; it erects a solitude. And herein lies the tension and the difficulty, in the continued presence of a desire that has ceased desiring, in the incomprehensible lacuna and silence that collapse sanity. For the pathetic cannot lie. It is beyond pretence, and hence beyond reason. It does not negotiate. It cannot negotiate. Its nakedness is antithetical to survival.

The pathetic's will to death remains untouched by proximity. The community Alphonso Lingis speaks of, the "community of those who have nothing in common," cannot be retrieved and salvaged.[1] The repeated encounter with one's own mortality in the face of an other's imminent death could lead, in an optimistic moment, to the compassionate richness of a layered resilience and sophistication. In another moment, in the pathetic moment, the paroxysm can only make way for fatigue and brittleness. The capacity to deny, to relegate to the periphery while retreating to the business of the inner core, dissipates. The capacity to deny presupposes a self-directed malleability and an agility the pathetic lacks.

The pathetic does not conquer fear. It feels no fear. It feels nothing. Patheticism is not about an active abasement of either self or external world. It is neither depression nor melancholia. Nor is it sadness, for that too presupposes the presence of a spirit or mood. Patheticism is emptiness, which is not to say alienation—Marxist, existentialist, or otherwise. It is the degree zero of intensity as Deleuze and Guattari would say, a two-dimensional body without organs that admits of no depth of feeling or desire.[2] Of course, it is a "botched" body without organs that prevents production, as Deleuze and Guattari would say, again, but this time lamentingly. But that is no longer a matter for

1. Lingis, Alphonso, *The Community of Those Who Have Nothing in Common* (Bloomington, IN: Indiana University Press, 1994).

2. Deleuze, Gilles, and Guattari, Félix, *A Thousand Plateaus*, trans. Brian Massumi (Minneapolis, MN: University of Minnesota Press, 1987).

mourning or even concern. Failure implies intention, responsibility, and guilt all of which Nietzsche has taught us, time and again, are nothing but the aftereffects of a petrified and sterile reason. The pathetic needs nothing. As one type of body without organs, and contrary to the misleading title of one of Deleuze and Guattari's plateaus ("How Do You Make Yourself a Body Without Organs"), the pathetic is not the culmination of a project or an agenda. For if one wills one's death, it is only after one has already died a thousand tiny deaths.

Stuck between Pathan—a courageous and fierce race in Afghanistan— and pathic—a catamite—the pathetic lends itself, but only mistakenly, to a reclaiming manoeuvre parallel to that undergone by the queer or the perverse, a reclaiming that often takes on the responsibility of exposing the arbitrariness and—dare one say it?—the pathology of the norm. But it should be clear by now that, unlike the queer, the pathetic carries with it no hope, no future deferred condition motivating an active participation in the present moment. Its depleted energies allow for neither earnestness nor irony. Its depleted energies are taken up almost entirely with the task of remaining alive in a mechanical fashion. This is not a will to life but a life by default. Suicide, too, requires earnestness and irony.

If the pathetic cannot speak the language of reason, of redemption or reparation, that is not because it has suffered the magnitude of a wrong that reduces it to silence. For if a wrong has been perpetrated, that wrong is not only the cause of silence but also a "reasonable" response to it. The pathetic does not share a compulsion to speak, nor does it submit to the imperative to speak. It is not a victim either in the current liberal sense of political disenfranchisement or in the sense used by Lyotard as the party that suffers not only the damage but also the loss of the means to prove that damage.

An aetiology of the pathetic would situate it at a moment of saturation. It is neither a breakdown nor an overload but the fullness of an inertia, an inverted ecstasy in which the mind and the body are absorbed in their own emptiness. The body no longer moves. It knows no shiver. It engages no relation. Anything can travel its surface. And for that patheticism is mistaken for submissiveness. And for that its mind is seen as meek, slavish, not quite human. But the pathetic is neither weak nor indifferently proud, though it is indifferent to what traffics its skin, to what uses or abuses its capacities. In a moment of crisis, not only the body but the mind, too, is stricken by a numbness that does not register, and hence cannot respond to, an urgent need for action.

But if the pathetic is not a programme, this does not foreclose on its

desirability. One can see this at work in the second principle of thermody-
namics on entropy and even, and especially, in Freudian pleasure. In one of its
ambivalent registers, outlined in *Beyond the Pleasure Principle,* this pleasure is
not the attainment of a goal but the cessation, or at least the containment and
diminution, of excitation.[3] Less abstract instances of such desirability also
abound. The psychiatric institution harnesses its chemical regimes in order to
check and reduce the extremes of a bipolar disorder, a manic-depression, to
the monotones of a cardiogram. The Nietzschean last man seeks the balance
of a predictable and uneventful existence. His Wagnerian outbursts of emotions are all the more evident in our hyper-frenzied attempts at accumulation
and consumption. Rather than indices of depth or wealth, they function as, at
times, justifications and, at others, symptoms.

To read such symptoms presupposes a familiarity with their drives and
logics, with the languages they speak. It is to share their "tastes" as Nietzsche
would say.[4] One must have already been there, or touched upon there, in some
fashion and to some extent. This is not an appeal to the authenticity of a lived
experience or to a privileged identity. Rather, it is a recognition of the perva-
siveness of the pathetic in however minuscule a dose it may manifest itself.
Freud could write about and treat neurosis only because, in the first instance,
the very fact of "civilization" is premised on the ubiquitous pathology of
repression.

It is not entirely clear, to me at least, whether this writing, my writing,
escapes or embodies the various permutations on either the psychotic split—
between pleasure and reality, affect and intellect—or, most importantly, on
those splits specific to the ego (dissociative as in multiple personality, disavowing as in fetishism, reflective or critical as in self-awareness). For this writing
is not just about the pathetic, a defence against it, or even an expression of its
author's fear of it. This writing is also, in part, and perhaps in spite of its
explanatory posture, a tending toward and a desiring of the pathetic however
untenable that may seem.

And that, indeed, is untenable.

The pathetic described here is a concrete limit, one of many that can

---

3. Freud, Sigmund, *Beyond the Pleasure Principle*, trans. James Strachey, in *On Metapsychology: The Theory of Psychoanalysis* (Harmondsworth: Penguin, 1984), pp. 269–338.

4. Nietzsche, Friedrich, *Thus Spoke Zarathustra*, trans. Walter Kaufmann, in *The Portable Nietzsche* (Harmondsworth: Penguin, 1983), III, p. 11.

circumscribe the activities of a force and define the terrains in which it may circulate. Much like the Deleuzo-Nietzschean active and reactive, the pathetic is not an attribute of individuals but of forces. But unlike the active and the reactive, the pathetic force does nothing. The use of the term "force" might be inappropriate in this instance in the sense that the notion typically invokes an intensity exerted upon an object for the purpose of producing an alteration in its position or constitution. But the intensity of the pathetic force is nil.

To think the pathetic is then to occupy a contradictory and tenuous position that yields neither doctrine nor principle. To think the pathetic is to think the nihil without its -isms, arbitrarily. To think the pathetic is to think the zero, as that which is made to distinguish between negative and positive, dead and alive. Zero is an annulus whose dual boundary always divides and severs. This, by the way, is one of the reasons why Nietzsche's circle, his eternal recurrence, *his* zero, could never be of the same since it is always already the production, and the recurrence, of the double.

Zero, however, is not the nihil of being, its castration or nothingness. Zero is not the excised one. It is almost a painless emptiness, a middle term that not only sets up the present polarity but also upsets and transforms it into an alogical plenitude. As Nick Land puts it, "[t]he nihil is not a concept at all, but rather immensity and fate."[5] But contrary to Nick Land, this immensity and fate are not always of a differentiating *amor fati*, a Nietzschean exuberance and affirmation of life. At times, they can be, and indeed are, the mute and inescapable expanse extending between the two borders life and death. Once again, this is merely an approximation since to characterise the pathetic as an intervention or a disturbance is to almost invariably define it in terms of an action and hence invest it with an energy that it does not seek, the same energy that we, in our attempts to distance ourselves from it, deny it.

II

Though an inexorable illness, AIDS need not be immediately catastrophic. Speaking of the long flight of steps leading from seroconversion to death, the late Hervé Guibert once wrote that the syndrome "gives death time to live and

---

5. Land, Nick, *The Thirst for Annihilation: Georges Bataille and Virulent Nihilism* (London and New York: Routledge, 1992), p. 19.

its victims time to die, time to discover time, and in the end to discover life. . . ."[6] The same thought is echoed by Eve Sedgwick in *Fat Art, Thin Art*:

> No good outcomes with this disease
> but good days, yes—that's the unit
> for now, the day: good day, bad day.[7]

But to watch someone take or even be dragged along the last of these steps where all that is left is just another comatose "day" prolonging a stillness punctuated by nothing except the faint and rhythmic whining of the morphine dispenser—for everything else had already been disconnected—to go through the routine of daily visits and conversations with the attending nurses, out of habit, mechanical, compulsive even, "good day" and "bad day" cease to have any reference. Action may still be possible, but it does become meaningless, if not for the dying person then at least for his or her witness. There are no more plugs to pull. And even if there were, one more or less "day" seems hardly to matter.

Time stops. The drama and melodrama unwind with the collapse of past and future. Instead of charging the moment with an overabundance of energy, whether fetishising or productive, this collapse is akin to an orgasmic release though with the simple but major distinction that the flattening and depletion that ensue in this case were never sought after and could never have been predicted. The machinery of the body without organs no longer responds to stimulus. With the collapse of past and future it is instead caught in a moment of anti-production that is prolonged into an eternity, the eternity of a void and unimpassioned grief.

Confusion and contradiction abound: zero intensities, vacuous plenitudes, and wayward, ungraspable, empty forces. One takes recourse in metaphor partly because the visibility and divisibility of language obscure the event. But even presence has its limits. At times, supposedly, the relevance of what is being said pales next to the fact that something, anything, is being said. I am thinking here of individuals, institutions, and texts that offer themselves as they stand alone for the most intimate of companions. Requiring neither

---

6. Guibert, Hervé, *To the Friend Who Did Not Save My Life* (New York and London: Macmillan, 1991), p. 164.

7. Sedgwick, Eve Kosofsky, *Fat Art, Thin Art* (Durham and London: Duke University Press, 1994), p. 9.

justification nor pretence, they beckon, in their openness, to be read, selectively, to be used for comfort and validation. The confusion of emotions comes across, bitterly at times, and at others with a faint sigh of relief. No compensation here, and no repose. Simply undemanding presence.

But what if that too ceases to carry resonance?

It would seem as if on some level, if not ultimately, to ask that the pathetic be accepted, or at least recognised, on its own inarticulate, unrepresentable, inconsistent, and, most significantly, irredeemable grounds is itself the mark of a pathetic abandon. Reason however cannot afford such luxuries. It can only surrender. And to abandon is not to surrender. The latter always generates a yield, a security of sorts, though the return here might be difficult to grasp. A higher authority—ideological, economic, or military—a higher authority steps in and deploys its repressive mechanisms in order to appease reason's neurotic frustrations. Henceforth, the pathetic is either denied or pathologised.

Equally dismissive, but perhaps more damaging, is the recuperating gesture that insists on locating and salvaging the pathetic from its pitiable mien. It becomes "food for thought." It is chewed upon, digested, defecated. Its nutritional content is made to bolster a moral, aesthetic, or psychological formula. It is transformed into a tragic sacrifice or a learned helplessness. It becomes redeemable for some, and for others the very signpost of redemption. Monuments—texts—are erected in its name as one begins to follow the protocols. Its event and spectacle will henceforth carry a truth and an intensity that locate it in a specific social and political order. It will point to a meaning, an efficiency, a purpose. Its sacrificial story will be registered in the history books—personal or institutional. Barometers of patheticism will be held by guardians of the faith adjudicating over quibbles between the various contenders to the throne. Who is the more pathetic? And is the pathetic "queer" enough, or "feminist" enough, or "coloured" enough? Schizophrenia has already met such a fate, if not at the hands of Deleuze and Guattari, then definitely at the hands of many of us, their readers.

It is not that the pathetic is loftier than such mundane concerns for the learned and the professional. It lies not beyond them, but alongside. And traversing the gap, and at times inadvertently bridging it, are the infrequent, frail, shriveled, and irresolute thoughts that still want to say "I am not alone," thoughts that have been tainted by the pathetic but are not pathetic themselves, or at least not yet.

4

One Train
May Be Hiding Another:
History, Memory, Identity,
and the Visual Image

Thomas Elsaesser

It has almost become a commonplace to say that our notion of history has entered a deep conceptual twilight zone, which seems to affect many of its traditional signposts and markers: our notion of temporality and causality, our notion of agency and veracity, our notion of absence and presence. Let's take an everyday example. I switch on the television to watch the evening news. A famous politician has just died, a terrible accident. But there he is, on the screen, making a speech, shaking hands, moving briskly to his waiting limousine. . . . Have I misheard, or is he speaking from beyond the grave? And if so, what is his message? Maybe his words are merely the echo of a cruel irony that escapes him, the better to strike me?

This irony is directed at history. Where once it was something one read about, one inspected through stone monuments and written documents, one drew lessons from or tried to leave behind, it now appears to exist in suspended animation, neither exactly "behind" us, nor part of our present, but shadowing us rather like a parallel world, hyper-real and unreal at the same time. With it, the famous phrase of "mastering the past" has changed connotation: today, cinema and television will master the past for us, principally by digitally remastering some sound and image archive footage, as in Woody Allen's *Zelig* or Robert Zemeckis's *Forrest Gump*. Neither distant nor near, history has become a kind of perpetual action replay, a Ghost Dance of the undead. Like a moving train, it seems to pass ours, possibly in the opposite direction, with human beings facing us through brightly lit carriage windows. Political or social events whose momentous significance we instinctively intuit, television turns into happenings, bizarre accidents, spectacular surprises, or terrifyingly surreal collages, only to return to them tomorrow as stories and narratives: with heroes and villains, conflicts and climaxes, and simple morals to be drawn. The fall of the Berlin Wall, the "velvet" revolutions in Eastern Europe, Mikhail Gorbachev's or Margaret Thatcher's forced resignations, Desert Storm, or civil war in Bosnia: no sooner do these events disappear from the nightly news bulletins than they become not just the past, but a past on which television networks or film companies have put a team of scriptwriters and researchers. History, it seems, has dropped out of sight and grasp between the newsflash of today and next month's miniseries. The irrational is tamed and compensated by the familiarly real of the docudrama. Future generations, looking at the history of the twentieth century, will never be able to tell fact from fiction, having the media as material evidence. But then, will this distinction still matter then?

Thus, the irony I referred to has to do not only with history's relation to truth and the real; it also affects our place in space and time, in short, our identity. This might be the second casualty of the media in history. We have learnt to put up quite happily with these metaphysical double takes occurring in our living rooms, taking for granted these effects of virtuality whose invention 100 years ago was greeted as a new conquest of reality. But if the cinema came into being as a way of recording the real and preserving time, its marriage with television and video has begun to bleed also into the sense of ourselves as creatures existing in a single spatio-temporal extension. While the dis-location of our selves in time and space is a fundamental aspect of modernity, especially where personal, cultural, or national identity compete with each other as so many intersecting circuits, we have yet to grasp what role the media are playing in this. Cause or effect, agent or consequence? Where identity once was the constantly affirmed sense of belonging to a geographical or linguistic community, the massive presence of the media have intervened and interposed themselves in paradoxical ways, exacerbating the rupture and healing it at the same time. One used to go to the cinema for a voyeuristic window on the world. Now, the ubiquity of television has changed the relation between the two media, making the cinema into a veritable identity-machine, a place to lose one's identity, in order to experience—in the form of fantasy, horror, or science fiction—the pleasures and terrors of otherness. Television is the exact opposite: it neither needs nor tolerates otherness, but makes the strange familiar, remaking the world in the image of the sitcom family. It socializes the self into identity by offering companionship and help, by being the perfectly behaved guest in the living room, the amiable host at the village fete, the show-master at life's birthday parties. In short, it wants to be the mirror-image of our fantasies of domesticity.

History and identity: these, then, may be two of the concepts around which to assess the impact of 100 years of cinema. And a first conclusion would be to suggest that the ambivalence which in our culture still meets the media stems from not quite knowing how to defend or redefine one's sense of selfhood and temporal coherence, in the face of ever more identifications substituting for identity, and ever more histories substituting for a past. My purpose in this essay, then, is to look at some of the strategies which film- and television-makers in the Netherlands have recently pursued, in order to engage with what one might call these "identity politics" of the media age, where neither national cinema nor national television, neither national identity nor national culture can be assumed unproblematically, because none quite encompasses the knowledge of living in ever more multifaceted societies and participating in ever more discontinuous histories, while still clinging to our belief in the singular and the individual.

One of the battlefields of these new identity politics is "memory." As history evaporates, becoming in the process the very signifier of the inauthentic, the false and the falsifiable, memory has gained in status, as the repository of genuine experience, the last refuge of what inalienably makes us who we are. What more appropriate instrument to record and preserve memory than sight and sound? "Let's work on our memories" was the call to arms of German filmmaker Edgar Reitz, when he undertook his momentous epic of rural life between 1919 and 1979 with the television series *Heimat* (1979–1984). In a remarkable piece of *Alltagsgeschichte* (the history of everyday life), Reitz set out to show how one can use the cinema and television as a site of memory and commemoration, and an enthusiastic public all over the world confirmed the power of his project. But nowhere else in Europe, perhaps, has the practice of using film as a medium of documentation for oral and visual testimony had such a long and fertile tradition as in the Netherlands. Kees Hin *(Na de Jodenvervolging,* 1985), Willy Lindwer *(Terug naar mijn schtetl Delatyn,* 1992), Frans Bromet *(Buren,* 1992), Marjoleine Boonstra *(Our Man in Kazachstan,* 1993), or Jos de Putter *(Het is een schone dag gewest,* 1994) are only some of the names that come to mind that have in recent years renewed traditions of documentary, drawing on history (especially that of the Jews in both the Netherlands and Eastern Europe), interviewing neighbours (exposing their dark passions and long memories when harbouring grudges against each other), or portraying the strength of mind and the frailty of body among remarkable (or indeed quite ordinary) individuals. Not only does the everyday attain a new dignity, humour, and poignancy in their films; many of the films give people a chance to speak about how they live their lives and see their world, who, prior to the electronic media, would neither have been given the word, nor have attained credibility as witnesses of their times and of the human condition. Faces and gestures, accents, the grain of the voice, landscapes and places come into view that demand a kind of respect, a commitment to the real and the authentic, for which Dutch filmmakers are justly famous. With them, another generation of documentarists, visual ethnographers and participant observers, armed with a camera and a Nagra tape recorder have followed in the tracks laid by Joris Ivens, Herman van der Horst, Bert Haanstra, and Johan van der Keuken.

Navigating between audiences in the cinema and finance from television, many a documentary has thus been made in the last decade that seeks to preserve for the medium a truly democratic dimension, while sacrificing none of the poetry for which their predecessors are deservedly known. By marking what is personal about the past, by bearing witness and giving testimony, such films add a new dimension to memory, connecting the speaking subject to both temporality and mortality, creating "pockets of meaning," in the sense that one can speak, in a guerilla war, of "pockets of resistance."

Remembering, giving testimony, and bearing witness can be tokens of a fight not only against forgetfulness, but also against history, doubly devalued as the mere residue when the site of memory has been vacated by the living, and as the carcass picked clean by the vultures of the media. Yet are the media not themselves the bearers of the flickering flame of memory, and impose on what they show the uncanny sense of "presence" that only a film achieves? It may be that the line where personal memory passes into public history is a thin one, being all too often crossed in either direction. These thoughts were provoked by three apparently unconnected film and television experiences, which however obliquely, responded to the initial question I posed myself about the place of the media at the end of a century. One was a film shown originally on television, entitled *Herinneringen aan Nederland* (*Remembering the Netherlands,* 1992) by Joes Roelofs and Jan Blokker. The second was a three-part television drama subsequently released as a cinema film, *Oude Tongen* (*Tongues Wagging,* 1994), by Gerardjan Rijnders, and the third a 1994 television documentary by Cherry Duyns about one of the most famous film images of the Second World War, *het meisje,* a female inmate of the Westerbork transit camp, destined for the death camps, briefly glimpsed on film. What connected these three programmes was indeed the relation between representation and memory, but in ways that neither quite confirmed my pessimism about history, nor my optimism about memory.

Herinneringen aan Nederland is a documentary about the village of Heiligerlee, site of a famous battle, where the Dutch defeated the Spanish and from which historians date the origins of Dutch national identity. In its search for the historical sites and places of the nation's memory, it was reminiscent of a French initiative, originally launched by the then minister of culture, but begun in earnest by the historian Pierre Nora, under the name of *lieux de mémoire* (places of memory). When the first volumes appeared in print, *lieux de mémoire* became the object of discussion among Dutch academics and writers, culminating in a series of articles in the *NRC Handelsblad*, asking whether a similar effort of gathering, inventorizing, and recording the customs and costumes, the food recipes and memorials should not also be undertaken on behalf of the peoples of Dutch Republic, before the ravages or modernization had obliterated all physical traces, and the pressures of tourism had Madurodamned each city and every last village. *Herinneringen aan Nederland* seemed almost to want to rise to this challenge. What Blokker's commentary notes is that the actual physical site bears few traces, if any, of this "history," but that, in another sense, Heiligerlee is so typically an average Dutch village of the 1990s that it can well stand as a symbol of the absence, today, of any specifically national memory. The film seems both glad and sad about what it finds. Glad that Heiligerlee has not been turned into the nation's historical theme park. Sad that so little remains by which one could commemorate the "birth of a nation." Looking for "real" history and memory, a documentary film, if it is honest, can only record absence. Mindful perhaps of Jean-Luc Godard's dictum ("the cinema creates memory, television is in the business of fabricating Forgetfulness"), *Herinneringen aan Nederland* seemed to hesitate between the two, not quite sure whether it was art cinema or a television documentary in the Dutch tradition: it may have wanted to be the former but did not have either quite the resources nor (happily) the necessary sense of self-importance. But it also seemed to take its distance from the documentary. Prominent were the stylistic marks of a certain idea of cinema: slow pans, static shots perfectly framed, empty vistas, long silences. One thought of Antonioni and *L'Avventura* or *Deserto Rosso*. By way of comparison to the filmmakers mentioned above, who had tried to created a kind of folk memory by recording the speaking voice and focusing on weather-beaten faces set starkly against sea and sky, *Herinneringen aan Nederland* tried to avoid all of this by almost voiding the frame of animated life, creating a kind of vortex into which eye and ear were drawn, thereby appealing the more strongly to the viewer to provide his or her own memories, becoming active in response to a gap—an absence the filmmakers had carefully prepared. As it happens, Bernardo Bertolucci's *Novecento* (a spectacular epic about the coming into being of Italy as a fascist nation) was scheduled against *Herinneringen aan Nederland* on one of the other network channels: zapping between the two, I could not help being struck by the stark contrast this opened up about fashioning national history as national identity, of memory as mythology, and history as spectacle.

The strategy of Roelofs and Blokker, of course, was directly related to their subject matter. For what witnesses and voices could be recovered for events dating back some 400 years? Yet it occurred to me that the filmmakers might also have gone about it in a different way, and that there were histories in Heiligerlee whose traces *Herinneringen aan Nederland* does not seem to be looking for, but which may nonetheless be *lieux de mémoire* for the nation as nation. If the Dutch people, as we are told by Blokker, do not have a national identity to which they feel an instinctive emotional allegiance ("champions of the short memory" he calls his countrymen and women), they are—as market researchers and opinion pollsters point out—extraordinarily loyal to their national television. This loyalty, too, must have left traces and thus constitute a history. It may not be the reference to a historical referent that makes up this history, which could then be conveniently recorded on television, but reference to television as creating its own remembered reality. About this, the inhabitants of Heiligerlee might have memories, sharper ones than even about Liberation Day in 1945. The big flood of 1953, for example, the first natural disaster in the Netherlands receiving media-saturation coverage, or the day their television set was delivered, or who they saw their first television show with (often, it seems, over at grandmother's house), the early Eurovision programmes (which coincided with the first televised soccer world championship in Switzerland), a Royal Wedding or a coronation.

Perhaps the sense of sociability, of coming together around shared feelings, which such a national media history might document, is after all not so different from what the peasants of Heiligerlee might have told Blokker had he been there at the time: about winters that destroyed the crops, or strange sightings, or soldiers looting and taking all the pickled beef. One thinks of Bruegel's *The Fall of Icarus* (and W. H. Auden's poem it inspired: "*Musée des Beaux Arts*"). When, one might ask, will media history have its *école des annalistes* locating such electronic *lieux de mémoire*? To speak about remembering and forgetting in the Netherlands today may risk forgetting about the surface, the ordinary, the everyday, of which television is, willy-nilly, our collective guardian. The fact that Western Europe has been without a war, a famine, a plague, or any other event that really went to the heart of everyday experience for precisely these fifty years of television, the lifetime of at least one if not two generations, means that we have had the luxury of building a culture and a cultural memory of the banal, the everyday, of what interests ordinary people, what amused them and what moved them, what they saw in the movies and on television: a history of leisure and of "killing time," alongside the history of all the killing fields on television.

So, once more, we may be deceiving ourselves when contrasting too sharply authentic memory with inauthentic (media-) history. A new authenticity may be in the making, or rather, with the audio-visual media not only writing their own history and creating a kind of second-order memory, representation itself may have become a second-order reality. When we ask: "Do you remember the day John F. Kennedy was shot," do we not actually mean "Do you remember the day you watched Kennedy being shot on television?" And not only once, but all day, or all week, as after the Challenger disaster, when the space shuttle seemed to explode into a starburst of white smoke on our retinas over and over again. For these moments, which we may well pass on to our grandchildren as authentic memories, the category of memory as I have been using it so far does not seem appropriate. Such images belong to a different kind of reality: that of obsession or trauma, to which correspond a different kind of action and placing of the self, based on re-telling, repeating, not working-on, but working-through. For this, television is indeed predestined, for otherwise, how to explain its most obvious feature, the compulsion to repeat?

Oude Tongen, too, is the story of a Dutch village, that of Oude Pekela. But the contrast with Heiligerlee could not be more marked, since Oude Pekela is notorious for a different kind of battle: that over the souls and bodies of a group of children, supposedly sexually abused by their parents, corrupted by satanic cults, and made to pose and expose themselves for pornographic videos. Going back to 1987, the *zedenaffaires* of Oude Pekela and de Bolderkar (where similar incidents were reported) at the time caused a predictable commotion: shock, horror, and outrage that such things could happen in the tidy world of dikes and tulip fields was followed by a more evenly divided, though no less emotional debate over whether anything had actually happened to the children, or whether, not unlike medieval witch-hunts, one was dealing with a case of village mass hysteria, with which the media had only too willingly colluded.

Here memory shows its other side, drawing attention to a problem that in recent years has stirred feelings all over the Western world: the debate over "repressed memory," over Freud's "discovery" of infantile sexuality, and the hesitation between crediting his (mainly female) patients with memories of incest or abuse by parental figures, or hypothesizing a basic fantasy scenario which children imagine as they pass through the traumatic phases from pre-oedipal to sexual identity and emotional maturity. With the strength of the women's movement, Freud's eventual assumption of the so-called "seduction fantasy" came to be challenged as a patriarchal cover-up, making the recovery of repressed memories of sexual abuse a major step in empowering women and thus in female "identity politics." Where such cases of child abuse either came to light or were rumoured to have occurred, entire families, whole communities came to be pitted against each other, with almost everyone a potential suspect of the most terrible transgressions, while social workers called in the police, who had children forcibly removed from their parents. But as Rijnders makes clear in an interview, when he first read about the Oude Pekela affair in *Vrij Nederland*, he was convinced that the children had been abused, but when he read a series of pieces in *de Haagse Post*, he was equally convinced that nothing of the sort had occurred, which in turn convinced him that his real subject as a filmmaker was not "the truth," but rather this hesitation around the question itself.[1] Consequently, Rijnders opted not for a documentary, but made a fiction film which combined the stylized social satire of a low-budget thriller with the comic exaggeration of a pantomime. Alluding to David Lynch's cult television series, *Twin Peaks* (on a similar subject, it will be recalled), Rijnders creates a dreamscape and fairy-tale world, which nonetheless has all of the chilling horror of a nightmare from which nobody seems to awake. What is particularly noticeable is that here is a village where the television set is always on, and where the VCR, glossy or pornographic magazines, and the corner shop videotheque have become standard features of daily life, giving a portrait of domestic sociability equally far removed from the rural idylls of Reitz' *Heimat* as from the prosperous ordinariness of Blokker's Heiligerlee.

In *Oude Tongen*, memory has become another country altogether: indistinguishable from bizarre dreams and surreal fantasy, from half-remembered

---

1. See "VPRO Gids," 7–14 May, 1994, p. 2.

scenes from childhood and images out of the television set, all of them fed by gruesomely realistic toys and the behaviour of gruesomely egotistical or sexually frustrated adults. To believe Rijnders' film, electronic images are indeed in one way or another set to supersede our own memory as recollection and a test for truth. While I had argued above that television, by creating memories we can share as a common culture, might be able to restore something like a sense of identity at once "individual" and "national," the media in Rijnders merely contribute to a generalized atmosphere of hysteria and fairy-tale horror. In the process, all manner of forces are "faking," "stealing" or "colonizing" individual memory, to the point where the question of recovery no longer even poses itself.

One may recognize in Rijnders' approach the theatre maker's delight in melodrama and Grand Guignol, and his correspondingly mixed feelings about television. But the dilemmas he raises in his treatment of both history and personal memory are nonetheless real enough, as one reflects on the fact that, given the proliferation of images as tokens of reality and as icons of history, our audio-visual culture has been brutally selective. Whether it is a matter of finding the image for a war, like the shot of a row of emaciated men behind barbed wire that has come to signify the barbarity of "Bosnia," or the face of a child covered with flies to signify a human disaster like the famine in Ethiopia, the media are always in need of visual shorthand, not caring what the "constructed" nature of such "representations" of the real suppresses, excludes, or simply keeps off-frame.

Put more sharply and more concretely, it is not only a question of whether the single image or frame can stand for an entire event, but also whether, quite generally, the one can stand for the many, whether one human being can give up his or her individuality to become a symbol, and whether one human being can represent a collective, can speak on behalf of others, in a medium where the single image and the individual voice have assumed a new power, often possessing the aura once bestowed only on the artist as the socially endorsed witness of society and the work of art as trans-individual, valid testimony.

The urgency of what I've called electronic or audio-visual *lieux de mémoire* coming under the same kind of scrutiny as more solidly physical monuments or documents was brought home to me by my third example, a detective film in the guise of documentary, which vividly illustrates how vital this struggle may be over collective images and individual identities. I am referring to *Gesicht van het Verleden* by Cherry Duyns. It is a film about *het meisje,* "The Girl," who for many Dutch symbolizes what the Germans did to the Jews in the Netherlands when they herded them together in the Westerbork concentration camp and then transported them to Auschwitz. First discovered in a documentary film shot on the orders of the German commandant to keep a trophy of his exploits and prove to his superiors his flawless efficiency as a dispatcher and executor of orders, the single frame has been reproduced a hundred times on book covers and posters, so much so that it has become, paradoxically, almost as common an icon as Churchill's victory salute, or — dare one say — James Dean. It is indeed an image to haunt the mind, never forgotten, and which the Jewish community, furthermore, is determined not to have forgotten. Pictured in the small opening of a cattle truck, just before the door is shut and bolted, she is the reason why I gave this essay its title, translated from the French *"un train peut en cacher un autre"*: a sign, familiar to anyone who has stood at a level crossing in rural France: "Attention! One train may be hiding another." For the girl from Westerbork, symbol of the Jews, of Auschwitz, and the Holocaust, was, and is, an individual with a name, an origin, an identity. And it turns out that her name is Settela, her origin not Jewish at all, her ethnic identity that of a Sinti, and her fate not Auschwitz, but Bergen Belsen. No doubt, she perished in Bergen Belsen as surely as she would have in Auschwitz, but the difference is not negligible. One Holocaust, as we have come to learn at our cost, hides others, one image's symbolic force may obscure another reality. To reclaim the truth of the suffering of the European Sinti and Romani is not to make it "compete" with that of the European Jews, however much the discovery of Settela's identity at first upset the sensibilities of Dutch Jewry.

On the contrary, it is the very force of the images of the Jewish Holocaust, and the work of memory subsequent generations of survivors and descendants have devoted to it, which should make us not only sensitive to genocide elsewhere and in our own time, but also to the power of the still image taken from a film, once reinserted into the flow of history, of sequence and consequence, to preserve a truth not available to the single image, or even the single voice. A historian and a filmmaker were able to open up this "face of the past" by painstaking work in the archives and the written records, the lab reports and eyewitnesses. Thus, by looking at the leaves on the trees, the chalk marks on the wagons, and the very boards from which the side panels were constructed, the researchers could determine that the transport was not the one in February, but must have been the one recorded for mid-May, which is to say the one that took the Gypsies in Westerbork to Bergen Belsen. A startling discovery, but also an object lesson.

For in a metaphoric sense as well as literally, any image is always more densely packed with information and resonance than the simple substitution of the one for the many—the icon for the reality—might suggest. The new truth of the face may have deconstructed the mythic force of the image, but in a sense it has restored another truth to the image, indeed, intensified its force as a symbol. Now when we see the image of "The Girl," we think of Jews *and* Gypsies, we think of history and its obliteration, we think of the one and the many, and we think of both our national and our European identity, hopefully in a new light.

After the gloomy picture I painted at the beginning, this seems to offer some hope: there may after all be reason to trust our audio-visual reality, which means to work at it, and work with it, so that one truth can not only cover another but also be recovered by another. A train may indeed hide another, as one image hides another, but alert to the histories and identities each carries with it, neither television nor the cinema need to be the train that runs us over.

Part II

Repetition

5

The Psychical Nature of Trauma: Freud's Dora, the Young Homosexual Woman, and the *Fort! Da!* Paradigm

Ellie Ragland

The burgeoning field of trauma studies in literature, occasioned, in particular, by Holocaust studies, as well as Women's studies and African-American studies, has led many literary critics to postulate trauma as itself a limit on representation. What makes this area of study particularly germane to literary critique and analysis is their finding there, not an extra-linguistic component which would seem to belong to the field of history. Rather, what appears in narrative accounts of trauma are the pathetic, suffering, passionate, and affective dimensions that literary language and genres have always sought to embody and recount. In Shoshana Felman's words, working with trauma in the classroom, whether through fiction, historical fiction, or poetry, has the pedagogical effect of "break[ing] the very framework of the class."[1]

Relating the descriptive words used by her students on the occasion of their having viewed a videotaped session of Holocaust testimony, Felman finds commonality between the students' words and those of various poets, such as Paul Célan and Mallarmé. Célan recalls "A strange lostness/Was palpably

---

1. Shoshana Felman, "Education and Crisis, or the Vicissitudes of Teaching," in *Trauma: Explorations in Memory,* ed., with intro. by Cathy Caruth (Baltimore, MD and London: Johns Hopkins University Press, 1995), p. 50.

present," while Mallarmé speaks of "the testimony of an accident."[2] But, the larger point to come out of trauma studies is that art cannot be seen as separate from life, or as separable from a certain normal affectivity which is the very domain of literary language.

The goal of this essay is to link the relation of trauma to memory in terms of its speech, displaced in symptoms, passion, affect; to unveil the nature of traumatic catastrophe as a literal, historical event; to argue that the limits of representation in trauma tell us something new about the affects (as opposed to cognition) which Lacan tried to explain by his category of the real. Further on, I shall relate my argument to Freud's Dora case, his "Fragment of a Little Hysteria" (1905),[3] his study of "The Psychogenesis of a Case of Homosexuality in a Woman" (1920),[4] and his comments regarding the trauma undergone by his young nephew in the *Fort! Da!* paradigm.[5] I shall reconsider these in light of Lacan's interpretation of Freud's theory of the object in reference to his *Seminar IV* (1956–1957): *The Object Relation.*[6]

Critics working in this new mode of literary and cultural studies have isolated certain features marking a clear set of *responses* that arise from trauma material. Dori Laub, for example, speaks of the *temporal delay* that carries one beyond the shock of a first moment of trauma to what inevitably follows; a *repeated* suffering of the event. Traumatic memories—whether recounted by Holocaust survivors, incest victims, survivors of rape, or any abuse—have the characteristic of reappearing with a literal repetitiveness that reminds one of Freud's discovery that, at the point where one would expect the pleasure principle to function, one discovers, instead, that *Beyond the Pleasure Principle* (1920) lies repetition whose fixities are on the side of the death drive.[7] Lacan put forth the theory that what is repressed in the real—the order of trauma, of the unsayable, unspeakable, the impossible—will return in the symbolic

2. Paul Célan, "The Meridian," trans. Jerry Glenn, *Chicago Review,* 29, no. 3: 29–40; Stéphane Mallarmé, *Oeuvres complètes* (Paris: Gallimard, 1945).

3. Sigmund Freud, "Fragment of an Analysis of a Case of Hysteria" (1905 [1901]), *Standard Edition* 7: 3–122. (Hereafter abbreviated as *SE.*)

4. Sigmund Freud, *The Psychogenesis of a Case of Homosexuality in a Woman* (1920), *SE* 17: 146–172.

5. Sigmund Freud, *Beyond the Pleasure Principle* (1920), *SE* 18: 3–64.

6. Lacan, *Le séminaire, livre IV (1956–1957): La relation d'object,* ed. Jacques-Alain Miller (Paris: Seuil, 1994).

7. Ellie Ragland, *Eassys on the Pleasures of Death: From Freud to Lacan* (New York: Routledge, 1995), cf. chapter 3, "Lacan's Concept of the Death Drive."

order of language. A trauma, in other words, will not just disappear. It cannot simply be forgotten. Not only will it remain recorded in the real as a limit point to memory, it will reappear as a symptomatic enigma which opens onto a certain anxiety. In his *Seminar X* (1962–1963): *L'angoisse*, Lacan stresses that the anxiety accompanying a trauma is not doubt.[8] Rather, its effects have remained inscribed as an unconscious system of knowledge which appears in conscious life as a concrete insistence, whose characteristic modes are repetition, passion, strong affect, or a suffering that one cannot simply and easily talk away or talk through. Trauma, in Lacan's estimation, is not only *not* doubt; it is, rather, the *cause* of doubt.

Lacan stresses an unfamiliar picture of the causality of trauma, then: it is a *kind* of certainty that can be known insofar as it is acted out. Put another way, behind an affect caused by trauma, one finds the movement of *cause* itself as a return of the real into the symbolic. Precise knowledge regarding the trauma's cause can, therefore, be ascertained at the point of the return: the name Lacan gave this particular kind of meaning was the *symptom*.

Yet, the symptom of a trauma seems not to be exactly the same as the symptom of a neurosis—as trauma studies show—nor of some biologically induced pathology. Not surprisingly, one learns that the characteristic features of trauma are the *secrecy* and *silence* that surround it. And, insofar as secrecy and silence are symptomatic of an event whose core meaning has been permanently displaced—is not known directly—or until such time as the truth of the unbearable can be spoken by the person traumatized and, subsequently, heard by others, the trauma can *only* enunciate itself as an enigma. It can only spawn the kind of *symptoms* that speak of what is not there, not sayable.

Without specifying any psychoanalytic category of neurosis, psychosis, phobia, and so on, Lacan, in his later teaching, evolved a theory of the *symptom* that may well be fruitful for trauma studies. His work here is of a piece with his theory of what knowledge is; of how the mental is structured. Having spent decades elaborating three interlinked categories which compose the base unit of meaning which he called the Borromean knot, Lacan added the fourth order of the *symptom* in the 1970s to his categories of imaginary, symbolic, and real exigencies,[9] arguing that the symptom knots together each

---

8. Jacques Lacan, *Le séminaire, livre X (1962–1963): L'angoisse,* December 19, 1962, unedited Seminar.

9. Jacques Lacan, *The Seminar: Book XX (1972–1973): Encore,* ed. Jacques-Alain

individual unit of real/symbolic/imaginary material into a vast, elaborate signifying necklace of associated images, words, and affects that produce the meanings we live by. The knot would be central to any interpretation of trauma, insofar as it ultimately resides in the real, while retaining properties of each of the other orders of meaning. Topologist and Lacanian analyst Jeanne-Granon Lafont writes that Lacan used the order of the knot as centered on the presence of a space where the object *a* writes itself, at the center of the Borromean unit, for example. The imaginary, real, and symbolic are placed one on the other such that the fourth exigency which knots them—what Lacan called the order of the symptom—represents the Freudian concept of psychic reality. But insofar as this reality rests on an unconscious fantasy, it remains invisible.[10]

Lacan, in other words, described the symptom as constituting the order of meaning that ties together the microstructures of each Borromean triadic unit: the symbolic order of language, the body interpreted as an imaginary consistency, and the affective real of discontinuities and cuts. Each person is not only a *symptom*, in a general sense, of his or her kind of desire—neurotic, normative, or phobic, for example—more importantly for Lacan, this fourth order of meaning marks the particularity of the concrete and literal events that give rise to trauma in an individual life. In 1987 Jacques-Alain Miller described the Lacanian concept of the symptom in *Joyce avec Lacan* as an enigma written in secret characters which in and of themselves say nothing to anyone. They are a message to be cyphered.[11]

In his concern to stress this particularity in each person's language, Lacan took recourse to the Medieval French spelling of the word *sinthome* to describe an enigmatic meaning that appears in any person's behavior or thought like a *knot*. While the symptom has the structure of a knot, its unique meaning(s) arise out of the memories that have been blocked at some limit point we recognize as trauma. By calling the knot real, Lacan means that it is extrinsic

---

Miller, trans. Bruce Fink (New York: Norton, 1998); cf. also *Le séminaire, livre XXIII (1975–1976): Le sinthome,* unedited Seminar.

10. Jeanne Granon-Lafont, *Topologie lacanienne et clinique analytique* (Cahors: Point Hors Ligne, 1990), p. 112; cf. also Jacques Lacan, *Le séminaire, livre XXII (1974–1975): R.S.I.,* unedited seminar; and the session of January 14, 1976, text established by Jacques-Alain Miller, *Ornicar?,* no. 3 (1975): pp. 96–97.

11. *Joyce avec Lacan,* ed. by Jacques Aubert, preface by Jacques-Alain Miller (Paris: Navarin, 1987), p. 11 of the preface.

to the units of meaning it ties together. It is put into language and identifications, as if from outside them. And it refers to the signifier for sexual difference—the signifier without a signified that Lacan denoted as a third term or the signifier for a Father's Name—which also has the properties of alienating the real of experience by the language that represents it. The more primordial experience of the cut belongs to a logic of the real as it marks the loss of objects-cause-of-desire as the first and most important traumatizing experience an infant must undergo as he or she assumes language and, later, sexual identity.

One might argue that all psychoanalytic resistance has the structure of a knot—an enigma or impasse—which proves that some limit point of blockage lies in a person's thinking *about* his or her life at a point which makes the first two traumas of life structural ones: infant loss of the partial objects that metonymically represent the *symbolic* mother as real[12] and *Oedipal* loss of an identification of Oneness with the mother as a difference that structures sexuation as a split between the object *a* and the law of interdiction to being One with the mother.

Lacan offers, I shall maintain, a theory that is not incompatible with contemporary trauma studies in the United States in his theory of the *symptom/sinthome*. It may even add another dimension to understanding the limit points in memory as themselves having a certain structure and logic. Cathy Caruth suggests that one exits from a trauma through a speaking of the truth, and a listening to that truth, *from the site of the trauma*.[13] Put in other words, the Other—the social order—must *hear* what is actually being said: a transference relation must be engaged such that a representative listener from the social order believes the *truth* that seeps through the imaginary dimensions of a narrative. The history of a trauma becomes not so much an accurate rendering of an event, then, as the actual belief of hearers that certain events can—and, indeed, have—produced unthinkable, unsayable, unspeakable, buried memories. Lacan called these the *sinthomes,* or opaque disturbances, whose limit is that of representation itself. The Other—whether the analyst as witness or some other—must, in some way, cease defending his or her (unified) concept of reality, and attend to the *picture* given by the traumatized person. Likewise, in literary texts, certain *symbolic insistences* on the truths

---

12. See Lacan, *Seminar IV,* p. 269.
13. See "Introduction," *Trauma: Explorations in Memory,* p. 11.

caused by a trauma—whether known consciously or unconsciously by the author—will remain buried in the density of language.

Freud made the point, again and again, that a traumatic event does not entirely disappear. It insists. A literal piece of it—a *bit of the real*, Lacan will say—continues to return into language and conscious life, beyond the law of the signifier which ordinarily states a recognizable (local universal) language reality. At the level of the traumatic real, something from *primary-process* thought enters the narrative realm of *secondary-process* conscious thought and language. Something that is discordant with a commonly held view of a reality event is heard by listeners who will assume that a certain set of conventions convey all the knowledge (or information) they need for the purpose of deciphering an enigma. Lacan argued that most subjects are constituted as a One-minus, placed between the dialectic of wanting and getting, first experienced in terms of the objects that are known as desirable when they are lost. This early experience makes of lack a structure in being, the inverse face of desire. And these early losses are experienced by infants as traumatic. The Lacanian concept of the real is of an order of meanings constituted by the inscription of unary traits that wind themselves around the edges of holes in the dialectic of loss and refinding of the object *a*—the object(s)-cause-of-desire—whose referent is the limit point of symbolic language and imaginary identifications. This early dialectic constitutes an Ur-lining of the subject *as unconscious subject of desire* ($). The object *a* will be, forever after, irretrievable in any pure form, although it will serve as the cause that marks limit points in memory as the real of the symptoms that speak the language of trauma, traversing the smooth grain of consistent discourse units.

In "On Traumatic Knowledge and Literary Studies," Geoffrey Hartman describes this feature of the symptom as the kind of perpetual troping of a memory, which "is inscribed with a force proportional to the mediations punctured or evaded."[14] Not only is it noteworthy that trauma enunciates itself continually in literary art, as well as in museums—not to mention the analyst's couch—this phenomenon also offers a paradox: when *real elements* of a trauma appear as artifacts in a museum, or as literary or artistic representations, they dramatize the paradox. *Distance* from the real—from its traumatic properties of loss, suffering, and anxiety—enables the looker or hearer

---

14. Geoffrey H. Hartman, "On Traumatic Knowledge and Literary Studies," *New Literary History,* vol. 26, no. 3 (Summer 1995): 537–563; cf. p. 537.

to *not see or not hear*. Distance enables the looker or hearer to discount, or, even romanticize, a visible, palpable trauma. Indeed, an artifact, archive, painting, narrative, or poem often gives the lie to a trauma by covering over the real of its suffering with images and words that *seem* to tame it, giving it the quality of *mere* art. In Lacanian terms, one could say that the passion of ignorance reveals its roots in the desire for homeostatic constancy—a drive that Freud and Lacan placed on the slope of *Thanatos*—that pushes individuals to avoid terror, horror, and pain at all costs. Any lie or deception becomes preferable, as long as it keeps subjects or societies believing their actions are consistent, unified, and stable. This same propensity to avoid the real—which Lacan equated with the *sinthome* of sublimation—also keeps artists concerned that their productions not be too unseemly.[15] Social unity works, then, by denial, thereby speaking what Lacan called a master discourse which represses fantasy, desire, or any lack-in-being:

$$\frac{S_1 \rightarrow S_2}{\$ \leftarrow a}$$

In this way, social unity works against the *truth* of the real of trauma which brings discontinuity and chaos in its wake.[16]

I shall argue, here, using the three textual examples I have chosen, that trauma appears to the one traumatized—or is grasped by the witness—at the point where *unconscious* fantasy objects can no longer suture the structural lack-in-being, thereby continually repairing a breach between the individual and the symbolic by the constant taking in of such objects.[17] At such a moment, the (Lacanian) real becomes knowable as anxiety produced by the existence of a void place *in being* and *in knowledge*. Anxiety has an object, Lacan taught; the void rendered palpable. Lacan argued, further, that the void can itself be reduced to a kind of object *(a)* that appears when the imaginary order ceases to fill up the concrete holes in signifying chains with the sem-blances—illusions of wholeness—which ordinarily keep individuals from having to fight or flee an unwanted truth. When the real does appear in a stark

---

15. Ellie Ragland, "The Passion of Ignorance in the Transference," in *Freud and the Passions,* ed. John O'Neill (University Park, PA: University of Pennsylvania Press, 1996), pp. 151–165.

16. Compare *Seminar XX,* ch. 2, "To Jakobson."

17. Compare Hartman, p. 543.

encounter with anxiety, it is knowable; but not as an historical fact or empirical event.

In "*L'hallucination: le rêve traumatique du psychotique,*" the Lacanian scholar Yves Vanderveken maintains that trauma is created by an encounter with the real that pierces the fantasy, confronting head on an emptiness or hole in meaning.[18] Indeed, such an encounter with the void causes a reliving of the trauma itself precisely because unconscious meaning ceases producing a signifying chain of unknowable—but ever functioning—fantasy interpretations of "reality." Lacan addressed this question as early as *Seminar I* when he described "History [as] not [being] the past. History is the past in so far as it is historicised in the present."[19] Lacan's statement recalls Freud's doubt that screen memories were actually original *memories*, continuous with the events they recorded. Rather, Freud opined, screen memories are reworked and revived memories that emerge only later in life.[20] Further clarifying his point here, Freud writes: "It may indeed be questioned whether we have any memories at all *from* our childhood: Memories *relating* to our childhood may be all that we possess. Our childhood memories show us our earliest years not as they were but as they appeared at the later periods when the memories were aroused. In these periods of arousal, the childhood memories did not, as people are accustomed to say, *emerge*; they were *formed* at that time. And a number of motives, with no concern for historical accuracy, had a part in forming them, as well as in the selection of the memories themselves."[21]

What emerges, in Dan Collins's estimation, is the primary repressed, the trauma.[22] Lacan's later teaching, his topological teaching that dovetails with what he calls his science of the real, demonstrates how pieces of the real return continually as the *sinthomes* surrounding the Ur-objects that first caused desire. In this purview, all returned memories would not be traumatic. A trauma would distinguish its return into the present from the past—bringing

---

18. Yves Vanderveken, "*L'hallucination: le rêve traumatique du psychotique,*" *Quarto: Trauma et fantasme,* no. 63 (1988): 53–56; 53.

19. Jacques Lacan, *The Seminar of Jacques Lacan: Book I (1953–1954): Freud's Papers on Technique,* ed. Jacques-Alain Miller, trans. John Forrester (New York: Norton, 1988).

20. See Dan Collins, "The Past Is Real: Psychoanalysis as Historiography," *The Journal of Affiliated Psychoanalytic Workgroups,* no. 2 (2001): 6–13.

21. Sigmund Freud, "Screen Memories" (1899), *SE* 3:322.

22. See Dan Collins, "The Past Is Real," p. 9.

the present into the symbolic from the radically repressed real—by the specific characteristics noted by the scholars in trauma studies: testimony of an accident; breaking of a frame of the seemingly normal; the catastrophic qualities of a literal, historical event; temporal delay; a repeated suffering of the event; the insistence of certain images; secrecy; silence. Such "break-throughs" place either the victim or a witness in a position to recognize the traumatic inscription of an affective knowledge which has dug its mark into the flesh.[23] The fact that such witnessing encounters the imaginary—the narcissistic domain of narrative—to a greater or lesser degree, is only of secondary importance here. In Lacan's view, a trauma distinguishes itself from its narrative, identificatory qualities, thereby becoming susceptible to treatment in analysis, literary interpretation, or social praxis, "a praxis . . . [being, for Lacan, that] places man in a position to treat the real by the symbolic."[24]

There are, for Lacan, traumas at the base of being that the social itself is constructed to protect against. These are the structural pinnings of being; not the catastrophic trauma encountered in abuse situations. Nonetheless, cata-strophic trauma can make an impact partially because its subject is not an inherently whole, unified being. For example, the trauma of the pre-mirror stage fragmented infant is that of progressively putting together an imaginary consistency of body. The mirror-stage infant builds a seemingly unified identity by linking images to words and its own proper name, as well as joining words and images to affect. In later life, when this unity is threat-ened—as in war experiences or an act of violence perpetrated—the fragility of the prior structuring is relived in the daily present if one encounters a hole

---

23. Charles Pyle, *On the Duplicity of Language.* In discussing the paradoxical logic of Charles Sanders Peirce's theory of duplicity, Pyle states: "As a function of the cut that engenders signs, all signs are duplicitous" (Ms. version [2/23/97]), p. 17. In *Lacan's Theory of Language,* Pyle brings together Lacan's three orders with Peirce's trinary logic, equating the imaginary with the iconic; the real with the indexical; the symbolic with Peirce's symbolic naming: "To cut indexically is to really cut, or interrupt, or shape, or otherwise impose some kind of extrinsic physical mark on some material thing" (Ms. version [6/24/97]), p. 65; all rights reserved to the author; forthcoming in *Proving Lacan: Psychoanalysis and the Evidentiary Force of Disciplinary Knowledge,* Urbana, IL: The University of Illinois Press.

24. Jacques Lacan, *Seminar XI (1964): The Four Fundamental Concepts of Psycho-Analysis,* ed. Jacques-Alain Miller, trans. Alan Sheridan (New York: Norton, 1978), p. 6.

rather than a symbol, a *gap* rather than an object *a* filling the gap.[25] Or, if one encounters the enigmata produced by a symptom or an affect in one's own thought, or in another's narrative, rather than that which is recognizable in terms of some would-be "corresponding" symbol—if this symbol is lacking—Vanderveken argues that this limit experience of memory is inseparable from anxiety. He describes *angst* as the non-symbolizable affect of the hole, at which point one encounters the horror of an unknown *jouissance*.[26] The hole functions, then, as a living piece of the real, bringing symptoms of trauma into conscious thought, the most recognizable one being anxiety.

Lacan, following Freud, described trauma as knowable in conscious life by the markings we have mentioned. Hartmann stresses that literary examples reveal the same thing as Freud's narrative cases.[27] The enigmatic meaning of suffering or passion in a story, play, poem, or case study is not an allegory or a myth that is disassociated from memory or affective life. An experience of trauma may be radically repressed in the real—attested to only by opaque symptoms—but this is not the repression of some base symbol, nor of a secondary reflective meaning. It is the repression of an actual event, doubled in an imaginary story, fleeting image, or vague affect. In other words, the symbol is realistic. One could even speak of the real dimension of symbols as that which gives poems, plays, or narratives the characteristic of "every truth [having] the structure of fiction," as Lacan wrote in *Seminar VII*.[28]

In the same Seminar, Lacan made a point he developed further in his Seminar on *L'angoisse*: "The structure [of fiction is] embodied in the imaginary [mirror-stage rapport of ego to ego] relation as such, by reason of the fact that narcissistic man enters as a double into the dialectic of fiction."[29] "The passage of the specular image to this double which escapes me [one]—that is the point where something happens by whose articulation, I believe, we can give to this function of *a* . . . its generality—its presence, in the whole

---

25. Charles Pyle, "Lacan's Theory of Language: The Symbolic Gap," in *Critical Essays on Jacques Lacan,* (Farmington Hills, MI: Gale Group, 1999).

26. Compare Vanderveken, p. 53.

27. Compare Hartmann, p. 544.

28. Jacques Lacan, *Le séminaire, livre VII (1959–1960): The Ethics of Psychoanalysis,* ed. Jacques-Alain Miller, trans. with notes by Dennis Porter (New York: Norton, 1992), p. 12.

29. See *Seminar VII,* p. 7.

phenomenal field and show that the function goes well beyond what appears in this strange moment."[30]

Lacan operates a conceptual subversion on the long-familiar idea that the ego develops by growth stages. Rather, he argues, the mirror-stage specular double is transformed into the fantasy object *a* which, in turn, supports the subject as a subject of the real by a binding of unary traits to an actual hole created by the collected, associated traits one might describe as an accretion of responses to the continual loss(es) of the object of satisfaction Lacan called the object *a*. Lacan's topology is a practice of the hole and of its edge, Jeanne Granon-Lafont points out, stressing that Lacan's use of topology is not an additional knowledge which elaborates itself in a series of concepts or fundamental texts.[31]

Effecting a similar conceptual subversion on the distinction long made between morals and ethics, Lacan maintained in *Seminar VII* that psychoanalytic thought defines itself in very different terms from moral thought, with which ethics is generally confused. While morals are concerned with good behavior and the rules of conduct which beget a socially desirable comportment, psychoanalysis is concerned, rather, he says, with

> *traumas and their persistence.* We have obviously learned to decompose a given trauma, impression, or mark, but the very essence of the unconscious is defined in a different register from the one which Aristotle emphasized in the *Ethics* in a play on words [meaning "to repeat"]. There are extremely subtle distinctions that may be centered on the notion of character. Ethics for Aristotle is a science of character: the building of character, the dynamics of habits and, even more, action with relation to habits, training, education.[32]

The Freudian experience teaches a different view of ethics; one related to *trauma*, rather than a *Bildungsaesthetik*. Just as the mirror double (of self/other relations) is perpetually transformed into the escaping, fading material of elusive fantasy, psychoanalysis pursues the cause of a suffering whose remnants bear little resemblance to a well-made story, or to a secondary-process product.

---

30. *L'angoisse,* January 9, 1963.
31. See Jeanne Granon-Lafont, *Topologie lacanienne* . . . , p. 13.
32. See Lacan, *Seminar VII,* p. 10.

That a literary work can carry traumatic effects in its weave, as can a real-life experience, makes sense insofar as the symbolic, according to Lacan, has the structure of a fiction. But such a logic only becomes available when one grasps that "fictitious does not mean illusory or deceptive as such. . . . Bentham's effort is located in the dialectic of the relationship of languge to the real so as to situate the good . . . on the side of the real. . . . Once the separation between the fictitious and the real has been effected, things are no longer situated where one might expect."[33] If, as Lacan teaches, the fictitious is a function of the symbolic, the exposure of *trauma* in art, the moment when the good turns from pleasure to displeasure, would unveil a truth, not a fiction. A given reality, an identity crisis, a concern for bodily integrity—these bind textual realities to the readers' imaginary reconstructions. But by functioning as literal, repeated—thus, objective—pieces of the text, traumatic elements, paradoxically, *resist* the subjective particularity of the reader's imaginary interpretations. In this sense, *knowledge of trauma* is not a premature knowledge, nor a radically absent one, but that which "stays longer in the negative and allows disturbances of language and mind the quality of time we give to literature."[34] Not only does traumatic material push imaginary reconstructions away, it unveils itself as a limit point to representations insofar as its insistences as textual realities have a certain objectifiable, formal quality.

In trauma theory, one is not dealing only with distortions of reality, then, nor with one catastrophe for all. Trauma, Freud said in *Beyond the Pleasure Principle* (1920), is more like war "neurosis"—a constant return to the scene of an accident. Although Freud notes what he called a fixation to a trauma in accidents, war frights, and hysteria—remarking that certain fear dreams bear this same traumatic, repetitive quality—he adds: "I am not aware, however, that patients suffering from traumatic neurosis are much occupied in their waking lives with memories of their accident. Perhaps they are more concerned with *not* thinking of it."[35] This is borne out in the memories of Holocaust survivors who prefer not to talk about that time.

In her introduction to *Trauma: Explorations in Memory*, Cathy Caruth defines trauma as a literality and its return. In other words, the trauma is its own history insofar as it has remained unassimilable. As an historical enigma,

---

33. See Lacan, *Seminar VII*, p. 12.
34. Compare Hartman, p. 547.
35. Compare Freud, *Beyond the Pleasure Principle*, p. 13.

trauma connects itself to a crisis of truth, revealing, in Caruth's words, not a trace on the psyche, but a hole in meaning.

Dora, The Young Homosexual Woman, the *Fort! Da!* Paradigm

When Dr. Sigmund Freud set up his clinic in Vienna in order to treat nervous diseases, he was in consultation with Dr. Josef Breuer, a friend several years older than he, who insisted that one could treat nervous disorders by an entirely new set of assumptions, assumptions which, off and on over the centuries, had been called "hysteria," a typically female suffering. Although many medical doctors thought of "hysteria" as the product of a psychical trauma, an "acting out" of some memory that had been forgotten (i.e., repressed) by the subject, such a view of hysteria often led to the kind of error Freud made in *The Aetiology of Hysteria* (1896).[36] Geoffrey Hartman has pointed out in "On Traumatic Knowledge and Literary Studies" that Freud's theory here could readily lead one to confuse *traumatic* hysteria with fantasy, particularly if one makes the error of equating fantasy with the repressed. Neither Freud nor Lacan made this error. In the late 1890s Freud thought he had discovered the element of trauma at the base of hysteria. He wrote: "At the bottom of every case of hysteria, there are one or more occurrences of premature sexual experience . . . which belong to the earliest years of childhood."[37] Yet, Freud's thinking about hysteria changed to the point that he split from Breuer, in large part, over their different explanations of the cause of hysteria. Freud's early opinion was that the cause of hysteria always had to do with sexual impulses.[38] Reminiscent of Charcot's use of hypnosis to prove that hysteria could be caused by verbal suggestion, Freud evolved a treatment which consisted of inducing in the hysteric a kind of state, not focused on external stimulii, that would enable the—overly excited, overly affected— woman or girl to recall the *supposedly* forgotten trauma at the base of her

---

36. Sigmund Freud, *The Aetiology of Hysteria* (1896), *SE* 3: 189–221.

37. Geoffrey H. Hartman, "On Traumatic Knowledge and Literary Studies," in *New Literary History,* vol. 26 (Summer 1995), no. 3: 537–563; quoted by Hartman on p. 539 from Freud's *The Aetiology of Hysteria* (1896), *SE* 3: 203.

38. Sigmund Freud and Josef Breuer, *Studies on Hysteria* (1893–1895), *SE* 2: ed. intro., xxv.

suffering. Breuer advanced a different idea. Remembering—for example, naming—the emotions appropriate to the nervous crisis was the key to cure. *"Hysterics suffer mainly from reminiscences,"* Breuer contributes to his joint text with Freud.[39]

This aspect of Breuer's theory seems to have more in common with contemporary work on trauma theory than does Freud's early theory of trauma. Breuer's stress on remembering—among a myriad other key concepts he advanced, although they are often attributed to Freud—was to change Freud's medical orientation, indeed, his entire system of thinking, culminating finally in what Freud called psychoanalysis, or the "talking cure." In Lacanian theory, however, the theory of reminiscences undergoes a reconceptualization. Reminiscences are not proximate to conscious thought and memory. They are, indeed, radically repressed in the real and can only be re-remembered in the enigmatic displacement of symptoms—physical or psychological. That is, they will *not* usually be found in the conscious memories of childhood events that make up an imaginary narrative.

But, insofar as the concept of trauma marked Freud's work from the beginning to the end, from his first encounters with hysteria to *Moses and Monotheism* (1939),[40] Freud maintained in his early work that in the case of hysteria, there were always three psychological determinant causes: "A psychical trauma, a conflict of affects, and—an additional factor which I have brought forward in later publications—a disturbance in the sphere of sexuality," particularly in his study of Dora.[41] Some Lacanian scholars, such as Vanderveken, maintain that the hysteric only dramatizes the experience every subject has of its initial assumption of "sexuality and its nonsense, which is traumatic in the measure where the signifier of a sexual rapport in the symbolic is lacking."[42]

While Lacan does not drop the idea of a traumatic cause of hysteria, he argues that the encounter with sexuality—and the assumption of sexuation—is traumatic for every subject. In other words, one defines oneself as masculine or feminine in reference to the mother's unconscious desire, the symbolic interdiction of a Oneness between mother and child given by the real

39. Josef Breuer and Sigmund Freud, *On the Psychical Mechanism of Hysterical Phenomena: Preliminary Communication* (1893), *SE* 2: 6–7.

40. Sigmund Freud, *Moses and Monotheism: Three Essays* (1939), *SE* 22: 3–137.

41. Compare Freud, *Dora*, p. 24.

42. Compare Vanderveken, *"L'hallucination,"* p. 56.

father, and in terms of other realities which are equally as enigmatic for the child who encounters confusions at the point he or she seeks the consistency and wholeness of a unified identity that will link together his or her being, gender, and sexuality. In stressing that sexual difference is not an innate knowledge, but rather is learned in bits and pieces from the Other, in reference to a signifier without a signified—the phallic signifier being the abstract signifier for difference itself—Lacan gave a reason why the encounter with sexual difference is traumatic for children. In any traumatism, Vanderveken writes, one finds a giving away of one's power to the Other. That is, the Other takes a certain portion of the subject's real—which Lacan describes in *Seminar XX* as a space opened up between the appearance and the reality—thereby creating the suffering.[43] This can occur because bits of the real lie outside the subject—as *sinthomes* that ex-sist or sit outside any particular ensemble of a seeming whole—such that the Other can see or hear them. When pieces of the object *a* that define one's *jouissance* in a condensed form, serving as a limit point to language and representations and, thereby, marking one's knowledge in the real, are touched by the Other—whether through insult, exclusion, or maltreatment of any kind—the Other traumatizes a subject by quite literally opening up a hole between the objects that usually suture any encounter with the lack-in-being and a concrete brush with the palpability of the hole.[44]

Insofar as the Lacanian concept of the real—defined here as the knowledge one cannot bear to know and which, for that reason, is radically repressed from conscious memory—concerns a knowledge that returns into conscious language via symptoms, passion, suffering, or affect, one can study its traumatic effects upon language at points where the image (imaginary ego identifications) ends and anxiety arises; or where consistencies and appearances are cut into by affect, and so on. Both Dora and the young homosexual woman, as well as Freud's little nephew, manifest anxiety at the moment of an encounter with the real which emanates from what Lacan designated as a void place in the Other. Furthermore, the appearance of anxiety in these three texts functions, I would argue, as a limit to memory and representation that bespeaks a meaning beyond *signification* that Lacan called the *sense* of a meaning.

Trauma experiences, as well as literary language, show that there are,

---

43. See Lacan, *Seminar XX,* ch. 7, "Knowledge and Truth."
44. Compare Vanderveken, p. 54.

indeed, two different kinds of logic in knowledge: conscious (secondary-process) and unconscious (primary-process) (Breuer's terms). Lacan made the innovation of bringing together Freud's concept of condensation and displacement as typical of primary-process functioning with Roman Jakobson's discovery that metaphor and metonymy are the two rhetorical tropes that govern language.[45] Metaphor/condensation allows one to make equivalency relations, to substitute one thing for another in a secondary-process way, because the substitute element already has a referent. It has already been inscribed in a primary moment as a "unary trait," Lacan's translation of Freud's *Einzige Zugen* of identification. Metonymy/displacement allows symptoms to move in language and thought as signs of a repressed knowledge that evokes enigmas and interpretations, rather than yielding transparent knowledge. Based on this bringing together of Freud and Jakobson, Lacan was able to elaborate a unique view of memory as an unconscious writing that represents its own signifying chain.

More precisely, Lacan's view of a traumatic cause at the base of hysteria offers a paradigmatic way to study primary-process or unconscious functions within conscious thought and language, giving us a way to grasp his concept of the unconscious as a present/absent knowledge. In "Group Psychology and the Analysis of the Ego" (1921),[46] Freud identified hysteria as the primordial mode of identification to which any being can be reduced through the effects of a traumatic event. He makes it clear, however, that such functioning is a breaking down from the seemingly unified and consistent functioning of ego to ego within a group, and the even higher level of identification of collective egos with a leader of the group. What I would like to stress in Freud's theory is that in primary identification, any subject is susceptible of being hystericized by trauma, of being traumatized. Here, hysteria and trauma are near equivalents.

In his *Seminar IV (1956–1957): The Object Relation*, Lacan introduces hysteria by giving full play to the unconscious meaning in the narrative text. According to his theory that the hysteric is troubled in her identity as a

45. Ellie Ragland-Sullivan, *Jacques Lacan and the Philosophy of Psychoanalysis* (Urbana and Chicago: University of Illinois Press, 1986), p. 242; compare also Charles Pyle, "Lacan's Theory of Language," (Farmington Hills, MI: Gale Group, 1999).

46. Sigmund Freud, *Group Psychology and the Analysis of the Ego* (1921), SE 18: 67–143; compare esp. ch. 7, "Identification."

woman, Freud announced this as a rule in the Dora case when he described the young woman's "conversion symptoms" as a physiological translation of a psychic response to the sexual advances Herr K. had made to her when she was 14 years old. At that moment, Herr K., having dismissed everyone so they could be alone, tried to embrace Dora in his store. Assuming that Herr K. excited her sexually, Freud maintained that the fundamental rule of the hysteric is to deny the sexual excitation she feels for a man. The hysteric's question, as described by Lacan, is quite different. It has little to do with sexual excitation, or even fear of male sexuality. The hysteric is troubled, Lacan argued, by an identity question: What *is* a woman? Lacan exits from Freud's impasse in thought, which ends up in his suggesting that the traumatizing element in Dora's case—and in other cases of hysteria as well—is the visual or tactile impact of the anatomical sexual difference.

Describing the scene in the store, Freud says Herr K. had ostensibly arranged to meet Dora and his wife at his place of business so as to view the church festival together. Meanwhile, he persuaded his wife to stay at home, sent away his clerks, and "set up a scene" where Dora could be surprised by him on a back staircase. He threw himself upon her and kissed her. She, in turn, fled in disgust. Freud implies that Herr K. wanted something more from Dora than a kiss. He wanted retribution. She had denied him a kiss at the famous scene beside the lake. Now, she has run away from him a second time, with no explanations to him. She, nonetheless, talks about these episodes to Freud. Some days later, the K.'s had planned an expedition which was to last for some days and on which Dora was to have gone. Not surprisingly, Dora refused to go along on the expedition.

But Freud was surprised and interpreted this as a *reversal of affect*, as well as a *displacement* of a symptom of sexual excitement from the genital area to the mucous membrane of the alimentary or digestive canal. Dora's *trauma* was attributable, in Freud's view in 1901, to Dora's sexual excitement which had been replaced by disgust.[47] On the prior page, he had written: "I should without question consider a person hysterical in whom an occasion for sexual excitement elicited feelings that were preponderantly or exclusively unpleasurable; and I should do so whether or not the person were capable of producing somatic symptoms."[48]

In light of Lacan's theory of the libido or *jouissance*—that not only is one

---

47. Compare Freud, *SE* 7: 29.
48. Compare Freud, *SE* 7: 28.

sexually excited by the myriad aspects of objects that cause desire, building up into meaning constellations of image/word/affect around each object—the breast, the faeces, the urinary flow, the (imaginary) phallus, the voice, the gaze, the phoneme, and the nothing—Freud's theory of physiological conversion symptoms would not be tenable.[49] Lacan teaches, furthermore, that at least three kinds of *jouissance* also produce a formalizable logic of meaning: in reference to the Father's Name signifier—located between the symbolic and the real—which one might equate with the superego or language; in reference to the identificatory material that enters the unconscious space— between the symbolic order of language and the imaginary order of ego and narcissistic relations—as unconscious meaning; in reference to memories buried in the radically unconscious Other, which are situated, topologically speaking, between the imaginary (body) and the real (of the flesh).[50]

Freud's thesis appears as biologically reductionist alongside Lacan's more finely honed picture of *jouissance*. The interest Freud's text sustains lies, I would maintain, in his sensing that sexual effects have the potential for producing trauma. But Freud does not come up with a theory to explain why Dora is disgusted by Herr K. before 1926 in "Inhibitions, Symptoms and Anxiety" when he speaks of a link between anxiety and sexual inhibitions arising out of repressed libido. I am more convinced, however, by his comments in the "Addenda" to that essay where he calls anxiety an affect that "has an unmistakable relation to *expectation*: it is anxiety *about* something. It has a quality of *indefiniteness and lack of object.*"[51] Yet, as the Frankfurt School, among others, has taught by example: if there are no inhibitions, there would be no law. In Lacan's conceptualization of this principle, there can be no law of language that enunciates a reality principle that signifies a difference

---

49. Jacques Lacan, "The subversion of the subject and the dialectic of desire in the Freudian unconscious" (1960), in *Ecrits: A Selection* (New York: Norton, 1977), p. 315.

50. Jacques Lacan, "La troisième" (1975), given at the VIIth Congress of the *Ecole freudienne de Paris* (Rome, 1974); *Le bulletin de l'Ecole,* no. 16 (1975), pp. 178–203.

51. Sigmund Freud, "Inhibitions, Symptoms and Anxiety" (1926), *SE* 20: 77–124, compare p. 164–165; Freud's theories regarding anxiety have largely been rejected by ego psychologists and analysts who emphasize the relation between an ego wound and anxiety. Compare Marvin Hurvich, "The Ego in Anxiety," "Symposium: Classics Revisited, Max Schur, 1953" (an addendum to Freud's theory of anxiety—Charles Brenner), *The Psychoanalytic Review,* vol. 84, no. 4 (Aug. 1997): 483–504.

between pleasure and reality unless that law is based on the paradoxical premise of there being an exception to the law on which law can be based.[52]

When Freud wrote up the Dora case in 1905, he spoke of the formation of symptoms. But his description remains at the level of positivistic descriptions of conversion or somatizing symptoms. He interprets Dora's disgust as a *literal* rejection of the sensation of pressure she felt on the upper part of her body when Herr K. pinioned her against the stairwell and tried to kiss her. Not only was the kiss disgusting, Freud opined, Dora also felt the pressure of Herr K.'s erect member against her body and was revolted by it. Her symptomatic response was to displace sexual excitement from her lower body onto her thorax. In a footnote, Freud defends the logic of such displacements.

Lacan supplied what Freud's argument lacks: a logic and a means. Because he lived in the milieu of the intellectual revolutions brought about by linguistics and cultural anthropology, starting in the 1930s, Lacan understood that a symptom displacement may well occur as a signifier substituting for some other thing, some image or effect, or some knowledge repressed from consciousness. Lacan emphasized, as Freud had before him, that anxiety is an affect that is not repressed. It wanders, inverts itself, takes myriad forms. But an affect is not repressed. What is repressed are the signifiers that anchor it.[53] In anxiety, Lacan teaches that the subject makes the most radical movements of trying to ascertain what the Other wants of him or her: *Che vuoi?* For, it is only by knowing the Other's desire that one can validate oneself in the scopic field of the gaze of others.

I would suggest that Lacan could offer a logical explanation for the way that anxiety responds to trauma, where Freud failed, because he had access to Saussure and Jakobson's discoveries regarding the laws that govern language, where Freud had only an affective symbology. An object-*cause*-of-desire has the structure of metonymy, Lacan argued. It serves first as a radically repressed cause and, subsequently, as a limit point to memory and conscious knowledge. But insofar as its displacement has a referential cause—one of the eight (corporal) objects-*cause*-of-desire which Lacan describes as constituting a real Ur-lining of the subject—it will always remain pre-specular.[54] Such material can, nonetheless, function by substituting one thing for another. But the substitutions themselves are made up of imaginary, symbolic, and real

---

52. Compare Lacan's theory of sexuation in "A Love Letter," *Seminar XX*.
53. See *Seminar X, L'angoisse*, Nov. 14, 1962.
54. See Jacques Lacan, *Ecrits: A Selection*, pp. 314–315.

material—remnants and remainders of unary identificatory traits. Following this logic, Lacan argued that the (re)found object *a* will always have the structure of metaphor; that is, its original traits can only be known in terms of its secondary traits in a dialectical movement around the object that brings both presence and absence into play in knowledge.

Freud proposed a logical series of relations at the level of meaning on which he based his biological conclusions regarding Dora's being traumatized by Herr K.:

> We have here three symptoms—the disgust, the sensation of pressure on the upper part of the body, and the avoidance of men engaged in affectionate conversation—all of them derived from a single experience. It is only by taking into account the interrelation of these three phenomena that we can understand the way in which the formation of the symptoms came about. The disgust is the symptom of repression in the erogogenic oral zone. . . . The pressure of the erect member probably led to an analogous change in the corresponding female organ, the clitoris; and the excitation of this second erotogenic zone was referred by a process of displacement to the simultaneous pressure against the thorax and became fixed there.[55]

But what would it mean to say a pressure became "fixed there?" Freud's concern is not to reduce a complex phenomenon to a simplistic notion of a biological, natural sexual knowledge:

> I took the greatest pains with this patient not to introduce her to any fresh facts in the region of sexual knowledge; and I did this, not from any conscientious motives, but because I was anxious to subject my assumptions to a rigorous test in this case. Accordingly, I did not call a thing by its name until her allusions to it had become so unambiguous that there seemed very slight risk in translating them into direct speech. Her answer was always prompt and frank: she knew about it already. But the question of *where* her knowledge came from was a riddle which her memories were unable to solve. She had *forgotten* the source of all her information on this subject. [p. 31]

---

55. Compare Freud, *Dora*, p. 30. Further citations to appear in the text.

Freud is so perplexed by Dora's forgetfulness that he goes to the most farfetched lengths to explain her reaction, saying that the taste of a kiss reminds one of genital functions, even to the point of the smell of micturition (p. 31).

Lacan depicts Freud as trying, rather, to figure out how the original object—the first memory—has always already, by definition, been lost or become absent. Freud knew the object could only be (re-)experienced as (re-)found. In his topological work, Lacan had equated the body with the imaginary—as that which has mutable, variable, plastic properties insofar as words, images, and events can sustitute themselves for other meanings, thereby creating a seeming consistency. This would mean that the illusion one has of having a whole *body* can be cut into—marked by affect—by the discontinuities and ragged, traumatic edges of the real. Once Lacan has made topological sense of the imaginary as an identificatory consistency—at least a logical one, if not an experiential one—commensurate with bodily identifications, Freud's biological interpretations of trauma and anxiety sound less farfetched.

That Dora's sexual curiosity has been stimulated by the relations between her father and Frau K. is doubtless. Not only had they taken bed suites, separated only by a hall, Dora surprised them in a forest together. The two families had, as if by chance, moved together to Vienna at the same time. When Freud said to Dora that she had been complicitous in the liaison between her father and Frau K. because she had acted amorously toward Herr K., she admitted the possibility right up to the scene at the edge of the lake.

More important for purposes of a study of trauma, however, is Freud's argument that some particular historical event is recorded and repressed, but remains concretely alive, even *insisting* on presenting itself in conscious life as an enigma. The particular character of hysteria distinguishes it from all the other psychoneuroses, Freud wrote, in that its *psychic* somatic complicity, whether offered by some normal or pathological process, is connected with one of the bodily organs:

> I am prepared to be told at this point that there is no very great advantage in having been taught by psycho-analysis that the clue to the problem of hysteria is to be found not in "a peculiar instability of the molecules of the nerves" or in a liability to "hypnoid states"—but in a "somatic complicance". But in reply to the objection I may remark that this new view has

not only to some extent pushed the problem further back, but has also to some extent diminished it. We no longer have to deal with the *whole* problem, but only with the portion of it involving that particular characteristic of hysteria *which differentiates it* from other psychoneuroses. [pp. 40–41]

At one level, Lacan makes a certain advance in enabling us to understand the logical interconnection of conscious and unconscious knowledge as a certain doubleness in meaning that can both keep a trauma secret, while enunciating it elsewhere. His theory of the object *a* serves as a connector, a limit point to memory and representation which can, nonetheless, be studied. The object *a* is a denotation for what remains of an object lost in the first place, constituting the desire for its return in terms of its earlier properties. Given that the desire for some object seems to emanate directly from the thing, or from an organ or body part—which makes it seem to Freud that the organs are direct causes of their own effects—Lacan's logical advance, here, depends on his topological grasp of how lines, points, and holes relate to structure meaning at the surface of an object.

The object is not *das-Ding-an-sich*, then, but the distance one must reach in space and time—*in the time it takes*—to place a substitute image, sound, event, and so forth, in an empty place. Moreover, a person's only knowledge of a lost object will be of some unary trait, some memory wisp, some stark image, which may bring trauma with it insofar as the memory is concretely bound to a hole created by a trauma experienced at the moment an object of pleasure or satisfaction was lost. Particular traits will have been repeated and linked associatively in memory—in reference to sound, image, and affect—thereby creating a literal piece of the real of unary traits that bind themselves to a hole. Indeed, these traits create the hole. Limit memories bring both things into play—the unary detail and the affect produced by the hole—offering a certain proof that a trauma has been recorded.

Freud maintained that the hysteric separates sexual feelings from bodily parts, disassociates them one from the other. Lacan argued that such a response would delineate a symptom and not a cause. We begin to see how traumatic memories can enter consciousness as pieces of the real. If an object that first caused desire can at a second remove—in a substitute form—fulfill a lack-in-being at the level of second remove, such an object will reveal the structure of the most basic layer of human thought; the particularity of fantasy. From the start of life, one *traumatically* loses objects that satisfy both corporally and psychically. Indeed, loss and trauma could be used inter-changeably. Each loss occasions an association—a memory—that implicitly promises to fill a lack-in-being, to make sure that no sense of emptiness registers itself in the body. By isolating parts of the body from the whole in hysteria, by showing the migration of symptoms as a traveling of symptomatic identifications, rather than medical maladies, Freud gave Lacan the basis by which to link his concept of reality as a One-minus to a dynamic structuration of inert fantasy circling around a limit object.

Dora is confused in her desire. Her games are complicity games in the sexual world of grown-ups. She has yet to engage her passions and find her place in her desire and in response to the requests and expectations the Other has of her. She leaves us with questions, not answers: Where is she in her desire? Where is she within the field of the scopic gazes that attract, repulse, and judge her? In Lacan's presentation of a structure to the discourse of hysteria, he places the subject of desire engaged in questioning as the speaking agent:

$$\mathcal{S} \rightarrow S_1$$
$$a \leftarrow S_2$$

Freud's young homosexual woman, on the contrary, has found The Lady she wishes to court. She is not questioning her desire. Rather, she is seeking her father's approval of her choice. And when she promenades her conquest in front of him, in an implicit question to him, and receives the answer of a scalding gaze, she throws herself over a railroad bridge. Although she only breaks some bones, she had risked suicide.

One could interpret the young homosexual's act simplistically. She cannot bear her father's rejection, so she throws herself over a bridge. But Lacan takes us further than this in understanding this act and, I would maintain, in understanding the nature of her trauma. Among his many statements about the cause of anxiety, Freud also noted that anxiety is always oriented toward the future and is one of the strongest manifestations of the kind of fear that can be engaged when one is unclear about what the future will be. Lacan argues in *Seminar IV* that each traumatic act resonates on the imaginary, real, and symbolic planes that come together in any production of consciousness. This theory of mind enables him, at the very least, to argue that trauma will always point to some aspect of the father's power in the *unconscious*. The traumatiz-ing *father* may be the real father of *jouissance*, the symbolic father of law and castration, or the imaginary father who functions as a kind of superego face of law; or some facet of one or more.[56]

Lacan's interpretation of the traumatic impact of the gaze, clearly ennunciating itself as a limit to language and understanding in this case, concerns the young woman's implicit question to her father regarding her place in his affections. Lacan stresses what Freud had emphasized: the mother has just given birth to a new child, a son. This event causes the young woman—whose sensibilities are heightened by her own self-questioning in what Lacan calls the third logical moment of Oedipal identifications—to doubt her privileged place in her father's affections. At this time she begins to court The Lady. Having been traumatized regarding her position in her symbolic order—her value or worth—the young woman reduces her father to an equation of imaginary father = symbolic penis. In this way, Lacan says, she makes herself the equivalent of the new brother who has stolen her affections.[57] Misreading her father's rejection of her relation to The Lady as confirmation that she has been replaced in the symbolic order by the new baby boy, she throws herself over the bridge. She acts out her *trauma* by casting herself out of the symbolic, into the void, so to speak, literally acting out the trauma she is undergoing affectively.

Lacan's interpretation of her "passing to the act" makes sense if one acknowledges that insofar as one is an object of desire, this pierces the narcissistic identifications that make up the imaginary ego, cutting their illusions by the truth of the real. What the young homosexual woman seeks to learn from her father, I would suggest, is not so much whether her sexual object choice is acceptable to him, as it is a topological question about her ontological value. And one's worth in the symbolic always concerns the position one occupies within the purview of the Other.

I shall conclude by referring to Lacan's reinterpretation of Freud's discussion of his little nephew's game with the bobbin reel in *Beyond the Pleasure Principle*. Lacan taught that a present-absent cause underlies the birth of language itself, a cause that bears on objects that are present only as lure objects, as stand-ins for an object that has been radically and traumatically lost. One might take Freud's text on the *Fort! Da!* incident as proof of Lacan's theory, even though Lacan disagrees with Freud's interpretation of why the little boy cried when his mother left. The 16-month-old boy was at the age

---

56. Compare *Seminar IV,* p. 269.
57. Ibid., p. 133.

where separation, individuation, and loss of the other are noteworthy events. His mother has gone away, temporarily. Lacan depicts this event as opening up a ditch of absence around him. Freud was interested in the fact that his grandson replaced his mother's presence by a repetitive game of rolling a bobbin spool back and forth, saying "Here! There!" (*Fort! Da!*). In that way, Freud says, he mixed pleasure and grief for the purpose of mastering the sorrow his mother's departure has occasioned. Lacan will later explain such a dialectic as the possibility for objects of all kinds to suture a structural lack-in-being.

Lacan takes a different tack in the *Fort! Da!* game than Freud. Although, like Freud, he agrees that the little boy has been traumatized by a loss, in Lacan's topological teaching, a ditch of absence is quite literally opened up in the scopic field that had anchored him as a solid subject within the sphere of his mother's gaze. When this gaze disappears, the little boy encounters a palpable void or hole which marks a limit to the perimeters of perception which seeks continually to affirm who and where one is in the imaginary/symbolic. When a trauma causes loss of position in those orders, the trauma demonstrates that loss of position in the symbolic/imaginary is experienced as loss of being.

Freud thought such inexplicable acts of repetition denoted a biological reality, usually occasioned by instinct. He writes in *Beyond the Pleasure Principle*: "*It seems, then, that an instinct is an urge inherent in organic life to restore an earlier state of things* which the living entity has been obliged to abandon under the pressure of external disturbing forces . . . the expression of the inertia inherent in organic life."[58] In other words, repetitions are performed at the behest of the id in order to provide pleasure, which Freud defined as the absence of tension or the maintenance of homeostasis. But Freud remained perplexed as to why there was also a "beyond pleasure" within repetition that was redolent of the death drive.

Lacan questions Freud as to how a zero-degree tension could be life-giving or pleasurable? He reinterprets the inertia which Freud equated with pleasure as some meaning placed on the biological organism from the world outside, rather than being something inherent in the organism. Since Freud did not understand that what repeats is the signifier, for lack of having had access to linguistics, he could not advance in his logic of the unconscious beyond a biological theory in which the body causes its own effects. The

---

58. See Freud, *Beyond the Pleasure Principle*, p. 36.

repetition of *Fort! Da!* in the bobbin reel game manifests, in Lacan's view, the passion of the signifier by which the little boy invests (cathects) the bobbin reel with a real piece of himself. In Lacan's interpretation of this incident, the spool or reel is not a (dual) symbol that represents the mother. Rather, it brings up the question of why children around approximately 3 to 18 months of age should need to master the temporary loss of their mothers in their daily comings and goings. Lacan concludes that the aim of the repetition is, rather, to reconstitute oneself as a being of consistency, recognizability, and unity; to reconstitute oneself as having a position or place within the symbolic and imaginary order of things and people. What the little boy must hide at all costs, Lacan will say, is the lack of the object.[59]

When the object (*a*) starts to lack, one confronts oneself as disunified, thereby encountering the catastrophe, chaos, and trauma that bespeak a limit to memory and representation to be found at the point where the real stops the ever-moving narrative of the symbolic/imaginary text. At this interface of lives and texts, I would propose that one can study trauma through the operation of the real on language; or language on the real.

---

59. Compare *Seminar IV,* p. 166.

6

An Interview with Jean Laplanche

Cathy Caruth

Jean Laplanche has long been recognized as a leading French thinker and psychoanalyst. His pioneering work on Freud's early writing first revealed the temporal structure of trauma in Freud and its significance for Freud's notion of sexuality. In his later work, Laplanche has elaborated on this understanding of what he called Freud's "special seduction theory" in a "general seduction theory," which examines the origins of the human psyche in the "implantation of the message of the other." I interviewed him in his home in Paris on October 23, 1994.

I. Trauma and Time

CC: The seduction theory in Freud's early work, which traces adult neurosis back to early childhood molestation, is generally understood today as representing a direct link between psychic life and external events.[1] When people refer to this period of Freud's work in contemporary debates, they tend to refer to it as a time in which Freud still

---

1. See, for example, Sigmund Freud, "Project for a Scientific Psychology," in *The Origins of Psychoanalysis: Letters to Wilhelm Fliess,* trans. Eric Mosbacher and James Strachey (New York: Basic Books, 1954), esp. pp. 410–413; Sigmund Freud and Josef Breuer, *Studies on Hysteria,* in *The Standard Edition of the Complete Psychological Works*

made a place for the reality and effects of external violence in the human psyche. In your understanding of the seduction theory, on the other hand, the theory does not provide a simple locating of external reality in relation to the psyche. As a matter of fact, your temporal reading of seduction trauma in Freud's early work would rather suggest a dislocating of any single traumatic "event." You say specifically, on the basis of your reading of the seduction theory, that there are always at least two scenes that constitute a traumatic "event,"[2] and that the trauma is never locatable in either scene alone but in "the play of 'deceit' producing a kind of seesaw effect between the two events."[3]

Would you explain what you mean when you say that in Freud, trauma is never contained in a single moment, or that the traumatic "event" is defined by a temporal structure?

JL: This question about the seduction theory is important, because the theory of seduction has been completely neglected. When people talk about seduction, they do not talk about the *theory* of seduction. I would argue that even Freud, when he abandoned the so-called seduction theory, forgot about his theory. He just dismissed the *causal fact* of seduction. When [Jeffrey] Masson, for example, goes back to the so-called seduction theory, he comes back to the factuality of seduction, but not to the theory, which he completely ignores.[4] To say that seduction is important in the child is not a theory, just an assertion. And to say that Freud neglected the reality of seduction or that Freud came back to this reality, or that Masson comes back to this reality, is not a theory.

Now the theory of seduction is very important because it's highly developed in Freud. The first step I took with [J.-B.] Pontalis a long

---

of Sigmund Freud, translated under the editorship of James Strachey in collaboration with Anna Freud, assisted by Alex Strachey and Alan Tyson, 24 vols. (London: Hogarth Press, 1953–1974), hereafter cited as *SE* 2; and Sigmund Freud, "The Aetiology of Hysteria," *SE* 3.

2. Jean Laplanche, *Problématiques III: la sublimation* (Paris: Presses Universitaires de France, 1977), p. 202.

3. Jean Laplanche, *Life and Death in Psychoanalysis,* trans. Jeffrey Mehlman (Baltimore, MD: Johns Hopkins University Press, 1976), translation of *Vie et mort en psychanalyse* (Paris: Flammarion, 1970).

4. Jeffrey Masson, *The Assault on Truth: Freud's Suppression of the Seduction Theory* (New York: Penguin, 1984).

time ago, in *The Language of Psychoanalysis*, was to unearth this theory, which has very complicated aspects: temporal aspects, economic aspects, and also topographical aspects.[5]

As to the question of external and internal reality, the theory of seduction is more complicated than simply opposing external and internal causality. When Freud said, "Now I am abandoning the idea of external causality and am turning to fantasy," he neglected this very dialectical theory he had between the external and the internal. He neglected, that is, the complex play between the external and the internal.

His theory explained that trauma, in order to be psychic trauma, never comes simply from outside. That is, even in the first moment it must be internalized, and then afterwards relived, revivified, in order to become an internal trauma. That's the meaning of his theory that trauma consists of two moments: the trauma, in order to be psychic trauma, doesn't occur in just one moment. First, there is the implantation of something coming from outside. And this experience, or the memory of it, must be reinvested in a second moment, and *then* it becomes traumatic. It is not the first act which is traumatic, it is the internal reviviscence of this memory that becomes traumatic. That's Freud's theory. You find it very carefully elaborated in the "Project for a Scientific Psychology,"[6] in the famous case of Emma.

Now, my job has been to show why Freud missed some very important points in this theory. But before saying that we must revise the theory, we must know it. And I think that ignorance concerning the seduction theory causes people go back to something preanalytic. By discussing the seduction theory we are doing justice to Freud, perhaps doing Freud better justice than he did himself. He forgot the importance of his theory, and its very meaning, which was not just the importance of external events.

CC: So you are saying that, in the beginning, Freud himself never understood seduction as simply outside, or trauma as simply outside, but as a relation between an external cause, and something like an internal

---

5. Jean Laplanche and J.-B. Pontalis, *The Language of Psychoanalysis,* trans. Donald Nicholson-Smith (New York: Norton, 1973), translation of *Vocabulaire de la Psychanalyse* (Paris: Presses Universitaire de France, 1967).

6. Sigmund Freud, "Project for a Scientific Psychology," esp. pp. 410–413.

cause. Are you suggesting, then, that when he said that he abandoned the theory, he himself forgot that complex relation? That is, when he told [Wilhelm] Fliess he was turning away from seduction by an adult to the child's fantasies,[7] that he himself misunderstood his own seduction theory as being only about external causality?

JL:　Yes, something like that. I think that when he abandoned the theory, he in fact forgot the very complexity of the theory.

CC:　You have just explained this complexity in terms of the relation between the first and second moments of the trauma: you say that in order to be psychic trauma the memory of the original implantation must be revivified. In your written work, you describe this relation between the original moment and its revivification in terms of *Nachträglichkeit*. This term, used by Freud, is usually translated as "belatedness" and is understood to refer to the belated effect of the traumatizing event. But you are careful to distinguish various interpretations and translations of the word. Would you explain the various meanings of *Nachträglichkeit* and your own alternative understanding of Freud's use of the term?

JL:　We translate *Nachträglichkeit* in French as *après-coup*, and in English I have proposed that it be translated as "afterwardsness," which is now gaining acceptance. After all, the English language can use such words with "ness." I read something about "white-hat-edness," so why not afterwardsness?

　　　Now this is not only a question of finding a word. Because in the translations of Freud, the full sense of *Nachträglichkeit* was not preserved. Even in Masson's translation of the Fliess letters, he doesn't preserve the full complexity of *Nachträglichkeit*.[8] This is very important because there are two directions in afterwardsness, and those two directions he translates by different words. The phrase "deferred action" describes one direction, and the phrase "after the event" describes the other direction. So even in Masson's translation the seduction theory is split.

CC:　So he splits what you have called the deterministic theory, in which

---

7. Sigmund Freud, *The Origins of Psychoanalysis,* Letter 69, pp. 215 ff.

8. Sigmund Freud, *The Complete Letters of Sigmund Freud to Wilhelm Fliess, 1887–1904,* trans. and ed. J. M. Masson (Cambridge, MA: Belknap Press of Harvard University, 1985).

the first event determines the second event, from the hermeneutic theory, in which the second event projects, retroactively, what came before.[9]

JL: That's it exactly, yes. Now, this is not so easy. Because even *après-coup* in French, and "afterwards" in English, have these two meanings. For instance, I can say, "the terrorists put a bomb in the building, and it exploded *afterwards*." That's the direction of deferred action. And I can also say, "this bridge fell down, and the architect understood *afterwards* that he did not make it right." That's an after-the-event understanding; the architect understood afterwards. These are the two meanings.

But you have to understand how those two meanings have been put into one meaning in Freud. I think even Freud did not completely grasp these two directions, or the fact that he put them in one and the same theory. Let me quote a passage I have referred to before. It's a passage from *The Intepretation of Dreams*, which is very interesting, because it's a long time after Freud has abandoned the seduction theory, and even the idea of afterwardsness. But afterwardsness came back again later on. This is his very amusing anecdote:

> Love and hunger, I reflected, meet at a woman's breast. A young man who was a great admirer of feminine beauty was talking once—so the story went—of the good-looking wet-nurse who had suckled him when he was a baby: 'I'm sorry,' he remarked, 'that I didn't make a better use of my opportunity.' I was in the habit of quoting this anecdote to explain the factor of deferred action [or as I would say, "afterwardsness"] in the mechanism of the psychoneuroses.[10]

It's very interesting because here you have both directions. That is, you can say, on the one hand, that there was sexuality in the small

---

9. Jean Laplanche, "Notes on Afterwardsness," in *Seduction, Translation, Drives: A Dossier Compiled by John Fletcher and Martin Stanton* (London: Institute of Contemporary Arts, 1992), pp. 217–227, reprinted in Jean Laplanche, *Essays on Otherness* (New York: Routledge, 1998). See also "Interpretation between Determinism and Hermeneutics: A Restatement of the Problem," in *The International Journal of Psychoanalysis* 73 (1992): 429–445.

10. Sigmund Freud, *The Interpretation of Dreams, SE* 4–5.

child, and afterwards, this man, who was once a small child, becomes excited again when he sees himself as a small child. That is the direction of determinism: sexuality is in the small child, and afterwards, as a deferred action, it's reactivated in the adult. Or, on the other hand, you can say that it's just a matter of the reinterpretation of the adult: there is no sexuality in the small child, the small child is just sucking the milk, but the older man, as a sexual being, resexualizes the spectacle.

So for Freud there were two ways of explaining afterwardsness, but I don't think he ever saw that there must be some synthesis of those two directions. Now the only possible synthesis is to take into account what he doesn't take into account, that is, *the wet nurse*. If you don't take into account the wet nurse herself, and what she contributes when she gives the breast to the child—if you don't have in mind the external person, that is, the stranger, and the strangeness of the other—you cannot grasp both directions implicit in afterwardsness.

CC: So to understand the truly temporal aspect of *Nachträglichkeit*, or afterwardsness, you have to take into account what is *not* known, both at the beginning, *and* later. What is radically not known.

JL: Yes.

CC: Whereas the other two models of afterwardsness imply either knowing later, or maybe implicitly, biologically, knowing earlier.

JL: Yes.

CC: There's too much knowledge, in a way, in the first two models, but in what you describe, there's something that remains uninterpreted or unassimilated.

JL: Well, what I mean is that if you try to understand afterwardsness only from the point of view of this man, being first a baby and then an adult, you cannot understand afterwardsness. That is, if you don't start from the other, and from the category of the message, you cannot understand afterwardsness. You are left with a dilemma that is impossible to resolve: either the past determines the future, or the future reinterprets the past.

CC: Another way in which you have talked about this position of the other in trauma is in terms of a model which is less temporal than spatial. You note (in *"Traumatisme, traduction, transfert et autres trans(es)"*) that the word "trauma," in its three uses in Freud (as physical trauma, as psychic trauma, and as the concept of the traumatic neuroses) centers around the notion of piercing or penetrating, the notion of "effraction" or wounding.[11] This notion of wounding seems to imply a spatial model, in which the reality of the trauma originates "outside" an organism which is violently imposed upon. You have suggested that the temporal and spatial models are complementery,[12] and I am wondering what the spatial model can add to our understanding of the role of the other in trauma.

JL: One might ask, since I have emphasized a temporal model of trauma, what need is there to go back to a spatial one, to what is called the structure of the psychic apparatus? Now the spatial model is first of all a biological model. That is, an organism has an envelope, and something happens inside, which is homeostatic, and something is outside. There is no need of psychoanalysis in order to understand that. Biologists understand that. But when I speak of "outside," I am not speaking of an outside in relation to this envelope, I am speaking of something very much more "outside" than this, that extraneity, or strangeness, which, for the human being, is not a question of the outside world. As you know, many psychoanalysts have tried to produce a theory of knowledge. We don't need a theory of knowledge. Psychoanalysis is not a theory of knowledge as a whole. The problem of the other in psychoanalysis is not a problem of the outside world. We don't need psychoanalysis to understand why I lend reality to this scale, to this chair, and so on. That's not a problem. The problem is the reality of the other, and of his message.[13]

CC: The reality of the other.

JL: The reality of the other. Now this reality is absolutely bound to his strangeness. How does the human being, the baby, encounter this strangeness? It is in the fact that the messages he receives are enigmatic. His messages are enigmatic because those messages are strange

11. Jean Laplanche, *"Traumatisme, traduction, transfert et autres trans(es),"* in *La révolution copernicienne inachevée: Trauvaux 1967–1992* (Paris: Aubier, 1992), esp. pp. 257 ff.

12. Ibid., p. 258.

13. See, for example, Jean Laplanche, "The Theory of Seduction and the Problem of the Other," in *The International Journal of Psychoanalysis* 78 (1997): 655–666. See also his "Seduction, Persecution and Revelation" in *The International Journal of Psycho-Analysis* 76 (1995): 663–682.

to themselves. That is, if the other was not himself invaded by his own other, his internal other, that is, the unconscious, the messages wouldn't be strange and enigmatic. So the problem of the other is strictly bound to the fact that the small human being has no unconscious, and he is confronted with messages invaded by the unconcious of the other. When I speak now of the other, I speak of the concrete other, I don't speak in Lacanian terms, with a big O or a big A. I speak of the concrete other, each other person, adult person, which has to care for the baby.

CC: So the figure of wounding or "piercing," as a model of trauma, does not have so much to do with, let's say, a metaphor of the body, but rather with this invasion of the unconscious of the other?

JL: Yes. Nevertheless the topographical model is very important, because the very constitution of this topography of the psychic apparatus is bound up with the fact that the small human being has to cope with this strangeness. And his way of coping with this strangeness is to build an ego. And as I have said elsewhere, Freud's topography is from the point of view of the ego.

So it is in relation to the seduction theory that the subject builds himself as an individual. He Ptolemizes himself, being at the very beginning Copernican, that is, circulating around the other's message. He has to internalize this, and he builds an inside in order to internalize.[14]

CC: So the trauma or the seduction, in your terms, anticipates or precedes or originates that envelope.

JL: Yes, that building of the psychic structure. So I don't think the ego is something bound to psychology in general. It is bound to the very fact that we have to cope with the strangeness of the message.

CC: And thus the ego is very closely linked to this temporal structure of originary seduction too.

JL: Yes, absolutely. It's bound, I would say, to the second moment, that is, the moment where the message is in some way already implanted, but not yet processed. And to process it, that is to translate it, the ego has to build itself as a structure.

---

14. "The Unfinished Copernican Revolution," in Jean Laplanche, *Essays on Otherness* (New York: Routledge, 1998).

CC: Is that why the ego is, after that, always open to the possibility of being traumatized again?

JL: Yes, yes. The other traumas of the adult, or later traumas, are to be understood with the ego already in place, and the first trauma, which is not trauma, but seduction — the first seduction — is the way the ego builds itself.

CC: So in every subsequent trauma there is always a relation between the specific event, whether it's a real seduction or a car accident or whatever, and the originary founding of the ego.

JL: Yes.

II. Sexuality and Trauma

CC: As you point out, in *New Foundations for Psychoanalysis,* after Freud "abandons" the seduction theory in 1897 he continues to develop various aspects of it in different ways throughout his work, but it no longer appears to have the same familial (or even sexual) character.[15] When trauma reappears in *Beyond the Pleasure Principle,* for example, it is linked to "accidents" and war events, first of all, and ultimately to foundational moments of consciousness and the drive.[16] In your own work, however, you insist that it might be possible, even in the example of the train accident, to link the seduction theory of trauma to a nonsexual theory:

> With any disturbance, even if it is not specifically sexual — for example the train trip, or the train accident — a sexual drive can be released and, in the case of the train accident, it is really an unleashing of the drive, traumatizing the ego from the inside on its internal periphery. In other words, it is not the direct mechanical impact that is traumatic; it requires a relay of sexual excitation, and it is this flood of sexual excitation that is traumatizing for the psychic apparatus.[17]

---

15. Jean Laplanche, *New Foundations for Psychoanalysis,* trans. David Macey (New York: Blackwell, 1989).

16. Sigmund Freud, *Beyond the Pleasure Principle, SE* 18.

17. Jean Laplanche, *Problématiques I: l'angoisse* (Paris: Presses Universitaires de France, 1980), p. 218.

Your insistence on the sexual dimension of the accident, here, seems allied to your own general interest in the language of seduction and the earlier seduction theory. In what way does *Beyond the Pleasure Principle* retain elements of the seduction theory?

JL: *Beyond the Pleasure Principle* is a very complex text, which must be completely dismantled. It is a speculative text, and it has to be interpreted from the very beginning to the end. It's a text which, I would say, follows the logic of the cauldron: the cauldron was not broken, you never gave me the cauldron in the first place, and so on. This is the logic of this text. So this text must be dismantled, it cannot be taken just as a form of reasoning; there are ruptures in the reasoning. And it's all in the ruptures.

For me, the significance of *Beyond the Pleasure Principle* lies in the fact that Freud was beginning to forget the destructive character of sexuality. This started with the introduction of narcissism. After the introduction of narcissism, sexuality was enrolled under the banner of totality and of love: of love as a totality, of love of the object as a totality. *Beyond the Pleasure Principle* is a way of Freud's saying, "sexuality is, in the end, something more disruptive than I thought in narcissism, which is only Eros, that is, the binding aspect of sexuality. Beyond this Eros, no, not 'beyond' but before—"

CC: *Jenseits*—

JL: Yes, *jenseits* of this Eros, this is what I first discovered: the fact that sexuality is unbound, in its unconscious aspects. In my opinion, that is the meaning of *Beyond the Pleasure Principle*.

CC: Is there also something new that he discovers as a consequence of his forgetting?

JL: Well, what he discovers, which is a very important discovery, is narcissism. That's one of the most important discoveries of Freud. The discovery in 1915 of narcissism.[18] But the danger of the discovery of narcissism as love of oneself as a totality, and love of the other as a total object, was precisely his forgetting that there is something not totalizing in sexuality.

CC: Doesn't he also introduce, in *Beyond the Pleasure Principle,* the importance of death, since now trauma becomes linked to death, to accidents that threaten your life?

---

18. Sigmund Freud, "On Narcissism," *SE* 14.

JL: The traumas that Freud treats there are adult traumas. And they are usually gross traumas, train accidents and so on. Now there are many interesting points in this regard, which have to be reinterpreted. First, he says, the dreams of the traumatic neuroses prove that some dreams are not the accomplishment of desire. But he did not try to analyze those dreams. He simply took them for their manifest content. That's very strange, to see Freud being fascinated by the manifest content of those dreams, and not being able to see that even those dreams could be analyzed. They are repetitive, but they are not completely repetitive; there are always some points where the analytic method could be used. And this he forgets completely. That's my first point.

My second point would be more positive. It's very interesting to take seriously the fact that when the trauma is associated with a wound, a corporeal wound, there is usually no psychic trauma. It's just trauma in the medical sense, as in an earthquake and so on; you also have traumas in the medical sense of the word. And the observation is very interesting that if there is some wounding the trauma does not become psychic trauma.

Now the other point which is important is that he says all traumas make sexuality active again, that is, by developing sexual excitement.[19] This question of adult trauma, I think, has to be examined through experience. One of my followers, Sylvia Bleichmar, who is Argentinian, was in Mexico at the time of the big earthquake in Mexico. She had a team of people trying to treat the post-earthquake traumas. And what was important even in that treatment was analytic work. Even in so-called physical trauma, the way to find a point of entry was in what was psychic, in how it revived something from infancy. If there weren't this revival of something personal and sexual, there would be no way of coping with those traumas. In this context she has made some important inroads concerning the resymbolization of trauma.

CC: When you say, "if there weren't a revival of something personal and sexual," what do you mean by "sexual"?

JL: I mean that, ultimately, a trauma like that may be—and this is very strange—in consonance with something like a message. After all,

---

19. As an extreme illustration, see the movie *Crash,* directed by David Cronenberg [Jean Laplanche's note].

even an earthquake could be taken in as a message. Not just something that is factual, but something that means something to you.

CC: And that message is, in some sense, linked to origins.

JL: Linked to earlier messages.

CC: Then it's a message that resists your understanding: the meaning of it is partly that you can't assimilate the message fully.

JL: Yes. But at the same time, if there is not something enigmatic in those gross traumas, something where you must ask a question — why this? why did this happen to me? — there wouldn't be a way of symbolizing them.

CC: Do you think that what is called flashback or repetition, the constant return of the message in dreams and so on, could be understood as the imposition of that question, *what does this mean?*

JL: Yes.

CC: In that case, if we could go back to the dream, you said Freud forgets that the dream can be interpreted. But could you reinterpret the dream, in this context as being, not exactly literal, but also not a symbol in the normal sense, because it has to do with this enigmatic message? I mean, isn't there a difference still between traumatic nightmares and other kinds of nightmares?

JL: Yes. There's certainly something that resists interpretation. But we have something similar in symbolic dreams, dreams that have an overtly symbolic content: there are dreams that impose on you by the fact that there are themes in which there is nothing to interpret after all. That is a repetition too. We have this experience in the dreams of our neurotic patients; sometimes they bring you a dream which is so real, which is a repetition of what happened yesterday, and they say, "there is nothing to interpret." So I'm very skeptical about the impossibility of interpreting those traumatic dreams.

CC: Could you say perhaps, though, that traumatic nightmares are linked in a more direct way to the originary traumatic message?

JL: Yes, there may be a shortcut between them. But in those shortcuts you always have to find the small details, the changing details in such dreams, and it's those changing small details that can be the starting point of the analytic method, which is interpretation and free association.

CC: You mean what changes in them —

JL: Yes, what changes even in these dreams as well. Freud said the repetitions are the same, but they are not always the same, and that's the difference that makes all the difference.

III. The Primal Situation

CC: This brings me to your own rethinking of what you call the "special seduction theory" of Freud in terms of a "general seduction theory," or the origination of human consciousness and sexuality in the "implantation of the enigmatic message of the other." Your own theory of seduction seems to involve the larger philosophical and foundational quality of Freud's later work on trauma, while insisting on the story of the "scene of seduction" from the earlier work. Would you explain what you mean by "primal seduction" and the "implantation of an enigmatic message," and why you insist on retaining, in this philosophical context, the language of seduction? What is the relation between a universal foundational structure or moment (the primal seduction trauma) and the contingency of the accidental or unprepared for that is so central to the notion of psychic trauma?

JL: For me, seduction must be understood as a primal situation. That is, it goes back to the constitution of the unconscious. And seductions— infantile seduction or adult seductions, seductions in everyday life— are derived from this original situation. This original situation, as I understand it, involves an adult who has an unconscious—I'm very realistic, I say "he *has* an unconscious," I'm not afraid to say that, I think that seems very strange to philosophers, "he *has* an unconscious," like a bag behind him—

CC: It's our baggage!

JL: It's our baggage, yes. So, the original situation is the confrontation of an adult, who has an unconscious, and the child or infant, who at the beginning has no unconscious—that is, he doesn't have this baggage behind him. (You must understand that I am completely against the idea that the unconscious could be something biological or inherited. I think the idea of an inherited unconscious is something that has to be forgotten.) The unconscious of the adult is very deeply moved and revived by this confrontation with the infant. And especially his perverse sexuality—in the Freudian sense of "perverse," that is, not perversity as an overt perversion, but the perverse sexuality of the human being that involves not only genitality but all the pregenital trends (I wouldn't say stages, but trends).

Now, you asked me why I keep sexuality in this. This question seems very odd to me because, at this very moment, sexuality in the United States is being put on trial, especially by the children who say that they were sexually attacked. And so sexuality is everywhere, it is in every court, in every trial. I would say that this is a way to forget the idea of generalized sexuality, which Freud has put forward. That is, sexuality cannot be identified with specific forms of perversity, it's not just something that can be isolated here and there. Perversion, rather, is in everyone, as an important component of sexuality. What Freud has shown, in the *Three Essays on the Theory of Sexuality,* is that in every adult's so-called normal sexuality, there is perversion: there is perversion in the means of taking pleasure, in the forepleasure, and also in the fantasies.[20] So why sexuality? I say that there is much more sexuality than they think in those trials. More sexuality, that is, in the sense that sexuality and perverse sexuality are everywhere in the most "innocent" relation of parent and child. And there is no reason to make a trial about that!

Coming back to this story of the wet nurse, something has been forgotten, I would say, not only in the United States (and France) but by all of psychoanalysis. Let's take the Kleinians for example. They speak of the breast, the good breast, the bad breast, the breast as the first object, and how you have to internalize it and so on. But there is more to understanding sexual life. Who before me has reminded people that the breast was an erotic organ for the woman? That is, the breast is something that is a part of the sexuality of the woman. And why is this sexuality of the breast now forgotten? When one speaks of the relation of the child to this breast, why does one forget this very fact of its sexuality? Now the fact that there is no reason to make a split between the sexual breast and the nursing breast has been noted by many pediatricians, who point out that many women have sexual pleasure in nursing, although they don't dare to acknowledge it. This has been noted by many gynecologists, pediatricians, and so on. Even ancient psychiatrists noted a long time ago those sexual feelings and sexual fantasies in the person who watched over the child. So why

---

20. Sigmund Freud, *Three Essays on the Theory of Sexuality, SE* 6.

sexuality? I say rather, why the forgetting of sexuality in the very fact of nursing?

CC: Why *do* you think there is a forgetting of sexuality?

JL: Well, the discovery of Freud was very important for generalized sexuality, but he did not go back to this point. Maybe there are some places where he touches on it, perhaps in the Leonardo essay,[21] but very few places where he deals directly with that issue. Freud talked about many erotogenic zones, but he never talked about the erotogenic zone of the breast. For me there's something missing there in the theory, including how the erotogenic zone develops in the woman (and also in men sometimes).

But what's important for me is not just the fact that the woman may have some pleasure in nursing, but the fact that something passes from the nursing person to the child, as an enigma. That is, something passes of what I call a message. And the most important thing is not the breast as a shape, as a whole, as an object, but the breast as conveying a message to the child. And this message is invaded by sexuality.

CC: And that would also mean, then, that it is invaded by something that neither mother nor baby can fully know.

JL: Yes, absolutely. Something that is unconscious, mostly unconscious sexuality. Sometimes it is also partly conscious, but there is always something going back to the unconscious and to the very personal history of the person.

CC: So in this case sexuality also means that which remains enigmatic.

JL: Yes, what remains unconscious, enigmatic.

CC: In regard to this role of the other, you have suggested that by introducing the mother (or the other) into the temporal scheme of trauma, the reality of trauma—as a temporal structure—can no longer be thought of in terms of a dual model: "[I]f one introduces a third term into this scene—that is, the nurse and her own sexuality—which is only at best vaguely sensed by the baby—then it is no longer possible to consider afterwardsness in dual terms."[22] What is the relation between the other and temporality in your model?

---

21. Sigmund Freud, "Leonardo da Vinci and a Memory of His Childhood," *SE* 11.

22. *Seduction, Translation, Drives,* pp. 221–222.

JL: In a paper of mine on temporality I speak of the other as immobile motor. Remember Aristotle's image of God . . . but I'm not a theologian. What I mean is that the temporality of afterwardsness develops in the child, but the message of the mother itself is not temporal. It is rather atemporal, simultaneous. That is, what is going to develop itself as temporality in the child is simultaneous in the mother. It is a simultaneity of the message, which, at the same time, and at the same moment—in the same message—is self-preservative and sexual. It is compromised by sexuality. And to go back to this model of the wet nurse, perverse sexuality is in the very atemporality of the adult. So I wouldn't say there is a passage of temporality from the adult to the child. I would say rather that there is a concentration in something that is not temporal, that is, the compromised message of the other.

CC: You say that the message in the adult is not temporal. If the message is enigmatic, which means it contains or conveys some of the unconscious of the mother, and if that unconsciousness in the mother is also formed around an originary seduction, what has happened to the temporality of that seduction?

JL: When sexuality has been repressed, let's say, in the adult, it becomes unconscious, and in the unconscious there is no temporality. So I would say there is something that is extracted from temporality.

CC: Is that why it's compromised?

JL: Yes. That's the reason why it's compromised. And I understand "compromised" as something not temporal, not bound to temporality. Except that our work, our psychoanalytic work is to retemporalize it. The very representations of signifiers that have been repressed are from then on subjected to temporality.

CC: So that's why, in order to be passed on, the message cannot be completely temporal.

JL: When it is passed on, it is passed on as something simultaneous. And from then on, the child develops a temporal dialectic, that is, a traumatic dialectic, first receiving the message and then reinterpreting it in a second moment.

CC: When you speak of the passing on of a compromised message, you are speaking of something repressed and unconscious. In *New Foundations for Psychoanalysis,* along the same lines, you suggest that the theory of seduction, or a traumatic model of sexuality, can be linked to the more general theory of repression in Freud through the distinction between primal repression and secondary repression. For most trauma psychiatrists today (in the U.S., at least), the theory of trauma and the theory of repression are opposed, since repression doesn't engage the same temporal structure as trauma. How do you link the two?

JL: I'm mostly interested in the humanizing trauma. That is, the first trauma, which most people wouldn't describe as trauma: the originary seduction of the normal, average subject or future neurotic subject (not the psychotic). So I have been much more interested in that aspect of trauma that ultimately leads to repression and restructuration, as opposed to something that has not been translated. Now, I completely agree that in the framework of the two-moment theory of trauma and seduction, one has to ask the reason why, in many instances, there is no second moment, or why the second moment is hampered or paralyzed. And that is really the trauma which cannot be reinterpreted, which is implantation, what I call *intromission*.[23] And here we come back to the question of psychosis, and to the question of the superego. Because I think that in some way the messages that become superego messages are messages that are not being translated. So I would speak of the superego as some kind of psychotic enclave in everyone, something that consists in part of messages that cannot be translated.

CC: Did you say that in some instances there is no second moment?

JL: Sometimes there is no second moment. In everyone. I think that there are some things that are not repressed after all.

IV. The Other and Death

CC: We have been speaking about the role of the other in trauma and primal seduction. In *Life and Death in Psychoanalysis,* your analysis of seduction trauma takes place within a larger framework in which you analyze, on the one hand, the relation between the vital order and sexuality (in the "Project for a Scientific Psychology" and in the *Three Essays on the Theory of Sexuality*) and, on the other hand, the relation between sexuality (now including the vital order) and death (in *Be-*

---

23. Jean Laplanche, "Implantation, intromission," in *La révolution copernicienne inachevée,* pp. 355–358, reprinted in *Essays on Otherness.*

yond the Pleasure Principle)—hence the title of your book, *Life and Death in Psychoanalysis*. In the introduction to that book, moreoever, you talk about the significance of death for Freud:

> Might it be that death—human death as finitude and not the sole reduction to zero of vital tensions—finds its place, in psychoanalysis, in a dimension which is more ethical than explanatory? . . . [Freud says,] "If you would endure life, prepare for death."
>
> More modestly perhaps in relation to the temptations of the heroic formulation, "If you want life, prepare for death" might be translated as "If you want life, prepare for the death of the other." If a certain ethic in relation to death might be evolved from the Freudian attitude, it would be in the sense of a distrust concerning every form of enthusiasm, and of a lucidity that does not hide the irreducible meshing of my death with that of the other.[24]

Is there a relation between the role of the other in the seduction theory and the relation between the other and death in psychoanalysis?

JL: I'm afraid that the more that I advance in my thinking, the more I disintricate the question of death, the enigma of death, and the so-called "death drive" of Freud.

CC: You take them apart?

JL: Yes. That's why I'm very critical about the term "death drive," and why I have called it a "sexual death drive," with the emphasis more on "sexual" than on "death." For me, the sexual death drive is just sexuality, unbound sexuality, the extreme of sexuality. And more than death, I would point to primary masochism. I see more of a sense of the sexual death drive in masochism or in sadomasochism than in death. And it was not on the side of sadism, but on the side of masochism, that Freud placed the core of his death drive.

Now as to the question of death—in the sense that we are all subject to the question of death and to the enigma of death—I wouldn't say it is as primal as some people would have it. We all know that infants up to a certain point in their development don't know

---

24. *Life and Death in Psychoanalysis,* p. 6.

death and don't have any questions about death. I see the issue in a very Freudian manner, or at least from a certain perspective of Freudian thought. I would say that the question of the enigma of death is brought to the subject by the other. That is, it is the other's death that raises the question of death. Not the existentialist question, *"why should I die?"* The question, *"why should I die?"* is secondary to the question, *"why should the other die?"*, *"why did the other die?"*, and so on.

CC: When or how does that question of the other's death get put to the subject?

JL: Well it's put at very different times in everyone's life. And it's also bound to absence. I don't think that metaphysical questioning about one's own death is primary. It doesn't mean it's not important, but I think it comes from the question, *"why should the other die?"*

CC: So would you say, then, that it is not necessarily linked to the implantation of the enigmatic message?

JL: I don't think it's bound to the very first enigmatic messages. But there are enigmas that come afterwards.

CC: By suggesting that the question of death is raised through the death of the other, you seem to be returning now to the notion that death is situated in an "ethical dimension." Can you say more about what that means?

JL: I am a little surprised to hear you ask about ethics, because in my opinion the alterity of the unconscious in everyone has very little to do with ethics. I would say that it is deeply antimoral.

CC: I am not referring to ethics in the sense of everyday morality, but rather in relation to your comments in the introduction to *Life and Death in Psychoanalysis,* where you say that death as a finitude might ultimately be placed in an ethical dimension, rather than an explanatory dimension in Freud. And I wanted to understand what you meant.

JL: Oh yes, sure, sure, yes. . . . I agree with you that an ethical dimension is introduced by the question of the death of the other. But I don't think there is a link to the primal seduction; I would see it a little after. Even in the oedipal situation, which includes the question of the death of the other.

CC: Maybe when you said to me, at the very beginning of this interview, that for psychoanalysis the question is not about knowing but about the reality of the other, perhaps that's what you mean by ethics. That is, it is not about epistemology, but rather about confronting the reality of the other.

JL: Yes. And especially in regard to knowing, I would repeat what I have said about knowledge as an intellectual process: when I speak of translation or interpretation by the individual, I don't mean an intellectual way of processing messages. Because they are processed in many languages, that is, also in an affective language or an image-language. I don't see the question of translating as having to do with intellectual translation.

CC: So there, too, it's not about knowing something, but about being linked to the other.

JL: Yes.

V. Translation and Detranslation

CC: When you discuss the role of the other in the original seduction, you also use a specifically linguistic terminology (the implantation of the "message" of the other). Likewise, your interpretation of repression and the drive, as well as of psychoanalytic work, is tied to what seems to be a linguistic terminology of "translation" and "detranslation." Can you say more about the meaning of these terms and about their specific significance as linguistic terms?

JL: I wouldn't say my view is a linguistic point of view; it is much less so than Lacan's and some others'. And up to now my linguistic vocabulary has been very minimal. But why do I use the term "translation"? When I use this term, it is a linguistic metaphor, in the sense that Jacobson speaks of translation. Which means not only verbal, linguistic translation, but also inter-semiotic translation, that is, from one type of language to another. So if I take translation as a model that is verbal, it's just a model. And for me, when Freud, in his famous Letter 52,[25] speaks of translation or the failure of translation, he doesn't mean translation into words. He means translation into what he sometimes calls drive language, or a type of drive language. You may also have a translation into a type of code which is internal to language, for instance, the castration code or the Oedipus myth, which is a type of code into which you can translate something.

---

25. *The Origins of Psychoanalysis,* Letter 52, pp. 173 ff.

So why do I speak of translation and not of interpretation? Interpretation may mean that you interpret some factual situation. Translation means that there is no factual situation that can be translated. If something is translated, it's already a message. That means you can only translate what has already been put in communication or made as a communication. That's why I speak of translation rather than of understanding or interpretation.

CC: It also has to do with the message and its enigma.

JL: Yes. I'm very interested, now, in the debate with hermeneutics. One of my last papers is called "Psychoanalysis as Anti-Hermeneutics," which suggests that the aim of analytic work is not translation but detranslation.[26] Translation is very important, but it's not an activity of the analyst. I'm not anti-hermeneutic in general, I'm anti-hermeneutic only insofar as people try to make analytic work a speciality of hermeneutics.

But the other point is that the only translator, the only hermeneut, is the human being. That is, the human being is always a translating, interpreting being. But what is he translating? That's why I'm using the word "translate" and not "interpret." Take for instance Heidegger's hermeneutic position. He says there is a proto- or first understanding, which is the understanding of the human condition. But as I see it, there is no translation if there is not something already being put into words, not necessarily verbal words. So I would go back to the idea of a hermeneutics of the message, which was also the first meaning of hermeneutics. Because as you know hermeneutics in the past was a hermeneutics of the text. And especially of sacred texts, like the Bible and the Koran and so on. So I think that we have to go back to a hermeneutics of the message. Not a hermeneutics of the message of God, but a hermeneutics of the message of the other.

CC: So you're saying that the modern notion of hermeneutics as a process of understanding has forgotten that hermeneutics originated as a reading and translation process.

JL: Yes, a translation process. Hermeneutics at the very beginning was a

---

26. Jean Laplanche, "Psychoanalysis as Anti-Hermeneutics," in *Radical Philosophy* 79 (1996): 7–12. See also "Temporality and Translation: For a Return to the Question of the Philosophy of Time," in *Stanford Literature Review,* vol. 6, no. 2 (1989), pp. 241–259.

hermeneutics of something being *addressed* to you. And in Heidegger, what is interesting is that it became a hermeneutics of the human situation. But he forgot that the human situation in itself cannot be translated. It's just facts, it's just factual. In the framework of the hermeneutics of the human individual, what is important is to go back to the idea that the first interpretation is an interpretation, not of one's own situation, but of the situation of receiving a message.

CC: If one can make an analogy with the original message from the mother, could one say that it is an address also?

JL: Yes.

CC: Is it a matter, then, not simply of translating any message, but a message that is addressed to you?

JL: Yes.

CC: So it's specifically then—which makes it more complex—the translating of an address, which is different from, let's say, the translating of a statement. Because an address takes a specific form.

JL: Yes. It's always the translating of an address.

CC: And so something of the enigma and the resistance has to do with that structure of address?

JL: Yes.

CC: In this context, how does "translation" help us understand what you have called "psychic reality"? You have commented that psychic reality is the "reality of the message;"[27] in what way is translation a rethinking of the general problem of the relation between reality and the psyche?

JL: My problem is not the old epistemological, philosophical problem of the reality of the external world. . . . On this point, I must say, I'm very much an empiricist, or, even if you want, I'm colored a bit by phenomenology—in the sense that every consciousness is consciousness of something. Even animal consciousness is consciousness of something. And there is no problem for me of rebuilding the external world, starting from something internal. I think that any living being is so open to the *Umwelt* that there is no problem of rebuilding the reality of reference starting from representations. The problem of representation and reference for me is completely wiped out by phenomenology.

---

27. *Seduction, Translation, Drives,* p. 75.

Now, my problem is not that. It's not a problem of the other world, the other thing, which is taken care of by phenomenology, and it is also not an analytic problem. As I said before, it's a very big error on the part of psychoanalysts to try to make a theory of knowledge starting from so-called psychoanalysis—for instance, starting from the breast and the reality of the breast. Or even Winnicott's starting from the first not-me possession and building the external world beginning with what he called the transitional object, and so on. The problem, on our human level, is that the other does not have to be reconstructed. The other is prior to the subject. The other on the sexual level is intruding on the biological world. So you don't have to construct it, it first comes to you, as an enigma.

CC: So it's the opposite problem. Too much other!

JL: Yes, the opposite problem. Too much other, exactly! And instead of saying the first not-me possession, the problem for the human sexual being is to have a first-me possession. That is, to build an ego starting from too much otherness.

CC: So your interest is in how that takes place.

JL: Yes. What I say in *The Copernican Revolution*[28] is that we are first Copernican, that is, on the sexual level, which is invaded by the other's messages, and the problem is to recover from that.

CC: Since trauma, at least later on, is connected with accidents, would you say that when the adult trauma interrupts like an accident, it is the reemergence of that too much other?

JL: Yes, absolutely. That too much other coming back. And there is a destruction of the ego. The ego cannot cope with it, or even is no longer there. So in that sense I agree with you. The otherness comes back full strength!

VI. The Practice of Psychoanalysis

CC: As a final question, I would like to ask you how you became interested in the problem of trauma in Freud, and if there is a link between your becoming interested in that and your philosophical training.

---

28. Jean Laplanche, *La révolution copernicienne inachevée*.

Would you say your interest in trauma grew out of your philosophical training?

JL: Perhaps my questioning came from philosophy; I went to psychoanalysis as a philosopher. I would say my main question is about psychoanalytic practice: not about clinical work as such, but rather the question, *what is the very invention of Freud in psychoanalytic practice?* Is it just a kind of role-playing? Or is there something else more fundamental? For me the understanding of analysis as just reconstructing some events that have not been constructed correctly, or as role-playing—that is, you play the role of the mother or father, but you must say that you are not exactly as they were—never seemed very interesting to me philosophically. Nor did it get at the true invention of Freud. I felt that the analytic situation could not be understood just as reviving a factual situation, but as reviving the situation of being confronted with the enigma of the other. So at the heart of my inquiry is really the analytic situation, and the question of what we are doing in it, and whether or not it is just something that any other kind of psychotherapy could do, which I do not think to be the case.

CC: You are also now going back, in your work, to the question of time, which you appear to believe is a crucial element of Freud's discovery. Is this also linked to your clinical inquiry?

JL: I think that there are at least two aspects of time in Freud, and I think he mixed them together. On the one hand, there is the question of time as the experience of the outside world, which is linked to perception and to what he calls the system of consciousness. But this, in my opinion, is the biological aspect of time. And that aspect of time is very limited; it is immediate time, immediate temporality. But what Freud tried to discover, through *Nachträglichkeit,* is something much more connected with the whole of a life. That is another type of temporality. It is the temporality of retranslating one's own fate, of retranslating what's coming to this fate from the message of the other. That's a completely different aspect of temporality.

CC: And that's what you're exploring in your clinical practice.

JL: Yes. That's what we're exploring in the analytic situation. Freud stressed the fact that psychoanalysis was first of all a method. And I think he was right. Not a method in the sense of a scientific method, not an objective method, but the method of the cure. That is, the method of free association in the frame of the address of the other, which remains enigmatic. That is something completely new in the experience of humanity, I believe. I think that's a new era in humanity.

CC: Do you think it would be important for people to continue to explore this relation to the address of the other in the psychoanalytic situation in the context of the current work being done on trauma?

JL: Yes, I think that the analytic situation, and the analytic understanding of how the human being responds to the message of the other, can also be extended to the question of why, in some instances, there is no translation. I was very interested in psychosis, although I don't have much experience with it anymore, but I think that psychosis can be understood as a negative of the seduction theory. A negative that says how the seduction theory doesn't work. In the treatment of children, as well, it's very important to understand that, before a certain point, interpreting has no meaning, if there is no unconscious yet. So the problem for the treatment of children would be to help to constitute an unconscious, rather than interpreting the unconscious as being there from all eternity.

CC: So hopefully psychoanalysis will be renewed through a different kind of understanding of the original insights of Freud that have been somewhat forgotten.

JL: Yes, but there is some strangeness in this seduction theory. For everyone of us it is difficult to give an account of this strangeness, and to face it. Think of it in terms of grammar. In grammar, you say, the first person is the person who speaks. The second person is the person to whom I speak. The third person is the person of whom I speak. But who is *the person who speaks to me?*

CC: And that is what . . .

JL: And that is what we have yet to cope with.

7

The Catastrophe of Narcissism: Telling Tales of Love

Charles Shepherdson

> *The water in which Narcissus sees what he shouldn't is not a mirror, capable of producing a distinct and definite image. What he sees is the invisible in the visible . . . a representation without presence . . . the nameless one whom only the name he does not have could hold at a distance. It is madness he sees, and death.*
>
> —Blanchot, *The Writing of the Disaster*

> *Credule, quid frustra simulacra fugacia captas? /Quod petis est nusquam.*
> —Ovid, *Metamorphoses,* Bk III, lines 432–433

I. Telling Tales: Of Philosophy and Literature

Can we believe that narcissism has a history?[1] Can we speak of an early form of narcissism, regulated by the ideals of Athenian democracy or the virtues of

---

1. This paper was written at the invitation of David Goicoechea for a conference on Julia Kristeva's *Tales of Love,* organized at Brock University. I was asked to comment specifically on this chapter of the text, and have therefore limited my remarks to that particular horizon here. I would like to thank the conference organizers for their hospitality. I would also like to acknowledge here the inspiration of

the Platonic city, and later transformed by the subtle revisions of Plotinus and the advent of Christian doctrine? Can we believe that there is, alongside the history of madness, "a new insanity," *novitasque furoris*, a new insanity of narcissism, born in the first centuries of the Christian era, and still living today, in a modified but essentially Plotinian form?[2]

For this is indeed what Kristeva suggests in *Histoires d'amour:* "Platonic dialogism," she writes, "is transformed, with Plotinus, into a monologue that must indeed be called speculative" (138–139/109). Neo-Platonism thus appears as the force capable of "setting into motion the internalization of reflection in order to transform Platonic ideality into speculative internality" (146/115). Plotinus would be located "as if at the start of a new era, the Christian era that led us to assume our humanity through the imposing suffering of Christ" (146/115). In the history of philosophical narcissism, Plotinus would thus inaugurate a decisive chapter—a new formation of the soul's interiority whose legacy we still retain today.

Alongside this philosophical trajectory, close by and yet distinct, in another neighborhood of thought or language, the same story would be echoed in the halls of literature. "Only in the beginning of the Christian era," Kristeva writes, "did the fable of Narcissus enter the domain of literature. We owe its first *complete* variant to Ovid (43 B.C.-A.D. 16)" (131/103). Let me stress these dates, and the idea of a datability of the proper name that accompanies this account. For the proper name of "Ovid," the properly "Ovidian" formulation of the myth, and indeed the very name of Narcissus as well, would be thereby situated *in time*, in a time that would already be given in the world and would not itself depend on the advent of the name, understood as the origin of time.[3]

Professor Claire Nouvet, whose scrupulous lectures on Ovid opened a far more labyrinthine path into this particular chapter of Kristeva's book than I would otherwise have taken.

2. Julia Kristeva, *Histoires d'amour* (Paris: Denoël, 1983). *Tales of Love*, trans. Leon Roudiez (New York: Columbia University Press, 1987), pp. 148/117. Unless otherwise noted, references to Kristeva will be to this text. Citations will be given to both editions, French first, English second. It should be noted that the epigraph to this chapter of *Tales of Love*—a quotation from Ovid that Kristeva leaves in Latin—appears in the English text in a form ("the strangeness of his infatuation") that conceals the connection between Kristeva's title, "The New Insanity" ("*la nouvelle démence*") and the original Ovidian line, "*novitasque furoris.*"

3. The whole of our question concerning Kristeva's exposition is already situated here: as Heidegger points out in *Being and Time*, one cannot avoid the problem of the

"Narcissism" here would not entail a psychic event whose character would bear on the very advent of temporality, but would simply fall within the already given time of a chronological succession. All this is quietly supposed by the opening gesture of Kristeva's account: the "first *complete* variant" of Narcissus in its literary form ("the fable of Narcissus") appeared with the work of one who is named "Ovid (43 B.C.-A.D. 16)."

The history of literature would thus echo the history of philosophy, or rather, would serve as the origin that philosophy itself would echo: for as Kristeva recalls, it is Ovid who precedes Plotinus, anticipating his thought and providing in advance the mirror in which Plotinus would be able to reflect (come to see himself). As Kristeva puts it at the conclusion of her account of Ovid's myth, "the *reflection* of which Narcissus became enamored and which led him to his death *became* [latter emphasis mine] the fundamental topos of a thought that parted with ancient philosophy to nourish speculative thinking" (134/105). This new thought would include both the gnostics, who "viewed the perceptible world as the result of a fault," and "Plotinus (A.D. 205–270)"—we again mark these dates, which resemble in their brevity the austere engraving on a headstone—for whom, in contrast to the Gnostics, "the *primary reflection* that created the cosmos is a necessary process" (135/ 105–106).

Thus, even if Plotinus will ultimately turn away from the world, like the Gnostics (and in accordance with a certain Platonism), even if, as he says in the *Enneads*, "we must close the eyes of the body, to open another vision," it remains the case that the perceptual world is not, for Plotinus, simply error and fallenness, since "form alone can penetrate into the soul through the eyes" (140/110).[4] The eyes of the soul cannot open, according to Plotinus, without

---

relationship between this apparently obvious chronological "datability" and its internal possibility, "the structure of datability" (Martin Heidegger, *Being and Time,* trans. John Macquarrie and Edward Robinson [New York: Harper and Row, 1962]). Pagination follows the seventh edition of the German text, *Sein and Zeit* (Tübingen: Neomarius Verlag, 1953), which is given marginally in the English text, in this case, p. 408. This problem is especially pressing insofar as the relation between chronological datability and Heidegger's question—"wherein is such datability grounded, and to what does it essentially belong" (407)—will be replayed at the very heart of narcissism itself, since the structure of narcissism, in Freudian doctrine, articulates not merely a momentary lapse, or a contingent pathological deviation, but the very coming into being of the subject.

4. As Kristeva's translator notes, there are "considerable discrepancies" (*Tales,*

the material ground of perception—"no more than reflection," Plotinus says, "can exist without a mirror or a similar surface" (135, n. 2/391, n. 3). The new formation of speculative interiority inaugurated by Plotinus—turned inward toward the psyche, rather than upwards toward the ideas—would thus be distinguished from Gnosticism insofar as it acknowledges a moment of absolute dependence on "form," which is not immediately ideal, but retains a sensory dimension, what Kristeva will go on to call an "objectal" dimension, an exteriority that will "penetrate . . . through the eyes" (140/110). Nevertheless, this momentary grounding of reflection in material exteriority does not fail to take a narcissistic turn when Plotinus insists, in a gesture marked by melancholy and anguish, on the *idealization* of the very process of reflection itself—what Kristeva calls the "luminous, reflective closure of psychic, auto-erotic space under the constituent eye of the One" (148/117). Thus, even Plotinus "did not seek an object to halt his anguish. He lashed himself down to the archetype or rather to the source of objecthood—image, reflection, representation, speculation . . . unifying them within the inner space of the Self" (149/117). And following in the steps of Narcissus, who likewise "is not located in the objectal or sexual dimension," so Plotinus will also find that "insanity comes from the absence of the object, which is, in the final analysis, the sexual object" (147/116).

On this account, or according to this story, literature would come before philosophy, providing the origin that philosophy would come to divide in half, giving us, on the one hand, an account of the perceptible world as fallen, shadowy, and erroneous—a world of sense-perception that will eventually be subjected to methodical doubt—and, on the other hand, a Plotinian account in which reflection, both sensory and psychic, is not simply error and fallenness, but rather the condition for the possibility of creation, as the imagination will be for Kant and Heidegger.

It is this genealogy and this double trajectory (of the object and its absence) that the translator of *Tales of Love* emphasizes at the beginning of his translation, while also inscribing *Tales of Love* within a history of Kristeva's work: "The sociological and cultural investigation of *Powers of Horror* is replaced with a philosophical and a theological one, which is conducted along two paths. One survey leads from Plato and the Bible through Ovid and Plotinus

---

391, n. 3) between the French and English translations of Plotinus. In this case, Plotinus (*Enneads,* I, 6, 8, 26) is rendered by Kristeva as follows: *"Echanger une manière de voir pour une autre"* ("exchange one way of seeing for another").

to Dante, Valéry, and Gide; the other goes by way of Paul, Bernard de Clairvaux, and Aquinas, to Mozart's *Don Giovanni* and Shakespeare's *Romeo and Juliet*" (vii). For the translator, Kristeva's trajectory thus passes from the sociological and cultural domain (*Powers of Horror*) to the philosophical and theological domain, each of these traditions being mapped in terms of its attachment to—or abandonment of—the object.

In the chapter entitled "Narcissism: A New Insanity," philosophy and literature would thus be intertwined in an intimate trajectory that preserves the identity of each, while also revealing their common destiny. We can therefore believe, and even narrate for ourselves, the history of philosophy and literature, which is also our own history. Such is the initial thesis linking Ovid and Plotinus in a chronological chain that will eventually bind us in turn, and lead to the present day: the "tragic, death-bringing solitude of Narcissus" is a new historical formation, "on which will be founded a man very different from the political and erotic animal of the ancient world" (150/118–119). And this new formation is a legacy that will be inherited, according to Kristeva, for "the Christly passion and the arts of all Churches have come to root into . . . that psychic space of love that the Narcissan myth and the neo-Platonic logos had actually just completed" (149/117).

II. The Place of Psychoanalysis

There would thus be a history of narcissism. And yet, we should perhaps reflect for a moment on the curious position that psychoanalysis occupies within this history—on the peculiar absence of psychoanalysis, or perhaps its omnipresence, in the chronicle and calendar of narcissism. Between literature and philosophy, various trajectories and traditions would be elaborated and transformed, as Kristeva passes from the "sociological and cultural investigations" of her earlier work to the "philosophical and theological" interests of the present volume. But in this history which passes through philosophy and literature, psychoanalysis would either be ignored, or else psychoanalysis would be present *at all stages of the narrative,* as if it did not submit to chronological time, as if narcissism did not need to wait for Freud to invent it, but were already waiting in the wings, or indeed fully present onstage, in the texts of Ovid and Plotinus, and even in the Platonic city, in the form of an *old insanity* which this "new insanity" would presumably displace. (A short parenthesis on reading, then: *"Novitas,"* the "new" in the title of Kristeva's chapter *("La nouvelle démence"),* would thus repeat the question that has already been posed by the datability of the proper name. Or more precisely—since this is really our question—the "new" in Kristeva's chapter would be a quotation that simultaneously conceals what it quotes: presenting itself as the assertion of a distinctive historical emergence, this "new" insanity would document itself by quoting an Ovidian phrase that, for its part, would seem to acknowledge less a new formation than a more ancient and mythical inheritance, a "new" insanity that merely echos and repeats the "old" insanity of the Platonic city. Ovid's *"novitasque"* would thus appear to remember what Kristeva's "new insanity" is tempted to forget. We close this short parenthesis.) Psychoanalysis would either have no place in the narrative, or else it would be *intertwined* from the very beginning with these other domains, in which case it is difficult to see what separates psychoanalysis from literature and philosophy, two disciplines or domains which would at least seem to be provisionally distinguished—capable of echoing or resonating with each other, but nevertheless not identical with one another. Psychoanalysis would either be left out of account, or else it would be *the medium* in which the entire genealogy takes place, the conceptual frame that allows us to grasp what is *really* happening in the history of subjectivity, behind the stories that philosophy and literature would tell about themselves. And since psychoanalysis is never simply ignored in Kristeva's work, we can only conclude that it serves as this general medium in which her account takes place. Not only her "sociological and cultural" work, but also her "philosophical and theological" analyses, would take place against the background of psychoanalytic theory, which elucidates and clarifies a trajectory of the subject that is usually lost in the standard histories of philosophy and literature. Psychoanalysis thus allows us to recover what is forgotten, or to remember what is concealed by the usual histories of literature and philosophy, insofar as it listens, neither to the story of the gradual emergence of truth and reason, nor to the history of the development of artistic forms, but to the subject who is speaking in philosophy and art, and whose destiny unfolds within those disciplines.

The difficulty that arises is therefore obvious: unlike all these other domains whose histories can be written, psychoanalysis itself would be the medium or ground of the narrative, the conceptual background or reflecting surface in which these other discourses would be brought to recognize themselves. Through the medium (and theater) of psychoanalysis, we would be able to see and recognize for the first time the truth that is hidden in the history of literature and philosophy. But as for psychoanalysis itself, it would not appear *within* the story: it would not be given in an image or a narrative, but would rather be like the watery pool which suspends before us on its delicate surface the image we are invited to contemplate, the image of philosophy or literature. The ungraspable liquidity of psychoanalysis, its watery invisibility and omnipresence, would thus be *the element* in which this history is formed. Psychoanalysis would be like water, like Cephissus and Liriope, the father and mother of Narcissus, the first a god of the river, the second a water nymph, who, anticipating Narcissus in advance, is herself transformed into a lily, "that other flower of moist areas," Kristeva says, "the funeral narcissus" (131/103).

Thus, between literature and philosophy, on the one hand, and psychoanalysis on the other, between that which enters into history and that which accompanies history without itself being inscribed in the calendar of time, a question would emerge—a question that not only concerns Kristeva's text, but ultimately bears on narcissism itself, insofar as one must eventually ask whether the event of narcissism is in fact a historical event, or whether, like psychoanalysis in this text, it flows alongside the entire course of historical time without belonging to a particular moment or a given temporal instant.

Can we believe, therefore, that we are really dealing with a history of narcissism in *Tales of Love,* as it might seem at first glance? Can we believe, moreover, that there is in fact a history of narcissism? Is this text in fact a history, and does the phenomenon of narcissism enter into history? And what would it mean to believe or doubt, that is, to enter into a debate in which doubt and belief, certainty and skepticism, are the organizing virtues? Is not the entire apparatus of doubt and belief, documentary evidence and theoretical vigilance, already part of the narcissistic story, in which recognition and misrecognition, seeing and believing, play their deadly game, mixing the imaginary and the real at the heart of the constitution of the subject? To doubt the story that is being told by Kristeva would already be to enter the arena of narcissism—of representation, evidence, and suspended belief. At the same time, however, if we were not to doubt, if we were simply to believe, taking Kristeva's history for granted, an entire network of questions and difficulties would have to be set aside.

III. The Catastrophe of Narcissism

In fact, this history of narcissism already puts in place a temporal structure that narcissism itself should not allow us to believe. For the time of narcissism is the time of a disaster, the time of an event whose traumatic character repeats itself at every moment, beyond the recovery of historical memory.[5] In its most basic structure, the event of narcissism would therefore resemble a trauma, an event that should not be too quickly inserted into the chronicle of ordinary time. The moment of narcissism would recall the experience of war and other traumas that Freud discusses in *Beyond the Pleasure Principle,* where he stresses the peculiar temporality of the traumatic event—not simply the fact that it repeats, refusing to pass away, and returning in dreams or nightmares that bring the subject back to the experience of trauma, in apparent violation of the principle of pleasure, but also the fact—far more enigmatic—that the trauma repeats because it was never experienced in the first place, never symbolized and made present as such to the subject. We must return here to the date, and the datability, of the event—the date of the "event" of narcissism. The experiences of war and other traumas do not belong to past time. They continue to intrude upon the present, blocking the experience of the here and now and asserting themselves in place of immediate experience—as if blinding the subject and interrupting vision with a kind of memory that does not appear as "memory," or as a recollection of the past, but rather *returns,* presenting itself in place of the present, so that the subject's own experience is lost. The flashback, the nightmare, the return of traumatic memory, is distinct from historical memory, insofar as it concerns an event that has not been integrated into historical time, ordered by a relation to the past and the future. Freud thus tells us that in traumatic events—if they can be called "events"—the past is *repeated instead of being remembered.* And if the trauma repeats in this way, Freud says, it is because the traumatic event was never experienced as such, never made present in relation to a future and a past, never given a place in any symbolic chain, or any network of protentions and retentions. What repeats is therefore something that somehow never "took place," a past that was never "present," which does not mean that it is merely nothing, a figment of the imagination or a purely mythical event, but rather that it happens without happening, as death happens for Heidegger, arriving without arriving, or like the murder of the father, the traumatic event

---

5. I take this phrase, "the disaster of narcissism," and some inspiration for my argument, from Claire Nouvet, whose lectures at Emory University pushed me in directions I would not otherwise have taken. See Claire Nouvet, "An Impossible Response: The Disaster of Narcissus," *Yale French Studies,* no. 79 (1991): 103–134.

that is recounted in the story of the primal horde in *Totem and Taboo,* an event which occurred, as Freud tells us, before history as such, before the beginning of historical time, in a mythical moment that explains how time in fact began.[6]

As the very structure of the "mirror stage" suggests, the traumatic event—the very advent of the ego—takes place before the subject is able to bear witness, before the "I" can utter any yes or no, and because it stands at the origin in this way, "before" the subject, we can only conclude that the trauma was never present to the subject as such, and *this* is why it cannot pass away, or belong to the past, as a present that once was. Because it does not belong to the past, moreover, the traumatic event is constantly expected to return from the future, like a catastrophe that is about to occur—a catastrophe (like object-loss in Kristeva's text) that must be avoided at all cost, avoided like madness itself, which, in Kristeva's account, already happened with Ovid and Plotinus, and yet must be avoided in the present age, where it emerges like an impending catastrophe, a "new malady" which may well be the defining catastrophe of our time, a narcissism that, although it was invented by Ovid and Plotinus,

---

6. It should be clear that, in speaking of narcissism itself as a "trauma," we are not attempting to condense into a single form the actual experiences of trauma—those, for example, that are linked in contemporary psychological literature to the definition and diagnosis of PTSD—and the "structural" or "constitutive" trauma of narcissism. Following Freud, we are rather suggesting that specific events (such as World War I, and its analogues in the theory of PTSD), insofar as they reveal a peculiar temporal return, might lead us to consider that the very structure of the subject includes and even requires a peculiar traumatic dimension, something "beyond the pleasure principle" that must be theoretically developed beyond the contingent examples of actual historical trauma. It is this very step that Freud takes in reformulating the theory of childhood incest, in quasi-anthropological terms, as he does in *Totem and Taboo,* where the "original murder" of the father is cast, not as a real event, but a structural characteristic that would account for the very emergence of historical time. See Monique Panaccio, "Notes on Freud's Concept of Trauma," *Clinical Studies: International Journal of Psycho-Analysis,* 2:1 (1996): 55–63. As Slavoj Žižek also observes, the concept of "trauma" in Freud progresses from an initial grounding in reality (an actual rape or seduction or violent accident), to a more generalized account of the traumatic constitution of the subject, which leads Freud to regard the trauma not as an actual event (one that might be interpreted and symbolized) but as a logical "stage" that can only be *constructed* and not *interpreted.* In this sense, the trauma corresponds to the second stage in Freud's presentation of the primal fantasy, "A Child Is Being Beaten"—a stage, Freud says, "that never had a real existence." See Slavoj Žižek, *The Plague of Fantasies* (New York: Verso, 1997), pp. 119–123.

is only on the verge of arrival. As Blanchot says, "We are on the edge of disaster without being able to situate it in the future: it is rather always already past, and yet we are on the edge or under the threat, all formulations which would imply the future—that which is to come—if the disaster were not that which does not come, that which has put a stop to every arrival."[7]

Is there a history of narcissism, then, and can we really believe that the name of Narcissus is datable in the way that Kristeva at least seems to suggest? Can we give Narcissus a date of birth in the works of Ovid and read its old age (its repetition or its end) in the contemporary world? This is a two-fold question, bearing on our knowledge of the past (or more fundamentally on our approach to it) and also on ourselves. Is Kristeva indeed willing, as she herself says, "to grant Narcissus such a crucial part in the history of Western subjectivity" (146/115)? Should we therefore stress, as Kristeva does, "the originality of the narcissistic figure and the very particular place it occupies, in the history of Western subjectivity" (134/105)? Should we, moreover, *see ourselves* as the heirs of this particular Western formation? Is the "new insanity" of her title intended to designate a historical invention, and one that we ourselves would inherit today? Is there a transmission and inheritance of narcissism, and can we give a history of this narcissism, *une histoire,* as Kristeva suggests in *Histoires d'amour?*

Or is it rather a matter of telling tales: *Ne faisons-nous que des histoires?* Are we only telling tales when we tell tales of love? Is the narrative therefore a fiction, a myth, a web of words designed, not simply to describe or document, but rather to contain and make more tolerable a narcissistic wound that accompanies the subject through all the various historical formations that mark its symbolic life?[8] Can we put narcissism on the calendar, as we would at least seem to be able to do with philosophy and literature, or is narcissism rather—along with psychoanalysis itself—the kind of watery event or possibility that haunts the time of the narrative at every stage of its development?

---

7. Maurice Blanchot, *The Writing of the Disaster,* trans. Ann Smock (Lincoln, NE: University of Nebraska Press, 1986), p. 1.

8. A "fiction" or a "myth," I write, as if there were no difference, or as if these differences, which are ultimately differences in genre, were trivial, a matter of indifference, when in fact it should be clear that the entire burden of our questioning may well come to rest on nothing other than this matter of genre—the forms of narrative (history, myth, fiction, and indeed developmental psychology, which is its own genre, and has its own narrative conventions) being precisely the many ways the subject has of relating to an impossible or traumatic origin.

On this view, the trauma of narcissism cannot be regarded as a historical event, an event in the history of thought or literature, with a beginning, a middle, and perhaps an end. Though capable of various transformations, of being cast in various versions or metamorphoses, with Ovid and Plotinus for example, narcissism itself would not have a historical birth or death. Instead, the event and the disaster of narcissism would repeat itself compulsively, like an original trauma that every narrative and every philosophy would bear within it, in a more or less visible way. The symbolic and cognitive presentation of this trauma—the philosophical and linguistic forms that appear to master and represent it (including Kristeva's historical rendering)—are certainly open to remarkable variation, but narcissism itself is not reducible to the images and words that offer to contain it. On this view, narcissism is not so much a "new insanity," as the insanity of a trauma that can only repeat itself. Plotinus would therefore not be (the father) at the origin (of a new insanity), but would only rework and transform the insanity of a more ancient Platonism that he cannot overcome or surpass—as if, true to the name of "neo-Platonism," he were telling a tale that was passed to him from his ancestors, from those who taught him to speak, to take up their story, a story that he repeats, but also figures as his own, through a language that makes it new. This would indeed be the "other" story told behind the narrative that we apparently find in *Tales of Love*: for as Kristeva in fact notes, the entire drama of shadow, sight, and reflection in Plotinus is constructed with "Platonic instruments" (137–138/108). The "new" insanity would thus be, at bottom, the transformation, and even the repetition, of a difficulty that was not invented ex nihilo by Plotinus or Ovid, but was rather inherited from an earlier time. Thus, contrary to first appearances, narcissism itself would not be a historical phenomenon—the invention of a particular moment, or the contingent product of a particular philosophical or literary outlook—but rather an event that compulsively repeats itself, as it passes from generation to generation.

For Ovid too, it is transparently clear that the story of Narcissus is already very old, its precise unfolding being in fact closely tied to a series of similar stories. Kristeva herself explicitly points this out. "Much emphasis," she writes, "has been placed on the morbid, narcotic, chthonian meaning of this legend," the "subterranean torpor" that "links the fable to the vegetative intoxication of Dionysus" (134/105). In fact, just as "Narcissus dies after he has seen himself," so also "Pentheus dies for having seen the mysteries of Dionysus" (134/105). In a parenthesis, Kristeva notes that the painter Poussin will later recall this connection "in his *Birth of Bacchus,* which pairs the two myths and the two heros" (134/105). Ovid's Narcissus is therefore not the first who sees what he should not, and who is punished for a kind of idolatry, a fascinated vision that sees what is not really there—an image that is neither another nor himself, but an illusion or mystery that blinds him, cutting him off from the other, and finally bringing about his death. These details about Dionysus and Poussin are not simply ancillary information, the sort of casual historical references that are supposed to characterize (the genre of) scholarly knowledge, a layering of incidental facts and information that would have no real bearing on the philosophical argument of the text. On the contrary, they register the entire difficulty of the historical localization that Kristeva would at first seem to have in mind.

The story was therefore not invented by Ovid, and its historical origin cannot be so quickly secured. As Maurice Blanchot points out in *The Writing of the Disaster,* and as Kristeva herself acknowledges, but without pursuing its consequences, there is already by the time of Ovid a well-established tradition of fables around Narcissus, in relation to which Ovid is in fact a notorious innovator and a quite self-conscious revisionist. As always in the *Metamorphoses,* the story being told is already an ancient one, and Ovid (like the Greek tragedians) is a latecomer, a commentator, and a receiver, whose task is to hear and understand anew what has already been said in a mythological past. "Mythologists do not fail to indicate," Blanchot writes, "that Ovid—an intelligent, civilized poet, upon whose version of the myth the concept of narcissism is modeled (as though his narrative developments indeed contained psychoanalytic knowledge)—modifies the myth in order to expand it and make it more accessible."[9] What is more, the explicit attention Ovid pays to the reception and repetition of antiquity is accentuated in a more general and systematic way, by the imbrication and layering of tales that we find in the *Metamorphoses* as a whole, every story introduced by another story, as if each tale were not really a new invention, but a commentary on another tale, the allegory or echo of the previous story, the whole series being linked in a symbolic chain—or intertwined like snakes.

So it is with the story of Narcissus and Echo, which Ovid introduces by recounting to us how it was that the prophet Tiresias, who can see the future, was blinded by Juno, as a punishment for having spoken against her. We recall very well how this came to pass: one day, Jupiter—who was drunk at the time and feeling pretty good, forgetting his cares and his anxiety (*diffusum nectare,*

---

9. Maurice Blanchot, *The Writing of the Disaster,* p. 125.

curas/Seposuisse gravis vacuaque agitasse remissos [lines 318–319])—turned to Juno and said "I'll bet that you women have more pleasure in love than we men." Juno disagreed (as often happened with these two), and in order to settle the dispute—each insisting upon the other's greater pleasure, without knowing in fact or by experience—they turned to Tiresias, for he alone knew what love was like for both the man and the woman. For one day, he had come upon two snakes intertwined in the woods, writhing together, and taking his stick, he pulled them apart, and was instantly transformed into a woman.[10] He thus lived as a woman for seven years, until one day he saw those snakes again, insinuating with each other, and thinking that the same cause might produce the same effect (or the reversal of that effect), he once more forced them apart, after which, he again became a man ("taking on again," as Ovid says, "the form and the image of his earlier self," *"forma prior rediit genetivaque venit imago"* [line 331]). And so, when Tiresias, having been appointed as judge, took the side of Jupiter, Juno punished him with blindness: *"Iudicis aeterna damnavit lumina nocte"* (line 335), Ovid says, "she damned his vision to eternal night, condemning the eyes of Justice to be blind." Like the story of Echo and Narcissus, and indeed like the story of justice that Oedipus brings upon himself, this too is a story in which blindness and sexual difference are brought together, and a story of punishment as well.

Thus, like the work of Plotinus, which fashions itself with Platonic instruments, so also the myth of Narcissus is not new with Ovid, but is rather inherited and repeated: the time of Ovid's "new" insanity is thus less easy to grasp than one might think, and it is not clear that this time will be datable in the way that one might date the signing of a treaty, a scientific discovery, or some other "historical" event. Nor is this difficulty restricted to the tale that Ovid tells about Narcissus. On the contrary, it extends to narcissism itself, for the "event" of narcissism—if one can speak of an "event" of narcissism, when it is really a question of something that never occurs, and at the same time never passes away, something that is impossible, a self-apprehension of the ego that is not a self-apprehension, a "splitting" that brings death at the very moment it brings the subject into being—already introduces a break with historical time and its sequence of localizable occurrences. Thus, while we have suggested that, for Kristeva, a provisional line might be drawn between

---

10. See Jacques Derrida, *Memoirs of the Blind: The Self-Portrait and Other Ruins,* trans. Michael Naas and Pascale-Anne Brault (Chicago, IL: University of Chicago Press, 1993), p. 17.

philosophy and literature on the one hand (insofar as their histories can be written), and psychoanalysis on the other hand (in its watery omnipresence), the historical datability of philosophy and literature is no longer so clearly secured.

At the same time, however, this is not to say that narcissism *simply* has no history, for as Kristeva observes, the "instruments" inherited from Plato are "dramatized, humanized, and eroticized by Narcissus," in a transformation that can be marked, only to be transformed or translated again, to "become with Plotinus *logical elements* of the elaboration, beyond narcissistic madness, of that Western consciousness of self" (137–138/108, emphasis added). Nevertheless, if narcissism repeats itself compulsively like a destiny or fate that every narrative and every philosophy would bear within it in a more or less visible way, this means that we cannot confuse the symbolic and imaginary presentation of this trauma with the enigmatic structure that essentially comprises it. And if narcissism points us toward this constitutive "event," the thinking that aims at narcissism itself would have to consist not so much in the documentary narrative that Kristeva appears to present, but in a task of thinking, whose effort would be to remember—to repeat, remember, and work-through—a trauma that has always already claimed it in advance. It would therefore be a mistake to believe that we are concerned simply with the invention of a new world, casting off (or doubting) everything that has gone before, and starting from a new ground of certainty; for indeed, given these temporal difficulties, and the fact that the true structure of the trauma would not consist in a localized chronological "event" that one might (secondarily) remember or forget, one can only conclude that the trauma itself is *in* the memory, in the structure of remembering and repeating, and nowhere else. As Plotinus himself says, explaining the origin of his own "new" invention, "the reunification of the soul within the ever-present unity of intellect": "Human souls rush down here because they have gazed at their images as in the mirror of Dionysus" (136/107)—a passage Kristeva does not fail to mark as "another mythical reference . . . in Plotinus." The "new" insanity of Plotinus is thus not to be confined to a historical moment, but is itself the memory, the echo, of a Dionysian myth, and Kristeva herself repeatedly stresses these "reflections" of archaic and mythical doctrine within Plotinian thought. Thus, commenting on the text of Plotinus, she writes: "Let us recall that, according to one version of the myth, Dionysus as a child allows himself to be seduced by Hera by means of a mirror, before undergoing the ordeal of the Titans, who cut him up into pieces that are then put together again by Athena and Zeus" (136–137/107).

IV. Of Narcissism Itself

Is there, then, a history of narcissism, with an origin in Plotinus or Ovid and an end or culmination in Modernity? Or is it rather a matter of telling tales when we speak of the formation of the subject? And if *the literary and philosophical exposition of narcissism* in fact reveals a structure that cannot be historically confined to a particular moment, what would this mean for *narcissism itself,* as it is understood not in literature or philosophy, but in the domain (and genre) of psychoanalysis—if one can pretend to suppose, after what we have just seen, that this psychoanalytic domain is "no longer" the domain of philosophy or indeed of literature, but a distinct and strictly separable genre?

In order to do justice to this question, we would have to ask not only about Kristeva's text, and the peculiar tension that marks it—narrating the history of subjectivity while at the same time taking back a certain number of formulations, as we have tried to show, with observations that acknowledge an archaic repetition. We would also have to ask about narcissism itself, about the story or history of narcissism, as it appears in certain versions of psycho-analysis, where we are told about the moment of the "mirror stage," which replaces a moment of bodily incoherence with a new unity, only to be again transformed (or metamorphosed) by the order of language. Does Freud himself (like Lacan, who only repeats what Freud has shown us) not speak of a "primary narcissism," and of its later transformation, through the oedipal conflict, into something like "secondary narcissism"? Does he not also speak of a period *before* narcissism, before the Lacanian "mirror stage," in which the subject's body would not yet be coherent—a stage before the constitution of the body? The essay "On Narcissism" is perfectly clear on this point: "We are bound to suppose," Freud writes, "that a unity comparable to the ego cannot exist in the individual from the start; the ego has to be developed. The auto-erotic instincts, however, are there from the very first; so there must be something added to auto-eroticism—a new psychical action—in order to bring about narcissism."[11]

---

11. Sigmund Freud, *The Standard Edition of the Complete Psychological Works of Sigmund Freud,* 24 volumes, trans. and ed. James Strachey et al. (London: Hogarth Press, 1953), 14, pp. 76–77. Further references to Freud will be by volume and page number.

Narcissism is thus not present at the beginning. A new psychical action would be necessary to bring about narcissism. That "new psychical action" is of course the "mirror stage," the "moment" (but in what kind of time?) when the child passes from bodily fragmentation to imaginary completeness, the inaugural moment in which the body is "given," by being transformed from a disorganized assemblage of bodily zones, each of which is capable of a certain pleasure, which Freud calls autoerotic, to another organization, in which the pleasure of the ego will become possible. Thus, as Lacan says, "we have only to understand the mirror stage as an identification, in the full sense that psychoanalysis gives to that term: namely, the transformation that takes place in the subject when he assumes an image."[12] And as we know, this initial "form" (with its captivating beauty, as the cognate *"formosa"* suggests) of the imaginary ego will later be subjected to yet another transformation, with the advent of language, which will allow the subject to identify with signifiers—a possibility harbored by the name, which will carry the subject beyond the realm of the image, toward something resembling the "other"—an alterity that, while it at first falls prey to the image (appearing only as an alter ego), can finally emerge as an "other" for the "subject." Lacan acknowledges this later transformation as well when he writes that the mirror stage reveals to us the I "in its primordial form, before it is objectified in the dialectic of identification with the other, and before language restores to it, in the universal, its function as subject."[13] In psychoanalysis too, there would thus be a history of narcissism—if not the history it acquires in Kristeva's text, then the series of stages that narcissism itself undergoes, according to psychoanalysis.

And yet, here too the matter is not so clear. Does Lacan not famously acknowledge that the moment of the mirror stage amounts to "the assumption of . . . an alienating identity, which will mark with its rigid structure the subject's entire mental development?"[14] On this view, the fundamental feature of narcissism would lie in its *constitutive* character, in the fact that it entails an initial formation of the ego—a first, traumatic rupture with natural existence—whose later re-deployments and translations will never overcome that constitutive foundation. In his essay "On Narcissism," Freud himself

---

12. Jacques Lacan, *Ecrits: A Selection,* trans. Alan Sheridan (New York: Norton, 1977), p. 2.

13. Ibid., p. 2.

14. Ibid., p. 4.

observes that the origin of the ego has a formative and structural character that no revision and no retroactive reworking will be able to forget (not only because of its constitutive character, but also because, as we have suggested, the inaugural "event" of narcissism cannot be, properly speaking, remembered). Narcissism will therefore never pass away, like an event that acquires a date, or a moment that eventually belongs to the past. Speaking of the projective identification that supposedly marks a stage in the "maturation" of the subject—what Lacan speaks of as the displacement of the first, bodily ego into a transitive identification with the alter ego—Freud writes that the subject now projects into the future another possible identity, an "ideal ego" toward which the present ego can aim. This will be a new formation in which the initial self-absorption of the child is supposedly transcended, cast off, and left behind, as a moment that now belongs to the past. And yet, no sooner has Freud deposited this notion into his text than he finds it necessary to explain that the process is not so linear:

> This ideal ego is now the target of the self-love which was enjoyed in childhood by the actual ego. The subject's narcissism makes its appearance displaced onto this new ideal ego, which, like the infantile ego, finds itself possessed of everything that is of value. *[Diesem Idealich gilt nun die Selbstliebe, welche in der Kindheit das wirkliche Ich genoss. Der Narzissmus erscheint auf dieses neue ideale Ich vershoben, welches sich wie das infantile im Besitz aller wertvollen Vollkommenheiten befindet.]* [SE 14:94][15]

Thus, contrary to first appearances, the so-called "primal" or "primary narcissism" is not a stage that is eventually given up. Indeed, as Freud adds in his laconic way, depositing the most obscure theoretical difficulties into a prose that is altogether misleading in its urbanity: "As always where the libido is concerned, man has here again shown himself incapable of giving up a satisfaction he had once enjoyed" (*SE* 14, p. 94). We cannot stop here, however, for the matter is still more complicated: it is insufficient to say that the primordial narcissism of the child ("the self-love which was enjoyed in childhood by the actual ego") remains present in its future transformation, in the form of the ideal ego which now attracts the self-love of the subject; for the

---

15. For the German original, see Sigmund Freud, *Gesammelte Werke* (Frankfurt am Main: S. Fisher Verlag, 1946), vol. 10, p. 161.

peculiar fact is that the origin itself, the very moment of the emergence of narcissism (the "satisfaction he had once enjoyed"), does not appear to lie at the beginning, but would seem to emerge for the first time *only through this "later" form:* for this is indeed the sense of Freud's meticulous phrasing, in which "narcissism *makes its appearance displaced*" (emphasis added). It is thus as if narcissism had to take place twice—through a certain repetition—in order to appear at all. Narcissism itself—not merely a later form or stage of narcissism, but the very thing itself: *Der Narzissmus*—would "first" show up and make its entrance [*erscheint*] only on the basis of this "new" form [*auf dieses neue ideale Ich verschoben*]. What Freud is saying here is that it is only on the basis of the "ideal ego" that the psychic economy is able (or we might say "condemned"), nostalgically, to produce for itself a backwards glance, a new temporal arrangement, that will allow this ego to speak to itself of a "former time," to represent for itself a mythical past which the childish ego once (as in "once upon a time") enjoyed. This is what it means, and this is the peculiar structure under consideration, when Freud writes that narcissism is *first born* (or "makes its appearance") the moment the ideal ego "now" receives (the auto-affection of) a self-love that is *construed as* the recapturing of a "lost enjoyment," a mythical satisfaction that is now attributed to an archaic time called "childhood" [*Diesem Idealich gilt nun die Selbstliebe, welche in der Kindheit das wirkliche Ich genoss*].

In fact, as the passage continues, the two moments of the ego we have just articulated in their peculiar temporality are further elaborated, and we find yet another moment, so that Freud's account would complete the same three moments already isolated by Lacan—the ego in its primordial form, the ego in its relation to the alter ego (identification with the other), and what Lacan calls the "restoration" (another word whose temporal dimension would lead us into difficulties) of the "subject" in the dimension of the "universal." It is precisely these moments which appear in the Freudian text, in the very passage we have just cited, where Freud speaks (as we have seen) of the "ego"—what he calls the "actual ego," *das wirkliche Ich*—the "ideal ego," and finally (as the passage continues) the "ego ideal," the last of which (corresponding to Lacan's "symbolic identification") opens a future in language that seems at first glance to amount to the only way out of narcissism. The passage from the ideal ego to the ego ideal (in Freud's language) would thus represent the passage into the universal, the order of symbolic mediation, which gives life to the statue that would otherwise be petrified by the Medusa-effect of the imago.[16] In short, with the arrival of the ego ideal, projected into the future through the symbolic apparatus (like a little spool of thread with its phonemic attachment), the image that was given in the mirror will no longer be sufficient, and the subject will desire something more, something else, an identity which might capture the recognition of others. Imaginary narcissism would thus be normalized and moderated by language and exchange, and by the mechanism of a newly social identification (the notorious "identification with signifiers"). *It is thus as if speech itself were the consequence and by-product of narcissism,* less a rational tool of communication between already existing "subjects," than a fantastic and desperate invention spewed forth by the human animal in an attempt to fashion an exit, or at least to heal the wound, of the narcissism that brought him into being. And again, this chronological mapping of stages is clearly irreducible to any historical sequence, for Freud notes that even with the ego ideal, the child

> is not willing to forgo the narcissistic perfection of his childhood; and when, as he grows up, he is disturbed by the admonitions of childhood and by the awakening of his own critical judgment, so that *he can longer retain* that perfection, *he seeks to recover it* in the new form of an ego ideal. *What he projects before him as his ideal is the substitute for the lost narcissism of his childhood,* in which he was his own ideal. [*SE* 14:94, emphasis added]

Infantile narcissism is therefore not actually *transcended* by means of social identification: on the contrary, it is *projected* into the future, so that it can be "found again," recaptured and preserved. Freud thereby suggests that the very formation of "conscience," the awakening of "critical judgment" that comes with the incorporation of the admonitions of others (an internalization of the law) and leads us to give up our infantile demands, is at the same time a repetition of the narcissism it promised to transcend. At every stage, it seems, the transformation of narcissism is less a sequence of discrete stages than a process of repetition and reiteration, all of which is set in motion by the "originally" narcissistic constitution of the subject.

---

16. For an extended discussion of the relation between the ideal ego and the ego ideal, see Jacques Lacan, *The Seminar of Jacques Lacan, Book I: Freud's Papers on Technique,* ed. Jacques-Alain Miller, trans. John Forrester (New York: Norton, 1988), pp. 107–142.

V. Sacrifice, Responsibility

We have tried to mark a tension in Kristeva's book, a peculiar vacillation between history and repetition, between the history that at least *seems* to characterize philosophy and literature in this text, and the watery omnipresence of psychoanalysis, which for its part does not enter into history, but accompanies its entire unfolding. This tension is apparent in Kristeva's title, in the very word *"histoires,"* which shuttles between "story" and "history." But the difficulty has not been restricted to the tale Kristeva tells about Narcissus. On the contrary, it extends to narcissism itself, in the sense that the "event" of narcissism (if one can speak of an "event" when it is really a question of something that never occurs) gives rise to a "past" that only emerges "later," as a lost origin—one that the subject, moreover, projects into the future, in order to "recover" and possess this time that never was. Like the moment of the glance that fixes Narcissus before the watery pool, so narcissism is also an event that is impossible, a self-apprehension of the ego that is not "self"-apprehension, but rather the figuring forth of an "identity" that is not the subject ("He did not know what he was seeing," Ovid's narrator tells us portentously [line 430]), an identity that brings petrification and death in the very moment when it brings the ego into being—only to promise, by means of this lure, an escape, another way forward, the possibility of attaining one day an existence that will recapture an original plenitude, a past that never was, or never was until the promise cast it forth, in the form of this absolute past.

The catastrophic character of the Ovidian story makes it less sanguine, perhaps, than Kristeva, or indeed than psychoanalysis, which holds out the promise of an end to narcissism or—if not an end—then a future for narcissism in which love is not altogether impossible. It is perhaps this promise that Derrida is willing, for a moment, to read in the sacrifice of Isaac, a story which shows us an Abraham whose decision (if it can even be called a "decision," any more than the look of Narcissus can be said to be the act of a subject) to accept this absolute loss paradoxically gives rise to a future, a "still-more-time," a possibility in which, despite (and because of) sacrifice and death, *time remains:*

> The instant in which the sacrifice is as it were consummated, for only an instant, a *no-time-lapse* . . . this is the impossible to grasp instant of absolute imminence in which Abraham can no longer go back on his decision, nor even suspend it. *In this instant,* therefore, in the imminence

that doesn't even separate the decision from the act, God returns his son to him and decides by a sovereign decision, by an absolute gift, to reinscribe sacrifice within an economy by means of what henceforth comes to resemble a reward.[17]

This "sacrificial" instant is precisely the time of the narcissistic wound, the time of the subject, which does not begin in identity with itself, but passes in an instant (the blink of an eye) from being "nothing" to being "something else," from incoherence to alienation. The *moment of representation* is the moment of a subject who is not a subject before he sees himself, and who is already lost the moment reflection begins—a subject who is nothing before the image gives him to himself, and who is already something else as soon as the image arrives. The time of the subject is thus an impossible time, the time of an instant of transition *(Untergang, metabole),* a moment that gives and takes away in a movement of constitution that is equally the destitution of the subject.

It is also the time of the voice of Echo, who calls to Narcissus and is never heard, who calls in words of love that are at the same time not her words, not the words of any subject, but only the borrowed words of the other, twisted and cut short in a mechanical reverberation, an echo that only repeats the desire of Narcissus—who in fact *has* no desire and *expresses* no desire—an echo that returns his words in an inverted form, which he is unable to hear. The voice of Echo thus repeats this impossible time, echoing a desire that does not (or not yet) exist, and returning it as an expression of "love" in which no voice of any subject is present. And yet, in an ethical gesture that could be inflicted only by psychoanalysis (as Ovid tells us in advance), *this* is what Narcissus is called on to "recognize." In fact, it is precisely for failing in response to this perverse and impossible call that he is punished by the gods and condemned to his mythical fate. The time of the voice is thus like the time of the gaze of Narcissus himself, who, looking into the pool, does not see or recognize himself ("*Quid videat, nescit,*" Ovid's narrator says [430]), but rather falls in love with an image, the simulacrum he mistakes for another—another to whom he then speaks, saying, "I can almost touch you; only the smallest distance stands in the way of love. Why do you deceive me, disappearing when I reach for you" [*Posse putes tangi; mimimum est quod amantibus obstat./ Quisquis es, hucexi; quid me, puer unice, fallis?/ Quove petitus abis?* (453–455)].

---

17. Jacques Derrida, *The Gift of Death,* trans. David Wills (Chicago, IL: University of Chicago Press, 1995), pp. 95–96.

What stands in the way of love is this image, an image that is neither of another nor of himself, an image that kills him, and that represents nothing— neither Narcissus nor the other—but rather hovers on the surface of a fragile pool, giving Narcissus to himself for the first time, but in a form that petrifies and brings death. The time of this representation that gives the subject would be a suspended time, an instant suspended between a subject who is not yet given and a subject who comes into being in an instant that brings his disappearance.[18] Between the traumatic advent of the subject and his disaster, there would be no time at all, as if origin and end were given in a strange simultaneity.

How then can we say that Narcissus is responsible for his failure to respond to the other? If the Ovidian myth is indeed an allegory of narcissism in the psychoanalytic sense (if the fable speaks to us, in Blanchot's words, "as if it already contained psychoanalytic knowledge"), how can we say that Narcissus has failed to recognize the other, to respond to the call of the other, or that he is in some way responsible, when there is no subject there before he arrives at the pool where he sees himself for the first time? How can we speak of Narcissus as already claimed by the other, already responsible, before the subject has even arrived on the scene? And still more sharply, how can we say that, in addition to being responsible in advance, responsible before he can "take responsibility," before he can subjectivize and internalize this relation to

---

18. Jacques Derrida, *The Gift of Death.* See also Blanchot, who writes of the peculiar way in which the Law produces this impossible situation, such that the Law must be covered over by ruses of narrative construction, which forget the Law they claim to represent, while also, at precisely the same time, preserving something of what they forget, just as Kristeva's history allows us to read, in spite of everything, the impossible structure of narcissism that is veiled by the tale she seems to tell us. Blanchot thus writes: "Laws—prosaic laws—free us, perhaps, from the Law by substituting for the invisible majesty of time the various constraints of space. Similarly, rules suppress, in the term 'law,' what power—ever primary—evokes. Rules also suppress the rights, which go along with the notion of law, and establish the reign of pure procedure . . . a manifestation of technical competence." And with Blanchot, too, we find not only this peculiar relation between the Law and laws, structure and history, but also an inevitable turn toward the question of genre: "Kafka's trial can be interpreted as a tangle of three different realms (the Law, laws, and rules). This interpretation, however, is inadequate, because to justify it one would have to assume a fourth realm not derived from the other three—the overarching realm of literature itself" (*Writing of the Disaster,* p. 144).

the other, he is also *guilty* for failing to respond, and even *due to be punished* as a result?

For this is indeed the harsh law that the Ovidian myth proposes in a story that unfolds in two stages, two scenes that have been admirably detailed by Claire Nouvet: one (the first) in which he fails to respond to Echo, and another (which comes second) in which he is given to himself in a first reflection.[19] In the logic of the myth, which clearly defies the linear time of narrative, Narcissus is already guilty in the first scene, before coming into being as a subject, before his "constitution in the mirror stage" of the second scene; and the second scene, which one might wish to read simply as the moment in which the subject is constituted, must in fact be understood as a punishment for an earlier, archaic or prehistoric crime. For it is his crime in the first scene that destines him for punishment in the second—his encounter before the watery pool being explicitly presented as a *punishment* for his failure to respond (according to a logic that enchains the destiny of Narcissus in a story that has already taken place with Echo, who for her part could not be heard as another, having been deprived of her voice for earlier crimes against the goddess Juno). The very advent of the subject, narcissism itself, in its "inaugural" moment and prototypical staging—a single figure suspended above the watery abyss—would thus have to be read, not merely as an inaugural moment, a beginning or constitution, but as a punishment, an extended moment or "stage" which therefore only takes place against the background of this divine Other, this Law that "already" destines the subject for exile and death, as a punishment for "earlier" crimes. This is the archaic justice of the myth, the harsh law that holds Narcissus responsible for an event—a relation or nonrelation—that occurred before any reflection took place, outside historical time, in a primordial or mythical moment before the advent of the subject, in a past that was never present, and that Narcissus will never remember. The moment of the look that is staged by Ovid, and by psychoanalysis as well, must be read against the background of this law. Indeed, the very look itself would capture the essence of this law. As Derrida says: "This look that cannot be exchanged is what situates originary culpability and original sin; it is the essence of responsibility."[20] Hovering for a moment before the pool, *Narcissus cannot remember* this "earlier time" that brought

---

19. See Claire Nouvet, "An Impossible Response: The Disaster of Narcissus," *Yale French Studies,* no. 79 (1991): 103–134.

20. Jacques Derrida, *The Gift of Death,* p. 94.

him to this place of origin and end. And yet, as we must also acknowledge, *his experience will also testify to this immemorial past,* as the second scene bears witness, after the fact, to the earlier scene.

This adds a final element to the operation of the law, allowing us to see the punishment of Narcissus somewhat more clearly. For the law of the gods may punish us for crimes we cannot remember, which took place before there was time for reflection; but the gods—however frivolous they may be, and however captivated by their own affairs—do not merely use us for their sport. Thus, while Narcissus will never remember the crime for which he has been punished, we must also acknowledge that he knows of his crime after the fact, and knows *because he is brought to justice* for his role in this archaic and immemorial event. In the logic of the myth: his punishment comes not as arbitrary brutality, but as evidence, indeed, as a memorial that something has taken place. If Narcissus is punished for a crime that took place "before the subject," then, and brought to a watery end, this punishment also gives, in the sense that it alone shows this relation to the other, an immemorial relation which—without this law and this punishment—would disappear without a trace. Thus, for an instant, and after the fact, Narcissus will recall this immemorial responsibility for us, *precisely because he is punished.* It is this divine law, this disastrous advent that gives and takes away, this "event" which occurs outside historical time, that the structure of narcissism confronts, and then reiterates at every stage, in a logic of repetition that will always be forgotten by narrative, which, for its part, at least offers, for awhile, a little refuge.

8

Trauma, Repetition, and the Hermeneutics of Psychoanalysis

Linda Belau

Translating the Symptom

Insofar as psychoanalysis attempts to address an impossible meaning at the core of traumatic experience, its hermeneutic activity is founded on a translation that is structured as an open practice of reading rather than a closed system of interpretation. Because the signifier is always marked by an inadequacy, psychoanalysis can never hold itself up as an idealism. For this reason, the "truths" it tells, and, in its clinical application, the hermeneutic practice it engages offer nothing to the analysand other than the awareness of the signifier's fundamental incompleteness. And even this final truth it embraces cannot be guaranteed. Psychoanalysis, then, does not tell the analysand the truth about his problems. It cannot excavate the original source of his troubles, hand it over to him, and suggest appropriate changes. That is, in addressing an analysand's particular problem or symptom, psychoanalysis does not make interventions at the level of the signified—an attempt, as it were, to create a content correlate to what the signifier cannot represent—but rather, it works at the level of the signifier—that it is inadequate.[1] Psychoanalysis, in other

---

1. For a further analysis of the relation between trauma and the inadequacy of the signifier, see my essay "Trauma and the Maternal Signifier" in *Post Modern Culture* 11:2.

words, does not try to overcome the split in the subject since it always structures its praxis around the inadequacy that characterizes the signifier. This materiality of the signifier is the only absolute knowledge that it posits, the only understanding that it embraces.

The most obvious product of the impact of the signifier, it is the symptom that is the starting point of analysis since the symptom shows us that the inadequacy of the signifier is not simply external to the subject as some prohibited or "lacking" content but, rather, that this inadequacy is proper to it. As a positive marker for the negating effect of the signifier on the subject, the symptom shows us that the lack suffered by the subject as he is constituted by the signifier into the symbolic is really an *excess,* a left-over piece from the passage through *creatio ex nihilo.* The passage from the presymbolic symbiotic relation with the mother to the differing relations of subjectivity creates a kind of presubjective *materia prima* that manifests itself as an uncanny presence for the subject of the signifier.[2] This lack in the subject is the remainder produced by the cut of the signifier. What is cut away, in other words, returns in the subject in the form of the unconscious repressed.[3] This does not simply mean that this remainder is inside the subject; the symptom, rather, as a formation of the unconscious, as an excessive remainder of the impossible primordial cut, exists *at the limit* of the subject. The symptom, then, is both inside and outside the subject: it is both prohibited and impossible since it marks both a lack and an excess. This is the extimate kernel around which subjectivity is constituted.[4]

In his seminar entitled "Extimacy" (1985–86) in which he offers a sus-

---

2. See Mladen Dolar, "Beyond Interpellation," *Qui Parle?* vol. 8, no. 1 (1994): 77.

3. The "material" of the cut also returns in the subject as the traumatic experience of *jouissance.* See my forthcoming *Encountering Jouissance: Trauma, Psychosis, Psychoanalysis* for a more sustained analysis of this point.

4. According to Dolar, "the remainder produced by subjectivation . . . is neither exterior nor interior, but not somewhere else either. It is the point of exteriority in the very kernel of interiority, the point where the innermost touches the outermost, where materiality is the most intimate. It is around this intimate external kernel that subjectivity is constituted. Lacan has, as always, coined a fine word for it: extimacy." Ibid., p. 78. "Extimacy" ("*Extimité*") is also the title of Jacques-Alain Miller's seminar of 1985–1986. A condensed exposition of this text, entitled "*Extimité,*" appears in *Lacanian Theory of Discourse: Subject, Structure, and Society,* ed. Mark Bracher et al. (New York: New York University Press, 1994), pp. 74–87. According to Miller, "the exterior is present in the interior. The most interior—this is how the dictionary

tained reading of the Lacanian concept, Jacques-Alain Miller considers the "phenomenon" of extimacy in terms of the real in the symbolic so that, as he says, one might "escape the common ravings about a psychism supposedly located in a bipartition between interior and exterior."[5] According to Miller, extimacy shows us that the intimate is Other. In this sense, it is like a foreign or alien presence, a kind of parasite.[6] This is precisely the status of the symptom: it is like an alien invader that is, despite its foreignness, most intimate to the subject. Without the symptom, the subject would never register the lack that marks its excess. And this mark, as correlate to the inadequacy of the signifier, is the only positive "content" the signifier has.[7] Without the symptom, then, no subject would "exist."

As the signifier cuts the body and emerges, *gleichzeitig,* as inadequate for filling the void opened in this cut, it is the symptom that attempts to positivize this negativity. This is why, according to Lacan, the symptom is to be understood as a metaphor. For Lacan, a metaphor is a signifier that stands for another signifier. It is a signifying substitution. Thus, the symptom does not have a fixed meaning but is, rather, the complicated effect of the signifier. And the signifier can never be reduced to its meaning. There is something of the signifier that exceeds meaning, something inadequate that is its very materiality. The symptom, therefore, as a positivization of this lack/excess, cannot be "cured" through an interpretation based on plumbing to its deepest meaning, its origin, since another symptom will always come in its place. Freud was not a little astonished to discover this in his practice with the treatment of women hysterics. The hysteric always has a symptom to display—a twitching eye, a pain in the shoulder, or an uncontrolled feeling of anxiety—that seems to point to some traumatic origin or meaning. In order to address the hysteric's symptom, Freud invented the "talking cure" so that his patients might be able

---

defines 'intimate' *(l'intime)* —has, in the analytic experience, a quality of exteriority. This is why Lacan invented the term 'extimate.'" See *"Extimité,"* p. 76.

5. Jacques Alain Miller, "Extimacy," in *Lacanian Theory of Discourse: Subject, Structure, and Society,* ed. Mark Bracher et al. (New York: New York University Press, 1994), p. 75.

6. See Ibid., p. 76.

7. Here we see that the "content" is really the form. Or, we might say, it is a form without content. This is what constitutes the signifier. The figure of a form without content also constitutes the symptom since it is always the form of the symptom in repression (as the return of the signifier's cut) and not its particular content that is significant for analysis.

to get to the bottom of their trauma. But, as Freud was soon to learn, getting to the bottom of the ailment, to its origin, so to speak, was precisely not the point of analysis. As soon as one symptom was talked though, summarily interpreted, as it were, another arose in its place. Thus, Freud quickly came to see that there was much more involved in discharging the symptom than a simple interpretation or translation of its seeming content. This insight would itself come to function as the basis of Freud's early theory of trauma and hysteria as well as the technique he would develop in order to address these problems and their attendant symptoms.

The question, then, for Freud will be how to translate the symptom. How can one symbolize what the signifier is not adequate to—the unconscious repressed? It is difficult to speak outright about the function of the signifier in relation to the problem of translating the symptom since it is possible to discern two different contexts or dimensions of this relation. First, there is the dimension of the signifier, and translation becomes a kind of method or tool for plumbing its depths. If there .is a certain inadequacy to the signifier, perhaps an extremely faithful act of translation can make this inadequacy good. The assumption here is that fidelity engenders truth. This is misleading, however, because this position implies that there is some content to the signifier, to its inadequacy, that translation can decode. The other dimension or perspective from which to consider the relation between translation and the symptom is, of course, the symptom. In order to get to the bottom of the symptom, it would seem, one has only to open one's mind and understand. The solution to all the suffering, then, is to treat the patient as a kind of lexicon of symptoms. One merely needs to be sensitive to the material of the symptom and to endeavor, as it were, to become a master of solicitude. In this manner, it appears simple enough to transmit the "foreign" material. Just as one translates a foreign language into another, the symptom might be translated into the vocabulary of hidden causes and buried aetiologies. The patient, then, is like an open book to a skilled translator, and the talking cure will give this translator the raw materials he needs to make the proper interpretation. This is also a mistaken assumption because the symptom is not characterized by its content. A patient may be suffering a particular ailment, but, as Freud was to discover early on in his studies on trauma and hysteria, there is no physiological explanation for the hysteric patient's symptoms.

Because the symptom is an expression of the unconscious repressed and the patient does not have conscious access to it, it both marks and exposes a splitting in the psychic functioning. Like the experience of trauma, then, the symptom is necessarily unavailable for translation since the unconscious repressed "content" which is pathogenically active (the symptom shows us this activity) is not consciously accessible for the patient. The patient, that is, is not able to symbolize the origin of his symptom because it is repressed—it belongs in the register of the real. When an element of "experience" is not psychically registered or elaborated, it is, properly speaking, not yet symbolically mediated—it remains embedded within the real and, thus, wields a traumatic, pathological impact on the subject. This pathological force, of course, is nothing other than the symptom as an expression of the unconscious repressed.[8] In order to understand the symptom in its relation to the mechanism of repression, then, Freud would have to invent the analytic strategy of construction since any analysis, interpretation, or translation of the symptom must necessarily engage a level of meaning that the analysand has not been aware of.

Construction: Accessing the Unconscious Repressed

There are, Freud tells us, certain scenes from infancy that are not reproduced during analysis as recollections. They are, rather, the products of construction.[9] Since we have no direct access to the time before the time of the subject—a time that nevertheless marks him in the most profound way—construction is the only technique at our disposal to access our unconscious recollections. Freud would turn to the phenomenon of fantasy in order to approach this possibility. In his 1919 essay, "A Child Is Being Beaten," Freud offers an analysis of the various stages of development of a common fantasy. The significant thing about this particular essay is the introduction of the strategy of construction for an analysis of the masochistic second phase of the fantasy since the child's fantasy of itself being beaten by its father is unavailable to consciousness. Freud is able to discern this second phase of the fantasy

---

8. According to Joël Dor, "the identity of a symptom is never anything but an artifact to be attributed to the effects of the unconscious. Diagnostic investigation requires us to find our support on this side of the symptom, in the intersubjective space that Freud (1912) described in his famous telephone metaphor as the communication of unconscious to unconscious." Joël Dor, *The Clinical Lacan* (New York: Other Press, 1999), p. 14.

9. Sigmund Freud, "From the History of an Infantile Neurosis," *Standard Edition of the Complete Psychological Works of Sigmund Freud,* trans. James Strachey (London: Hogarth Press, 1955) volume 17, pp. 50–52. Hereafter abbreviated as *SE*.

as the only logical link between the other two conscious parts.[10] There is, in other words, a gap in consciousness that Freud would have to address in order to make sense of the entire fantasy. And it is the analytic strategy of construction that he would use in order to give some form to the lost material of this gap. Because this gap is correlate to the gap in the signifier, construction, like the symptom, can be said to function as a positivization of the negative "content" of the unconscious repressed, of the second phase of the fantasy. According to Freud, "this second phase is the most important and the most momentous of all. But we may say of it in a certain sense that it has never had a real existence. It is never remembered, it has never succeeded in becoming conscious. It is a construction of analysis, but it is no less important on that account."[11] Because of its negativity, this second phase is what counts for the fantasy. And it is also what counts for subjectivity, structured in and through a lost or impossible event. Thus, it is construction, as a practice of reading the negative, that will emerge as the most adequate technique for addressing the symptom in the signifier.

In an attempt to remember an elusive memory that resists representation—a disturbing dream or a traumatic experience, for example—Freud turns to construction in order to access the lost material. Working off conscious material, Freud will have to engage a reading practice that reconstructs the missing part of these memories. Shifting from an emphasis on the interpretation of resistances to the unconscious repressed, Freud introduces construction to account for this "forgotten" stage. In a sort of historical overview of the development of analytic technique, Freud opens chapter 3 of *Beyond the Pleasure Principle* with a call to this new hermeneutic practice:

> Twenty-five years of intense work have had as their result that the immediate aims of psycho-analytic technique are quite other today than they

---

10. The first phase of the fantasy, which is conscious, is of an adult beating another child. This phase, Freud says, is represented by the phrase "My father is beating the child whom I hate." The third phase, also conscious, contains neither the father nor the child who is producing the fantasy (as in the second phase), and usually a number of children are present. According to Freud, patients typically see themselves as entirely separate from this stage and usually declare "I am probably looking on." See Sigmund Freud, "A Child Is Being Beaten," *SE* 17, pp. 184–186.

11. Ibid., p. 185. When Freud says that this phase "never had a real existence," he is clearly pointing to an instance of the Lacanian real. It is precisely these moments in our existence, according to Lacan, that are real. Everything else is mediated.

were at the outset. At first the analyzing physician could do no more than discover the unconscious material that was concealed from the patient, put it together, and, at the right moment, communicate it to him. [This is the early function of the talking cure]. Psycho-analysis was then first and foremost an art of interpreting. Since this did not solve the therapeutic problem, a further aim came in view: to oblige the patient to confirm the analyst's construction from his own memory.[12]

As a practice of reading the unconscious, construction would jettison Freud beyond the art of interpretation and the efficacy of the talking cure. The analyst's construction, however, insofar as it is remains unconvincing to the analysand (as it typically does), opens the space for a repetitive acting out. Freud continues:

> The patient cannot remember the whole of what is repressed in him, and what he cannot remember may be precisely the essential part of it. Thus he acquires no sense of conviction of the correctness of the construction that has been communicated to him. He is obliged to *repeat* the repressed material as a contemporary experience instead of, as the physician would prefer to see, *remembering* it as something belonging to the past.[13]

The analysand recoils from the presentation of the unconscious material, Freud claims, precisely because it strikes a chord. There is no negation in the unconscious, and any time a patient exclaims "That's not it!" the analyst can be sure that it *is* it.[14] The analyst's construction, Freud tells us, always hits the analysand with an "unwished-for exactitude."[15] Perhaps this is also why the analysand always recoils from the analyst's constructions. In them, interpre-

---

12. Sigmund Freud, *Beyond the Pleasure Principle, SE* 18, p. 18.

13. Ibid., p. 18.

14. In a footnote added in 1923 to an earlier essay, Freud writes that "There is another very remarkable and entirely trustworthy form of confirmation from the unconscious, which I had not recognized at the time this was written [1901]: namely, an exclamation on the part of the patient of 'I didn't think that'. . . . This can be translated point-blank into: 'Yes, I was unconscious of that.'" See "Fragment of an Analysis of a Case of Hysteria," *SE* 7, p. 57. See also Freud's essay "Negation," *SE* 19, pp. 234–240 and the first two sections of his "Constructions in Analysis," *SE* 23, pp. 255–265, for a more detailed discussion of the lack of negation in the unconscious.

15. Sigmund Freud, *Beyond the Pleasure Principle, SE* 18, p. 18.

tation hits the traumatic real. Whether Freud's constructions are correct or
not is precisely not the point, since they are more concerned with creating a
scenario in the present than interpreting some past event.[16] The analysand,
therefore, cannot put the repressed material in the past, he cannot simply
refuse it as incorrect—even if he does, lingering doubts will return—or
abreact it as a memory—if he does, it will be a false memory (or the wrong
memory) since it has never been psychically registered in the first place. The
analysand must, instead, repeat the repressed material in the present. This
repetition of the forgotten past in the present exposes the analysand to the
metaleptic structure of his missed (traumatic) experience; it bares the real.
Thus, repetition makes the analysand attentive to another level of meaning
beyond the signifier—to a level of meaning, that is, which the signifier is not
adequate to. Here we see how the analytic strategy of construction introduces
a whole new structural practice into psychoanalysis. With the introduction of
construction, Freud essentially opens psychoanalytic practice up to the very
logic of repetition. Through this strategy, Freud exposes his analysand to the
abyssal structure—the impossible origin—of the symptom, to its elusive and
traumatic meaning beyond the signifier.

Moving beyond the talking cure as a mode of discovery to what he will later
come to call "the bedrock of castration," Freud begins the arduous process of
pointing us toward this elusive meaning. In the conclusion of his 1937 essay
entitled "Analysis Terminable and Interminable," Freud argues that the
terminal point of analysis lies in the subject's recognition of its own essential
structure inaugurated in castration and the Oedipus complex.[17] This is the

---

16. As Bruce Fink points out, "insofar as interpretation hits the real, *it does not so
much hit the truth as create it.*" See Bruce Fink, *A Clinical Introduction to Lacanian
Psychoanalysis: Theory and Technique* (Cambridge, MA: Harvard University Press,
1997), p. 158.

17. While Freud came to a seeming impasse with his notion of the "bedrock of
castration" as the terminal point of analysis, this is not necessarily the case since the
subject's recognition of such a structure can only open him up to the indeterminacy of
his very identity. Freud himself admits, however, that once analysis brings the
analysand to the point of discovering castration, a kind of barrier is erected, a bedrock
beyond which analysis can penetrate no further. Lacan moves beyond this barrier as
he aims the terminus of analysis at a traversing or reconfiguration of the fundamental
fantasy. In *The Four Fundamental Concepts of Psychoanalysis,* Lacan writes that a
subject who has traversed his most basic fantasy can live out the drive. In this sense, he
is able to move beyond the seeming impasse of the bedrock of castration. See Jacques

impossible origin of the symptom that the analysand comes to: the structure of the subject and the inadequacy of the signifier. With this development of his theory of the talking cure, Freud has thus come to the realization that one can move no further in analysis than this impossible origin.[18] This position is radically different from the notion that the talking cure might return one to the source of his troubles. So, while Freud never abandons the talking cure with its emphasis on interpretation, he does envision its function differently, suggesting that the treatment of the symptom should revolve around the repetition of the subject's impossible origin. This will be the essential point he makes, at any rate, with the introduction of repetition and the death drive in *Beyond the Pleasure Principle*. Freud would have to make, however, a number of adjustments to his theory of hysteria, in particular, and to his understanding of the notion of the aetiology of traumatic experience, in general, before he could come to shift his practice toward a sustained analysis of the level of meaning that is beyond the signifier and the logical limits of speech: this will be nothing other than the traumatic meaning of the death drive.

Freud's Turn

According to most accounts, Freud's *Beyond the Pleasure Principle* marked a revolution in his thought. In the 1919 text, Freud radically revised his theory with the introduction of the death drive and of his understanding of trauma and dream interpretation.[19] One can read an account of Freud's turn in Paul

---

Lacan, *The Seminar of Jacques Lacan, Book XI: The Four Fundamental Concepts of Psychoanalysis,* trans. Alan Sheridan (New York: Norton, 1981), p. 273. For an explanation of Lacan's strategy of traversing the fantasy and how it relates to the terminus of analysis, which Lacan calls the "pass," see Bruce Fink, *A Clinical Introduction to Lacanian Psychoanalysis: Theory and Technique* (Cambridge, MA: Harvard University Press, 1997), pp. 212–214.

18. Concerning the efficacy of this analytic strategy, Freud writes that "It would be hard to say whether and when we have succeeded in mastering this factor in analytic treatment. We can only console ourselves with the certainty that we have given the person analyzed every possible encouragement to re-examine and alter his attitude to it." Sigmund Freud, "Analysis Terminable and Interminable," *SE* 23, pp. 252–253.

19. In his introduction to the Norton reprint edition of Freud's *Beyond the Pleasure Principle,* Gregory Zilboorg, for example, comments on the development of Freud's

Verhaeghe's *Does the Woman Exist?* In this insightful and instructive reading of the development of Freud's theory of hysteria, Verhaeghe reads the later Freud (which he calls Freud II) as the truth of the early Freud (Freud I). Following the shift from Freud I to Freud II, Verhaeghe points to the development of Freud's second theory of hysteria, which, according to Verhaeghe, essentially centers around the question of a structural impossibility and, consequently, is organized by the traumatic return of *jouissance*. While Verhaeghe specifically locates this shift from Freud I to Freud II in the 1914 text "Remembering, Repeating, and Working Through," one can always see how Freud, at much earlier points in his work, was already flirting with the kind of structural reading of trauma and the symptom that "Remembering, Repeating, and Working Through" inaugurated. And here, of course, one could otherwise choose to follow Zilboorg and Gay and say, instead, that, although it is with *Beyond the Pleasure Principle* that Freud introduced the structural change into psychoanalysis, one could always see these structural elements exhibited in earlier works.[20] The point, however, is not to find the correct site or time of the turn—somewhere in the pages of the text of either *Beyond the Pleasure Principle* (1919) or "Remembering, Repeating, Working Through" (1914). The point, rather, is to see how the interpretive practice that

---

thought up to the 1919 text, maintaining that this work is "one of the first great landmarks in Freud's ways of changing his mind." See Gregory Zilboorg, MD, "Introduction," in Sigmund Freud, *Beyond the Pleasure Principle,* trans. James Strachey (New York: Norton, 1961) p. xxviii. Peter Gay's biographical introduction also points to *Beyond the Pleasure Principle* as a turning point in the development of Freud's theory since the introduction of the death drive had irrevocably impacted his thought. According to Gay, "once Freud had adopted this construct, in which the forces of life, Eros, dramatically confront the forces of death, Thanatos, he found himself unable to think any other way." See Peter Gay, *Freud: A Brief Life,* in ibid., p. xx.

20. Through a kind of biographical detection, however, one can claim that Freud was already developing the raw materials for his new theory of repetition and the death drive as early as 1915, within one year's time of the appearance of "Remembering, Repeating, and Working Through." Knowing that the mother of the famous baby of the *Fort! Da!* game was Freud's daughter Sophie and knowing that she died early in 1920 when, as Freud himself tells us in a note in *Beyond the Pleasure Principle,* his grandchild was five and three-quarters years old, one can see that the *Fort! Da!* game, which appeared as the emblematic example for repetition in *Beyond the Pleasure Principle,* was probably the first observed in the Freud household some time in 1915 when the child was, as Freud again tells us, one and a half years old. (See *Beyond the Pleasure Principle, SE* 19, p. 16, n. 1 and p. 14 respectively.)

Freud abandoned for the more sophisticated reading practice of construction was, on some level, always marked by the later practice, although Freud may have been less aware of it in the early years.[21]

The 1914 text, however, does mark a certain development in Freud's thought where, among other things, his understanding of the function of hypnosis opens onto the possibility of accessing a lost memory as present to the scene of analysis.[22] Freud's realization of this particular point will be monumental for psychoanalysis, since it will show him the way to understanding the abyssal logic of the symptom and, ultimately, of the practice of psychoanalysis itself. What Freud will essentially come to recognize is the traumatic dimension of the symptom: that the repression of an event or memory does not precede its return in the symptom. This, essentially is the logic of repetition and of trauma. This insight will also undoubtedly become the foundation for a more sophisticated interpretive practice in relation to the patient's resistances. And it will not be much longer (1919) until Freud will be able to claim in *Beyond the Pleasure Principle* that a successful transference will allow the analysand to embrace the validity of construction.[23] Insofar as construction—as a strategy for addressing the symptom—makes the lost memory or the "portion of forgotten life" present to the scene of analysis, it engages the symptom on the level of reading rather than interpretation. And it is a successful transference that allows this act of reading on the analyst's part to take

---

21. This, however, might also explain Mladen Dolar's clever variation on Freud's title "Remembering, Repeating, and Working Through as "remembering, repeating, and reconstructing the repressed." See Mladen Dolar, "Beyond Interpellation," *Qui Parle?* vol. 8, no. 1 (1994), p. 85.

22. See my comments concerning hypnosis as a (failed) strategy for returning one to the primal source of one's troubles in the introduction of this collection.

23. According to Freud, "these reproductions [constructions], which emerge with such unwished-for exactitude, always have as their subject some portion of infantile subject life—of the Oedipus complex, that is, and its derivatives; and they are inevitably acted out in the sphere of transference, of the patient's relation to the physician. . . . The physician cannot as a rule spare his patient this phase of the treatment. He must get him to re-experience some portion of his forgotten life, but must see to it, on the other hand, that the patient retains some degree of aloofness, which will enable him, in spite of everything, to recognize that what appears to be reality is in fact only a reflection of a forgotten past. If this can be successfully achieved, the patient's sense of conviction is won, together with the therapeutic success that is dependent on it." See *Beyond the Pleasure Principle, SE* 18, pp. 18–19.

hold. Through the mechanism of construction and the transference, then, Freud could focus on the abyssal structure of the symptom—as the positivization of a radical negativity—rather than simply on its content.

In order to further consider Freud's move to an analysis of the symptom in relation to the impossible origin of the subject, we have to look at some earlier interpretive devices, especially those related to hysteria and the aetiology of trauma. As we stated above, one need not locate the shift in Freud's focus on the symptom from a straightforward interpretive stance (the early emphasis of the talking cure on the content of the symptom) to an analysis of the structure of the symptom only in *Beyond the Pleasure Principle*. As early as 1898, in his first development of the theory of sexuality and the neuroses, one could argue that Freud had already made this formal move from interpretation to an analysis of repetition and, by extension, the traumatic death drive.[24] As he further developed the theory of infantile sexuality (the Oedipus complex) and the function of fantasy in psychic life, Freud was compelled to drop the earlier seduction theory, which was the first theory he developed to explain the emergence of hysterical symptoms.[25] The seduction theory essentially held that all hysterical neuroses were the result of premature sexual activity. Since Freud presumed that the child was not a sexual being, he came up with the seduction theory to explain how the hysteric comes to have a relation to sexuality. In this sense, the origin of the symptom was locatable in

---

24. See Freud's 1898 essay "Sexuality in the Aetiology of the Neuroses," *SE* 3.

25. In his 1905 essay, "My Views on the Part Played by Sexuality in the Aetiology of the Neuroses," Freud separates himself completely from the seduction theory: "in the course of ten years of continuous effort at reaching an understanding of these phenomena, I have made a considerable step forward from the views I then held, and now I believe that I am in a position, on the basis of deeper experience, to correct the insufficiencies, the displacements and the misunderstandings under which my theory then labored. At that time my material was still scanty, and it happened by chance to include a disproportionately large number of cases in which sexual seduction by an adult or by older children played the chief part in the history of the patient's childhood. I thus over-estimated the frequency of such events (though in other respects they were not open to doubt). Moreover, I was at that period unable to distinguish with certainty between falsifications made by hysterics in their memories of childhood and traces of real events. Since then I have learned to explain a number of phantasies of seduction as attempts at fending off memories of the subject's *own* sexual activity." See "My Views on the Part Played by Sexuality in the Aetiology of the Neuroses," *SE* 7, p. 274.

some concrete external event. According to this early theory, the analyst could directly address the hysteric's symptom: he simply had to return the hysteric to the traumatic sight of her attack and show her that all her troubles emanated from this unfortunate incident. Psychoanalysis was then primarily an interpretive technique that allowed analysands to understand their problems in terms of their origins.

This theory began to seem somewhat improbable, however, especially as it held to the extremely limited claim that only the rape of an innocent child by a sexually predatorial adult could be the cause of the neuroses. If sexuality is so foreign to the child, then why or how is a seduction experienced as traumatic? There must already be something inherently sexual about the child, Freud surmised, in order for the affect that is associated with the first stage of a hysterical trauma to take hold.[26] This is the point Freud will come to in his essay "Infantile Sexuality." Here Freud writes that "seduction is not required in order to arouse a child's sexual life; that can also come about spontaneously from internal causes."[27] In this essay, Freud was also beginning to develop his theory of the Oedipus complex and the notion of the infant as polymorphously perverse. Freud's adaptation of this excessively sexualized prehistoric period of the subject's adult sexual life put an end to the preponderance of the theory of "innocent victim" hysterics. And along with the hysteric's victim status, the possibility of an external and readily locatable cause for the hysterical symptom would also have to be abandoned. With the possibility of an internal aetiology for hysteria, Freud began the first turn toward an analysis of the symptom that is grounded in the abyssal structure of the subject. Interpretation would no longer stand as the cornerstone of analytic practice.

From Infantile Sexuality to the Death Drive

Through the demise of the seduction theory and, with it, the possibility of an exclusively external cause for hysteria and the traumatic neuroses, a new

---

26. See Breuer and Freud's *Studies on Hysteria, SE* 2, for an extended explanation of the splitting of affect and meaning that inaugurates the sexual trauma that will be so important for the analysis of hysteria. In this early theory, Freud essentially argues that a sexual experience without sexual meaning or understanding leads to a registering of affect without meaning. It is precisely this unanchored affect that returns in the form of the hysterical symptom.

27. Sigmund Freud, *Three Essays on the Theory of Sexuality, SE* 7, pp. 190–191.

problematic was to arise for psychoanalysis: where does the misery come from? That would be the essential question for Freud as he developed both a new theory of hysteria and a more nuanced understanding of traumatic experience. That was also the question Wilhelm Reich was to place at the center of his disagreement with Freud concerning the aetiology of the neuroses. In a 1952 conversation with Kurt Eisler, Reich boasted that "while Freud developed his death-instinct theory which said 'The misery comes from inside,' I went out, out where the people were."[28] With this claim, Reich places himself squarely on the side of seduction and the external cause. Reich, in other words, believes that social rather than psychic determinants are responsible for the neuroses. Working off Reich's position, Jeffrey Masson also takes issue with Freud's dismantling of the seduction theory. Masson goes a bit farther than Reich, however, and his sharp critique of Freud, outlined in his book *The Assault on Truth: Freud's Suppression of the Seduction Theory,* attempts a political indictment of Freud.[29] Masson argues that, with the seduction theory, Freud's psychoanalysis was politically charged. It focused on the victim, and, apparently, this attention to the status of the victim had real potential to shake things up in turn-of-the-century Europe. With its focus on the victim's rights, the seduction theory might also go a long way to expose the hypocrisy of the sexual predators responsible for the victim's suffering. Masson argues that Freud abandoned this political edge in order to save his reputation in the field of psychoanalysis. With the seduction theory, Masson claims, Freud uncovered a politically explosive element and then abandoned it for fear it would derail his career.[30]

---

28. Wilhelm Reich, *Reich Speaks of Freud: Conversations with Kurt Eisler,* Mary Higgins and C. M. Raphael, eds. (New York: Farrar, Straus, and Giroux, 1967), pp. 42–43. See also Jacqueiline Rose, "Where Does the Misery Come From? Psychoanalysis, Feminism, and the Event," in *Feminism and Psychoanalysis,* ed. Judith Root and Richard Feldstein (Ithaca, NY: Cornell University Press, 1989).

29. See Jeffrey Masson, *The Assault on Truth: Freud's Suppression of the Seduction Theory* (New York: Farrar, Straus, and Giroux, 1984).

30. This, it seems, is a strange claim to make about a man whose career *began* as derailed. With the extremely marginal cases he saw at the beginning of his physician's career (the cases that would not stand up to neurological scrutiny and that, incidentally, would later become the seminal cases for the new practice of psychoanalysis—a practice which Freud would invent out of this very failure), Freud was never able to establish himself as a neurologist (the field of his training). He thus began his career in psychoanalysis as a failed neurologist. For an especially insightful account of Freud's

Where, then, does the misery come from? Although these words are uttered by Reich in the 1950s, they will also form the kernel of Freud's concern as he abandons the seduction theory for the psychically more nuanced and less socially determined theory of fantasy and the part played by infantile sexuality in the subject. Despite Masson's claims to the contrary, Freud's interest in the role that psychic processes play in the development of the neuroses is driven by his concern for his patients, especially as he comes to the problem of the traumatic neuroses. This question concerning the source of misery certainly parallels our concern with the aetiology of trauma: where does trauma come from? Is trauma the effect of an external event, some unknowable and, therefore, "unrepresentable" experience, or does it come from within (which, incidentally, would not make it any less unrepresentable)? How is it that we are able to undergo the experience of trauma at all?

As he moves toward the Oedipus complex—that universal family tri-angle—and the part played by the subject's prehistory in the development of the neuroses (and, thus, the development of the subject), Freud will embrace the very radical idea that it is the internal structure of the subject that is inherently traumatic. This structure is necessary to the experience of trauma. Without it, it seems unlikely that external events would strike us as traumatic at all. Traumatic events do not strike us as "impossible" or " beyond represen-tation" because of anything inherently transcendental about these events themselves. A traumatic event that persists beyond representation will only emerge as such because of our relation to the signifier, to the way the signifier inadequately covers the cut it makes on the body of the subject.

External events, therefore, are what one might call necessarily contingent to the experience of trauma. Some sort of event is surely necessary to provoke a traumatic neurosis, but what this event, in particular, turns out to be is entirely contingent. The external event emerges as an experience of extrem-ity—as traumatic—because of an internal structure; the external event is merely (necessarily) contingent. Freud makes his first step toward an under-standing of the significance of internal and external causes as he embraces the cornerstone of his theory of sexuality and of the subject: the Oedipus complex. With this move, he allows a place for the unconscious in the theory of trauma. The full force of this realization will not take hold, however, until he revises

---

early career status as "a neurologist without a job," see chapter 1 of Paul Verhaeghe, *Does the Woman Exist?: From Freud's Hysteric to Lacan's Feminine*, trans. Marc du Ry (New York: Other Press, 1999).

his theory of dreams in *Beyond the Pleasure Principle*. Allowing for a new category of dreams that do not function as wish fulfillments, Freud will be able to fully embrace the theory of an internal determinant for traumatic experience. This is the traumatic death drive, the abyssal internal cause of traumatic experience.

With his position concerning seduction, Masson essentially maintains that traumatic experience is exclusively externally provoked. Rather than viewing misery as proper to the subject (the subject suffers the signifier), Masson sees misery as an imposition from the outside world. The mechanisms of the *subject's* psychic processes have nothing to do with the aetiology of trauma or the neuroses although, according to Masson's position, the outside has direct effects on psychic processes. In this sense, Masson's seeming desire to see the subject as sympathetic and worth fighting for backfires as the very ground he stands on to make this claim essentially demands that the subject be a completely passive agent, acted upon by external forces but not itself making any effect on these same processes. Freud saw the subject as much more complex as the viability of an external source gave way to the internal vicissitudes of the Oedipus complex and the death drive. Since new symptoms always arose in the place of symptoms that were cathected through interpretation and the talking cure, Freud had to face the possibility that symptoms could be generated from within, independent of any external cause.[31] Therefore, the empha-

---

31. Given the place that Aristophanes's myth of the prehistoric human being would come to have in Freud's work, both for the theory of infantile sexuality and for his theory of the death drive (which will be discussed below), it may be no accident that Aristophanes was the one reveler in Plato's dialogue who understood the nature of symptoms: one symptom always stands in the place of another. In the *Symposium*, one recalls, Aristophanes was inclined to give his turn to Eryximachus due to an uncontrolled hiccough that was hindering his ability to speak. While the narrator attempts to ascribe this gastric anomaly to the amount of alcohol consumed, he misses the point of its psychic significance: this is a classic hysterical symptom if ever there were such a thing. Once Eryximachus finishes his part, however, Aristophanes is ready to begin, though not until he overcomes a fresh symptom: a fit of sneezing. As Aristophanes observes, the one symptom seems to cure or displace the other: "the hiccough is gone [Aristophanes says]; not, however, until I applied the sneezing; I wonder whether the principle of order in the human frame requires the sort of noises and ticklings, for I no sooner applied the sneezing than I was cured." While the hiccough might be attributed to excessive drinking, there is no way to trace the cause of the sneezing to the same source. This is precisely the kind of symptomatic substi-

sis on the origin of the hysterical symptom would necessarily shift from consideration of an external to the exploration of an internal source. This shift would initially be reflected in Freud's turn toward the significance of infantile sexuality, the theory he specifically works out in *Three Essays on the Theory of Sexuality*.

An unconscious and internal source of excitation, infantile sexuality would emerge as much more traumatic for the subject than any external event since it evokes something of the subject as the root of its problems. Pointing the way toward an analysis of an "earlier state of things," Freud's theory of infantile sexuality would pave the way to his later, more ambitious theory of the death drive. In "Sexual Aberrations," the first essay in *Three Essays on the Theory of Sexuality,* Freud suggests that deviations in respect of the sexual object have everything to do with the sexual prehistory of the subject, the polymorphously perverse child. Because infantile sexuality is not directed toward any particular object, it is possible that any sort of object other than the customary one might become the chosen object. Introducing the notion of a sexual instinct as a biological need, Freud begins this essay with an invocation of Aristophanes's myth of the original united human being, the tale Aristophanes tells when it becomes his turn to speak of love in Plato's *Symposium:* "The popular view of the sexual instinct is beautifully reflected in the poetic fable which tells how the original human beings were cut up into two halves—man and woman— and how these are always striving to unite again in love."[32] Freud will take this same tale up again at the end of chapter 6 of *Beyond the Pleasure Principle.* Commenting on the fact that science has so little to teach us about sexuality,

---

tution that Freud was faced with in his practice. (See Plato's *Symposium,* in *Lysis, Phaedrus, and Symposium: Plato on Homosexuality,* trans. Benjamin Jowett [New York: Prometheus Books, 1991], p. 120.)

32. Sigmund Freud, *Three Essays on the Theory of Sexuality, SE* 7, p. 136. Aristophanes's tale begins as follows: "the original human nature was not like the present, but different. In the first place, the sexes were originally three in number, not two as they are now; there was man, woman, and the union of the two having a name corresponding to this double nature; this once had a real existence, but is now lost." One can quite easily see that the earlier state of things Freud invokes is represented in this little tale: the original human nature is a primal myth. Aristophanes's myth is also instructive for our understanding of the prehistory of the subject—the symbiotic relation with the maternal—as lost. (See Plato's *Symposium,* in *Lysis, Phaedrus, and Symposium: Plato on Homosexuality,* trans. Benjamin Jowett [New York: Prometheus Books, 1991], p. 120.)

Freud again turns to Aristophanes's myth since it so effectively shows us something of the impossible origin of the species that Freud's meditation on the death drive is also concerned with. "It traces," Freud tells us, this time in *Beyond the Pleasure Principle,* "the origin of an instinct to *a need to restore an earlier state of things.*"[33] After a brief summary of the tale, Freud continues: "Shall we follow the hint given us by the poet-philosopher, and venture upon the hypothesis that living substance at the time of its coming to life was torn apart into small particles, which have ever since endeavored to reunite through the sexual instincts?"[34] What might this tearing up of the life sub-stance be other than an allusion to the traumatic cut the subject suffers upon entry into language, to the impossible loss of the primal symbiotic relation with the mother, to the subject's exile from the "earlier state of things" that is the aim of the traumatic death drive?[35] Thus, it is in *Beyond the Pleasure Principle* that Freud comes full circle with his theory of infantile sexuality as the traumatic internal cause of the symptom. The compulsion to repeat, which drives the subject, is a compulsion to repeat a prior impossibility, an earlier state of things. This is the compulsion the subject suffers as the logic of its own impossible genesis, and it is where the misery comes from.

The Misery Comes from Within: Trauma and Repetition

It is also in *Beyond the Pleasure Principle,* of course, where Freud first intro-duces his theory of traumatic repetition and its function in dreams. Freud's revised theory would encapsulate a new category of dreams that radically subverted the famous thesis that all dreams are wish fulfillments and, thus, are characterized by a content that is accessible through interpretation. In "Supplements to the Theory of Dreams"—an address delivered before the International Psycho-Analytical Congress at The Hague in September, 1929, introducing the publication of *Beyond the Pleasure Principle*—Freud publicly reverses the position he had taken concerning the special content of what he

---

33. Sigmund Freud, *Beyond the Pleasure Principle, SE* 18, p. 57.

34. Ibid., p. 58.

35. For further development of the significance of the impossible loss that subject suffers as the advent of language, see chapter 2 of my forthcoming book *Encountering Jouissance: Trauma, Psychosis, and Psychoanalysis.*

had discovered as "punishment dreams," as he manages to subsume what at first glance appeared to be a new category of dreams under the general category of wish fulfillment.[36] The fact that Freud was able to include a category of dream that was characterized by an unpleasant, punishing experience in his theory of wish fulfillment already shows how well this interpretive device can appropriate any content, regardless of how paradoxical or contradictory to the theory of wish fulfillment it might, at first glance, appear to be. While Freud knew that there is nothing overtly fulfilling about being punished, or that most normal (only mildly neurotic) people do not actively wish to be punished, he pushes beyond this commonplace to another consideration of fulfillment that might be constituted by a kind of substitute satisfaction. Thus, he only need to remind his audience of the functioning of another agency of the ego (what one can easily recognize as an early articulation of the superego) in order to show how any new psychical discovery can be appropriated by his interpretive strategy, reflected in the theory of wish fulfillments.

Freud pushes beyond the systematic and seemingly closed theory of wish fulfillment dreams, however, as he introduces a radically new kind of "traumatic dream." These traumatic dreams will become the basis for the theory of trauma and its relation to the death drive in *Beyond the Pleasure Principle*.[37] Here one sees the traumatic experience determined both by an external cause

---

36. Because the essay is supposed to appear as an external review of *Beyond the Pleasure Principle,* Freud refers to his findings through a strange kind of parabastic gesture: "The speaker explained that, alongside the familiar wishful dreams and the anxiety dreams which could easily be included in the theory, there were grounds for recognizing the existence of a third category, to which he gave the name of 'punishment dreams.' If we took into account the justifiable assumption of the existence of a special self-observing and critical agency in the ego (the ego ideal, the censor, conscience), these punishment dreams, too, should be subsumed under the theory of wish-fulfillment; for they would represent the fulfillment of a wish on the part of this critical agency." See Sigmund Freud, "Supplements to the Theory of Dreams," *SE* 18, p. 4.

37. In the "Supplements," Freud writes: "Another class of dreams, however, seemed to the speaker to present a more serious exception to the rule that dreams are wish-fulfillments. These were the so-called 'traumatic' dreams. They occur in patients suffering from accidents, but they also occur during psycho-analyses of neurotics and bring back to them forgotten traumas of childhood. In connection with the problem of fitting these dreams into the theory of wish-fulfillments, the speaker

("they occur in patients suffering from accidents") as well as through an internal structure ("they also occur during psycho-analyses of neurotics and bring back to them forgotten traumas of childhood"). Later, in the actual text of *Beyond the Pleasure Principle,* however, Freud seems to back off this doubled necessity as he considers the primary significance of the element of fright (*Schreck*) in the development of a traumatic neurosis. As Freud maintains that a wound or an injury is usually a hindrance to the eventual development of a traumatic response, the external cause loses its importance and the significant source of excitation for the trauma is necessarily internal to the subject, not an external force as had typically been surmised.[38] According to Freud, the experience of fright is a purely internal phenomenon since it is not a reaction to a definite object. It is, rather, the *fixation* on some internal impossibility. Therefore, what Freud emphasizes as a "fixation to the moment at which the trauma occurred" is a fixation on nothing at all, on something irrevocably lost, missing, or void of place.[39]

Because they repeat something of this fixation, or they are themselves a kind of fixation on the void, the traumatic dreams that Freud analyses do not bring their sufferers back to a place; they do not return the subject to an earlier event. Rather, Freud says, the dreams *bring something back to the dreamer,* something excessive that cannot be contained in the essentially interpretive theory of wish fulfillments. The new traumatic dreams, that is, cannot be appropriated by the interpretive strategy that classifies all dreams as wish

---

referred to a work shortly to be published under the title of *Beyond the Pleasure Principle.*" Ibid., p. 5.

38. According to Freud, "a condition has long been known and described which occurs after severe mechanical concussions, railway disasters, and other accidents involving a risk to life; it has been given the name of 'traumatic neurosis.' The terrible war which has just ended gave rise to a great number of illnesses of this kind, but it at least put an end to the temptation to attribute the cause of the disorder to organic lesions of the nervous system brought about by mechanical force. . . . In the case of the war neuroses, the fact that the same symptoms sometimes came about without the intervention of any gross mechanical force seemed at once enlightening and bewildering. In the case of the ordinary traumatic neuroses two characteristics emerge prominently: first, that the chief weight in their causation seems to rest upon the factor of surprise, of fright; and secondly, that wound or injury inflicted simultaneously works as a rule *against* the development of a neurosis." See Sigmund Freud, *Beyond the Pleasure Principle, SE* 18, p. 12.

39. Ibid., p. 13.

fulfillments. There is something unrepresentable about these dreams. As such, they suggest to us something of the impossible structure of the subject. There is something of the subject, that is, which is not available for interpretation and which returns in the material of the dream.[40] It is precisely this return that will become the touchstone for Freud's new theory of the death drive: the "earlier state of things" the drive aims toward is no state at all; it does not exist anywhere or any time in the subject's past. It is, rather, an impossible time. And it is precisely this impossibility that the subject repeats in traumatic experience.

Traumatic repetition means that the misery comes from within, and a simple interpretive approach will never bring one to what is essential in traumatic experience. In order to access that lost or forgotten material, Freud would have to turn to the strategy of construction as a means of reading the unconscious repressed. A reading strategy that essentially is able to positivize the negative, construction would become the very approach Freud will utilize in order to articulate the text of *Beyond the Pleasure Principle*. Thus, it is no surprise that Freud turns again to myth to lead him into a theoretical space that is concerned primarily with articulating an impossibility. As he reaches the limits of scientific inquiry, Freud turns to the literary, to myth, to teach us something about impossible origins:

> science has so little to tell us about the origin of sexuality [and the death drive] that we can liken the problem to a darkness into which not so much as a ray of a hypothesis has penetrated. In a quite different region, it is true, we *do* meet with such a hypothesis; but it is of so fantastic a kind—a myth rather than a scientific explanation—that I should not venture to reproduce it here, were it not that it fulfills precisely the one condition whose

---

40. With the discovery of such dreams, Freud once again is in a position to shift his practical engagement from the art of interpretation to a strategy of construction. One already sees the stirrings of the impossible structure of the subject reflected in the fabric of dreams as early as 1895, however, when, in a note appended to his analysis of the dream of Irma's injection in *The Interpretation of Dreams,* Freud discovers the hidden, abyssal truth of dreams: "I had a feeling that the interpretation of this part of the dream was not carried far enough to make it possible to follow the whole of its concealed meaning. If I had pursued my comparison between the three women, it would have taken me far afield. There is at least one spot in every dream at which it is unplumable—a navel, as it were, that is its point of contact with the unknown." (See Sigmund Freud, *The Interpretation of Dreams, SE* 4, p. 111, n. 1.)

fulfillment we desire. For it traces the origin of an instinct to *a need to restore an earlier state of things.*[41]

Freud's positing of this state is purely speculative, guided not by science and empirical data but by myth and a literary sensibility. Here, Freud uses myth as a statement about the impossible. This is not a weakness in his approach. Rather, it is how he manages to intersect the space of the unconscious. Itself a negative space, the unconscious cannot be empirically proven. Freud's theory of the unconscious, then, can only be pursued through a reading practice that embraces the mythic side of understanding and existence, through a practice of reading otherwise. This is why Freud offers his disclaimer at the beginning of chapter 4: "What follows is speculation, often far-fetched speculation, which the reader will consider or dismiss according to his predilection."[42] With the introduction of the death drive and a model for traumatic repetition that is essentially grounded in an impossibility as the only means for accessing the Other scene of the unconscious repressed, Freud shattered the possibility that psychoanalytic technique could be appropriated through either empirical study or a straightforward practice of hermeneutics.

Repetition, Reading, and the Failure of Interpretation

In her essay entitled "To Open the Question," Shoshana Felman opens the question: What does it mean to read otherwise? How does reading open onto the possibility of an Other scene (here, the scene of psychoanalysis), exposing the radical alterity inherent in any discursive act? How is reading intimately related to the movement of repetition? It is most certainly true, after all, that the unconscious, insofar as it exceeds our subjective grasp, always opens onto an other scene. This scene, which we could call the unconscious, appears as the signifier's difference to itself: that is, what the signifier is both not adequate to as well as what the signifier cannot adequately address. It is precisely the point of this difference that is significant for Freud's reading of the unconscious repressed and the function of the death drive in the structure of the subject.

   Felman's brief essay is a compact meditation on the relation between literature and psychoanalysis. How is it, she wonders, have literature and

---

41. Sigmund Freud, *Beyond the Pleasure Principle, SE* 18, p. 57.
42. Ibid., p. 24.

psychoanalysis come to be read together and what, exactly, is the significance of this relation? Rather than thinking the relation as one of subject to object, Felman invites us to think the possibility of reading literature and psycho-analysis together, not as different forms of the same thing, but as different from each other, insofar as each compromises what Felman calls "the interi-ority of the other."[43] Here Felman calls for a reading of the movement of psychoanalysis as a reading of the unconscious (or limits) of literature, while literature can also be read as the borderline element, the unconscious, of psy-choanalysis. Thus, she calls for a reading that might address a level of meaning to which the subject is not always immediately attentive. This, of course, is nothing other than a call for a reading of the unconscious repressed, a practice which Freud had devoted the entire field of psychoanalysis to. As a kind of materialist mystic, suspended between the rigors of empiricism and the wonder of myth, Freud forged a practice of reading the unconscious repressed through the strategy of construction and the movement of repetition.

Both Freud and Felman are looking to open the relation between two different types of discourse — science and myth or psychoanalysis and litera-ture — in order to consider the function of the unconscious repressed and, especially, of repetition in the life and language of the subject. To further consider the function of repression and repetition in trauma and for the subject, we can turn to the field of literary theory and to its earliest represen-tative: Søren Kierkegaard. In this turn, we should also remember that Lacan compares Freud to Kierkegaard in *The Four Fundamental Concepts of Psy-choanalysis.* In the final chapter of the first section, entitled "The Unconscious and Repetition," Lacan points out that, while Freud had painstakingly come to the solution of the problem of the unconscious repressed — what Lacan here calls the *Vorstellungsrepräsentanz* — through his theory of repetition, Kierkegaard had already covered that ground in his little epistolary book

---

43. According to Felman, "each is thus a potential threat to the interiority of the other, since each is contained in the other as its *otherness-to-itself,* its *unconscious.* As the unconscious traverses consciousness, a theoretical body of thought always is traversed by its own unconscious, its own 'unthought,' of which it is not aware, but which it contains in itself as the very conditions of its disruption, as the possibility of its own self-subversion. We would like to suggest that, in the same way that psychoanalysis points to the unconscious of literature, *literature, in its turn, is the unconscious of psychoanalysis.*" See Shoshana Felman, "To Open the Question," in *Literature and Psychoanalysis: A Question of Reading: Otherwise,* Shoshana Felman, ed. (Baltimore, MD: Johns Hopkins University Press, 1982), p. 10.

entitled *Repetition*.[44] In this text, Kierkegaard shows us that repetition is not about the return of something tenable. It is about the new. This is also the significance of repetition for Freud and the field of psychoanalysis.[45]

Repetition creates the past in the present as it creates the new; it engenders the unconscious repressed as something belonging to the present (to the scene of analysis), not to the past. Kierkegaard's *Repetition* brilliantly demonstrates this return of the repressed insofar as it exposes the limits of the scientific through the limits of the poetic. In the collapse or failure of the scientific, the poetic emerges, tracing itself not only as different from the scientific, but also as *the difference of* the scientific. The poetic engenders a repetition on the side of the scientific that is radically beyond, yet profoundly intimate, to it.[46] It is the poetic, in other words, that exposes another level of meaning for the scientific. In this sense, we would say that the possibility that Kierkegaard's young man glimpses (what Kierkegaard calls the ethical stage) is precisely the limit of the scientific as the objectifying gaze of the observer collapses into the madness of the poetic. This relation, one might argue, encompasses the very notion of repetition in Kierkegaard's text. This relation, that is, is the form of repetition. And, just as it stands with Freud and his engagement in and with the unconscious repressed, the "in-itself-more-than-itself" relation between the observer and the poet that Kierkegaard demonstrates engenders the kind of text which must be *read* in the movement of repetition.

Such a practice of reading that emerges out of the movement of repetition reminds us of Freud's use of construction and the role that transference plays in psychoanalysis, especially as transference becomes the primary mode of transmitting the truth of the analyst's readings to the analysand. In an act of reading—when interpretation hits the real—the truth of the unconscious is created. This elicits the very limits of interpretation and meaning. This is precisely why an act of reading in psychoanalysis is not about plumbing to the secret depths of the true content of the unconscious repressed. It is, rather,

---

44. See Jacques Lacan, *The Seminar of Jacques Lacan: Book XI, The Four Fundamental Concepts of Psychoanalysis,* trans. Alan Sheridan (New York: Norton, 1981), pp. 60–61.

45. This might help explain, *après coup,* the meaning of Kierkegaard's subtitle for his text: "A Venture in Experimenting Psychology." See Soren Kierkegaard, *Repetition,* trans. and ed. Howard V. and Edna H. Hong (Princeton, NJ: Princeton University Press, 1983).

46. Following Lacan, we might here say that the poetic has an extimate relation to the scientific.

about engaging the extimate limit of the signifier and the abyssal structure of the subject.

In the movement of repetition, the hermeneutics of psychoanalysis opens up the possibility for reading something of the unconscious repressed. This is what psychoanalysis teaches us as an open practice of reading rather than a closed system of interpretation. This is precisely why psychoanalysis is necessary for an adequate understanding of trauma since the very mode of interpreting the trauma is disrupted in the movement of its representation. Since the subject repeats rather than reports the traumatic event, translating the experience (in the sense of remembering) itself becomes a kind of exercise in withdrawal. While the traumatic encounter emerges through the withdrawal of the identity, the subject engages in a kind of impossible reading or a failed translation of the event. As the subject attempts, and fails, to understand the truth of his or her traumatic experience, this very failure stands in as the true experience of trauma. Through the failure of understanding, the subject succeeds in accessing something of his or her traumatic experience. Something of the repressed returns, *après coup,* to the scene of this failure, and a certain knowledge is forged. It is precisely such knowledge, however, that strikes the subject as traumatic and, therefore, is not directly accessible. The subject must engage again in a kind of impossible reading or failed translation in order to access this knowledge. And this is precisely how the forgotten—or missing—past is played out in the present scene of the analysis. In repetition, then, nothing succeeds like failure. This is the meaning of traumatic repetition and the essential logic of the hermeneutics of psychoanalysis.

Part III

Working-Through

9

In the Future . . . :
On Trauma and Literature

Petar Ramadanovic

There is now a substantial body of writings focusing on the intersection between history, traumatic memory, and literature. Yet in few of these works has a basic proposition been interrogated—that there is a narrative of trauma. The question I would like to ask, then, is simple enough: what does it mean to say that a literary work is "on trauma"?[1] If, for example, there is a traumatic event in Toni Morrison's *Beloved,* how is it that it is there?[2] That *Beloved* represents, or repeats, or transmits, or actualizes a trauma is not a given, but a

1. For their generous help in the realization of this text I would like to thank the Virginia Foundation for the Humanities and the Center for the Humanities, University of Virginia, where I spent a year (1996–1997) as a Rockefeller Fellow ("Institute on Violence, Culture, and Survival"), and the Society for the Humanities, Cornell University, where I spent a year (1997–1998) as a postdoctoral fellow. Special thanks to Catherine Peebles and Roberta Culbertson for their help in thinking through the problem of the representation of trauma.

In memory of the year in which we have enjoyed mutual challenges, I dedicate this text to the fellows at Cornell's Society for the Humanities: Teresa Brennan, Jonathan Elmer, Bruce Fink, Maria Antonia Garcés, Max Hernández, Mary Jacobus, Biddy Martin, Tim Murray, Herman Rapaport, Mark Seltzer, Suzanne Stewart, and Lyndsey Stonebridge; the Society's director, Dominick LaCapra; and the Mellon Fellows: Sarah Banks, David Brenner, John Carson, Eleanor Kaufman, and Joseph Reed.

2. Toni Morrison, *Beloved* (New York: Penguin, 1988); hereafter cited as *Beloved*.

proposition whose meaning and condition of possibility this text will seek to examine.

What we learn from *Beloved*'s critics is, in short, that there was a traumatic event in the past that was not fully incorporated by either the survivors or their descendants and that, consequently, this trauma is acted out and repeated, both within the novel on the level of its narrative, and *as* the novel itself (the novel as one particular manifestation of the transmission of trauma). Recent critical texts, especially those influenced by Cathy Caruth's *Unclaimed Experience,* see this literary repetition of trauma as constituting a history that is itself regarded as a testimony to the difficult, interminable process of working through a traumatic legacy.[3] But what is it that makes this arrangement, this entanglement between trauma and literature possible? (As will be made more apparent below, this question of the relation between trauma and literature implicates, necessitates, an inquiry into the very existence of literature: how come there is literature?)

One need only glance at any literary history to see that literature has played an important role in the mourning of catastrophic events. Today, it is common knowledge that telling a story about a traumatic event helps to work through the experience. But, how is trauma present—presented again—in a literary work of art? How, in other words, does trauma—by definition constituted through repetitions (the event, in Freud's terms, both causing and consisting of the compulsion to repeat)—become representable? How can one distinguish between representation (of trauma) and compulsive repetition (in or as a novel)? At stake here is the relation between history, memory, and literature, and equally, the natures of literature and trauma—that is, what they are—as well as the possibility for the constitution of an identity in the wake of

---

3. My text also draws on Caruth, not so much on the possibilities for history she probes as on what she calls the "literary resonance" of Freud's examples. For example, in *Unclaimed Experience,* Caruth introduces her analysis of trauma by suggesting that the "dramatic illustration of repetition compulsion" in Tasso's epic "exceeds, perhaps, the limits of Freud's conceptual or conscious theory of trauma" in that there is also a "*voice* that cries out." Cathy Caruth, *Unclaimed Experience: Trauma, Narrative, and History* (Baltimore, MD: Johns Hopkins University Press, 1996), p. 2 (Caruth's emphasis). Is this voice, which is released through the wound and which Caruth calls the "voice of the other," in some sense the voice of literature in a psychoanalytic work? For another of Caruth's elaborations of the relation between literature and trauma, see her earlier work *Empirical Truths and Critical Fictions* (Baltimore, MD: The Johns Hopkins University Press, 1991).

a traumatic event. So that my question about the presence of trauma in *Beloved* is asked as part of a general concern regarding the possibility for the future (after a traumatic event).[4]

In suggesting a reading of *Beloved* in this context, I am beginning an inquiry into that which is at once beyond trauma and part and parcel of what is today classified in mainstream clinical discourses as Post-Traumatic Stress Disorder (PTSD). Which is to say, I am beginning an inquiry into haunting, not only on the level of *Beloved*'s plot—the return of Beloved as ghost—but haunting also insofar as it marks the status of this novel: on the one hand, the way its story is told and the effects this story has, and on the other, the way its literariness, the fact or the phenomenon of *Beloved* being literature, is constituted. As if this novel about haunting, this novel bearing in its title the name of a ghost, were itself a ghost. A ghost-writing, written by another hand. Written by the hand of another, Beloved. Another Beloved.[5]

The encounter with trauma in a critical essay such as this one on haunting in *Beloved* is not spared its own entanglement with and repetition of that which cannot be fully repeated or fully disengaged: namely, (another) trauma.[6] What I hope to show is how the repetition of trauma, or precisely, haunting in *Beloved,* repeats also something that is otherwise (in a political, historical, and ethical sense) than trauma, something that is otherwise than the compulsion to repeat.

---

4. Among the attending questions that will not be explored here are, for example, the terms in which African-American identity can be seen today. Does, for example, the ghostly appearance in *Beloved* compel us to put quotation marks around the word "black," implying, among other things, on the one hand, a moment in the U.S. history of racism, perhaps even racism's breaking point, and, on the other, the limitations inherent in the construction of a collective identity? I also want to suggest that the question "how come there is literature?"—how come *Beloved* was/could have been written?—is posed together with that of the possibility for the future, because, if posed alone, either of the questions threatens to end up in abstraction: as if there were literature as such, on its own, unrelated; as if there were a future, on its own, unrelated.

5. In this conjuring of the ghost, *Beloved* follows a tradition of African-American women writers. See Marjorie Pryse and Hortense J. Spillers, *Conjuring: Black Women, Fiction, and Literary Tradition* (Bloomington, IN: Indiana University Press, 1985).

6. The possibility of a different understanding of trauma will be reviewed in the third part of this essay.

Beloved

There is some doubt as to whether Beloved, the one who returns, is the ghost of Sethe's murdered baby daughter or a living young woman, an ex-slave whom Sethe mistakes for her daughter. Whichever of the two be the case (and the novel contains textual evidence for both identities), Beloved is the strangeness of a "disremembered" (Morrison's term) past. A past, that is to say, which has been neither remembered nor forgotten and which returns in the shape of a ghostly young woman. What is strange about her, then, is not the place she comes from—a "dark" place, "[h]ot. Nothing to breathe down there and no room to move in. . . . A lot of people is down there. Some is dead."[7] Nor who she is: Sethe's daughter, a young woman, or even a fictional version of the historical Margaret Garner's child.[8] What is strange about her is the comeback.

The strange is, according to Freud in his essay "The Uncanny," that which brings the familiar into an unfamiliar relation with itself, and is an aspect, a reflection of the familiar.[9] In this sense, the ghostly guise under which the past returns is not, so to speak, the body of the past, the past as such, but is the form the repressed or disavowed past acquires in the present—a displacement of the past in the present and also a displacement of the present. Beloved is thus not a murdered baby, a corpse, or a mistreated young girl. But neither is she a person with a proper name like Sethe's other daughter, Denver. Beloved is rather between the two, between the object-like character of the corpse and a person with a proper name, neither fully present nor absent, at once human and not entirely so. It/she is both the same (that which went away) and the different (that which comes back).

---

7. *Beloved,* p. 75.

8. The events in the life of Margaret Garner, a runaway slave who killed her infant, serve Morrison as a model for *Beloved.* In an interview Morrison says: "I did not do much research on Margaret Garner other than the obvious stuff, because I wanted to invent her life, which is a way of saying I wanted to be accessible to anything the characters had to say about it. Recording her life as lived would not interest me, and would not make me available to anything that might be pertinent." Marsha Darling, "In the Realm of Responsibility: A Conversation with Toni Morrison," in Daniel Taylor-Guthrie, ed., *Conversations with Toni Morrison* (Jackson, MS: University Press of Mississippi, 1994), p. 248. Darling's interview was originally published in *Women's Review of Books* 5 (March 1988): 5–6.

9. Sigmund Freud, "The Uncanny," trans. Alex Strachey. *Collected Papers* Vol. IV. (London: The Hogarth Press, 1956): pp. 368–407.

Beloved is what others see in her. For Sethe, she is a lost daughter. For Denver, a sister with whom she identifies almost completely. For Paul D, she is both a potential lover and a rival in his attempt to gain Sethe's affection. For some readers, she is the embodiment or the symbol of African-American suffering. But, whatever she may be in the eyes of people around her, Beloved is also always the tension between the absent and the present, between that which we project onto her and that which she (it) reflects back, between the same and the different, the alive and the dead, the human and the inhuman. In a word, Beloved is a reminder of a certain past.

In terms of this analysis, the ghost can introduce into the house at 124 Bluestone Road only what is and has already been there in some form or another. With Morrison and Freud we have the possibility to see, then, what it is that gets repeated in the return that the spectral appearance both provokes and is a product of. Where does the path back through the ghostly place of "Sweet Home" (the farm where Sethe was a slave) and through the haunting period of slavery lead to? Does the coming and going of Beloved allow for an opening onto a beyond of the compulsion to repeat the traumatic experience—for Sethe, for Denver, for those who come later? And what would it mean to say that *Beloved* helps its contemporary audience work through the trauma of the past? And, in light of that question, is a truly critical essay on *Beloved* possible?[10] An essay which would, in the terms Freud made available (presuming that *Beloved* transmits trauma), narrow the neurosis and allow for the remembering or reinvention, as opposed to the repetition, of trauma?[11]

To ask these questions today is not to devalorize the extant essays on *Beloved*. The essays are "truly" critical toward *Beloved* in the sense that they show—in one way or another—what seems to be the crucial point: that the haunting in *Beloved* bears a structural *analogy* to a traumatic experience. However, I do find that most of them overidentify the loss; that is, they are too quick to name the ghost, thereby covering over or disavowing its disturbing character. Because of this, they miss the juncture between *Beloved*'s haunting, *Beloved*'s literariness, and historical trauma. We still have to ask, for example,

---

10. The implications of this last question reach far beyond the ambition of this essay, since what it asks concerns racism in America and *Beloved*'s place in respect to it. I hope, however, that my analysis of the possibility of detachment from trauma may offer a basis for a detailed pursuit of this problematic. What is the meaning of "true" and "critical" in a context which is racially biased, unjust, or discriminatory?

11. See the second and the third chapters of Sigmund Freud, *Beyond the Pleasure Principle,* trans. James Strachey (New York: Norton, 1989). Hereafter cited as *BPP.*

whether the ghost *can* be named? Can a traumatic memory be either remembered or forgotten? In what way (if any) is the past related to the present?

But, instead of arguing against existing interpretations of *Beloved,* let me offer a few additional introductory remarks which should situate more precisely the stakes and conditions of an inquiry into haunting. I want to begin from the assumption that the task of literary analysis cannot be reduced to discovering what a text means, symbolizes, or represents, nor to showing its underlying, unconscious structure, but involves the analysis of the way meaning, showing, and uncovering take place both in the literary work *and* in the critical intervention. I emphasize the taking-place-of-meaning because, finally, it is not the "historical time of the plot" that concerns us here, but the historical moment in which the meaning of *Beloved* is constituted, that is, conjured. In this sense, the historical moment proper to *Beloved* is the moment of its manifestation as literature. This becoming of the novel—or if you will, the moment at which transference is established through reading—is a condition for the novel's being a representation.

Also, with Freud, we have introduced the distinction between the traumatic event emerging in (conscious) memory and its (unconscious) repetition. This distinction, like some of Freud's other differentiations—pleasure principle and death drive, mourning and melancholia—fails to indicate how to work through trauma and not end up subverting one's own task. (If the relation between repeating and remembering is dialectical, when does the sublation take place? If there is no sublation, what is the relation between them?) It does, however, offer the valuable explanation that trauma is situated both within and without the topoi Lacan will call the imaginary and the symbolic. Trauma involves, in other words, an incapacity of imaginary identification and a (constitutional) inability of the ego to incorporate the event which remains on the side of unbound, disturbing, freely floating energy. Hence the compulsive repetition and the intention of the analyst to make the analysand remember, for example, reimagine, the event. This reinvention of the event—Freud implicitly suggests in the second chapter of *BPP*—has everything to do with play and with artistic creation, as well as with the constitution of identity. Consequently, to draw on the possibility of reinvention suggested by Freud is to presume that one is tracing the emergence of literature as the (ghostly) substitute for a traumatic experience. This substitution also obliges us to be careful in deciding what *Beloved* can substitute, and what kind of substitute it is. To suggest that there is an identity which emerges in *Beloved* presumes that one ask what kind of identity can emerge in literature. Similarly, the notion that *Beloved* reclaims a memory from oblivion requires us to stop and ask how literature can claim, and who would be claiming in its name.

I am not proposing to embark upon a full-fledged detour into the nature of literature, but rather to take a shortcut. For us here it is not necessary to elaborate what literature is, but to raise this question on the occasion of reading *Beloved* as a narrative of trauma. The very gesture of raising this question should in itself suffice *to bind* one's writing on *Beloved* to a certain responsibility toward the facticity of this work (as a literary work of art). And then, if in reading *Beloved* one's task is to attempt to bind the underlying trauma[12] that evades naming and appears as an excess of signification; if this is what is at stake in reading a trauma narrative, then this attempt to bind has ethical and aesthetic, not merely psychological, implications.

Haunting

Beloved opens with an epigraph from Romans 9:25:

> *I will call them my people,*
> *which were not my people;*
> *and her beloved,*
> *which was not beloved.*

In Romans, these words are Paul's citation from the Old Testament Book of Hosea. In Hosea, the same lines are spoken by Hosea who is despairing over the actions of his adulterous wife Gomer whom the husband refuses to abandon, despite her infidelity. Metaphorically, commentaries often emphasize, God in Hosea's book behaves like a jealous lover toward Israel. That is, he promises loyalty and patronage despite Israel's betrayal. For Paul, on the other hand, the same words offer guidance (for Christians) on how to pursue righteousness. Not all who follow God's word, Paul claims, attain the good, especially if they follow the law blindly as Israel does. In the New Testament version of Hosea's words, the emphasis is on the idea that the now outcast will be gathered to God, whereas those who follow the law to the letter are not guaranteed salvation. The difference between Hosea and Paul, then, consists

---

12. To, in Freud's parlance, bind the surplus energy.

of two different understandings of God's love and the way a people becomes "His," that is, chosen. In terms of Paul's usage of the citation, the question is whether they are chosen because they are "God's" even in betrayal, or whether people become "His" because they pursue Christ in a certain (that is, Christian) way and are, thus, chosen.

In Morrison's epigraph, the Bible is invoked as a witness to the deaths of more than sixty million enslaved African people. The "sixty million and more" to whom this book is dedicated constitute a community in the sense that they shared a common destiny which, belatedly for their descendants, becomes formative of a people. In becoming a part of a context that is politically and historically different from those in Romans and the Book of Hosea, *Beloved*'s epigraph—which is also an epitaph—makes, in fact, a claim against a certain Christian lineage, the one which approved, organized, and maintained the enslavement of African people. At the same time, as in both the Old and New Testaments, these words, devoted to *my people* and a *beloved,* allude to the very possibility of testimony. A possibility which is inseparable from the possibility of betrayal—including here the betrayal, or the willful change, of the context from which the epigraph is taken. Beloved and my people are hence necessarily invoked as neither mine nor beloved. This is what the epigraph says: that a certain kind of negation is inherent in the process of giving a name to somebody or something (even if it were a self-naming). The work of the giving/taking hand of God, operative in the epigraph, is accented throughout the novel and especially in Baby Suggs's litany: "'God take what He would,' she [Baby Suggs] said. And He did, and He did, and He did and then gave her Halle who gave her freedom when it didn't mean a thing."[13]

To be sure, *Beloved* has the power to create a history where there is not one, or to forge a historical link where one is missing, as it can also give rise to "my people" where there is not one to be called by that name. And it attempts to do so using the words of Paul, who used the words of Hosea—words that testify to the original covenant with the Creator and mimic His creation of the world in the act of naming.[14] In reference to this tradition that cannot be called by one name (Judeo-Christian), *Beloved* dedicates itself to the unremembered

---

13. *Beloved,* p. 23.

14. However, when in *Beloved* Morrison speaks of the beginning of the beginning she writes, "[i]n the beginning there were no words. In the beginning was the sound, and they all knew what that sound sounded like" (p. 259).

past of sixty million and more. The dedication here stands as a promise of the present to the past and as an invocation of that past in the present. It displaces both (past and present) yet also brings them into a relation—into a ghostly, haunting relation. The purpose of the dedication, then, is almost clear. At any rate, the need underlying it is apparent: the need for the symbolic burial of the slaves whose lives and deaths, loves and sorrows, birthplaces, names, and graves remain unknown. I say that the dedication's purpose is *almost* clear, for it seems to me that the beginning of the novel is necessarily situated at a crossroads between the symbolic and the literal, between memory as repeated experience and memory as imagination, between past and present, a crime and its haunting effect. Neither here nor there.

At this historical crossroads, *Beloved* opens, raising questions about the past, justice, and inheritance, and also about love, community, and the place of literature vis-à-vis a historical event. Raising them, in the sense of raising the curtain of the past and letting its return bear upon the present. Raising, also, in the sense of the raising of the dead whose strange return is prompted by the dedication itself. The danger that ensues when the gates of the past open threatens primarily, Morrison suggests in an interview published in *City Limits,* the way America is used to remembering.[15] One can expect (only) the unpredictable.

The novel begins with Beloved's return wreaking havoc at 124 Bluestone Road. With her arrival, Beloved brings memories that the ex-slaves, now living in Ohio, resist being reminded of. She brings pleasure as well, to Sethe's daughter, Denver, whose sexual awakening takes place in Beloved's proximity, to Sethe whose terrible memories of Sweet Home nevertheless overflow with beauty. Beloved leaves just before the closing pages of the novel, when Sethe is sick and Denver is forced to leave the house. After Beloved's departure, this novel which might have been about a crime and its redemption in a communal gathering ends with a scene at least as puzzling as the legacy and the covenant that the epigraph alluded to. Morrison writes:

By and by all trace is gone, and what is forgotten is not only the footprints but the water too and what it is down there. The rest is weather. Not the breath of the disremembered and unaccounted for, but wind in the eaves,

---

15. Toni Morrison, "Living Memory," *City Limits* (31 March–7 April, 1988), pp. 10–11.

or spring ice thawing too quickly. Just weather. Certainly no clamor for a kiss.

Beloved.[16]

At the end, we may presume, Beloved's trace disappears and the forgetting of her sets the stage for another arrival of a ghost. As if no one is mindful any longer that there was a ghost, as if all shy away from the discovery of the un-remembered past, as if the mourning that began with the epigraph suddenly stops. It seems, however, that it could not have been otherwise. For Beloved's return cannot place properly that which was displaced, nor can it recuperate or gather that which was fragmented, nor, which amounts to the same thing, can it represent the past. What her or its appearance can do is to recall this community of ex-slaves to the past. What *Beloved* does, in other words, is to actualize a long-gone event, perform its remembering and forgetting, and hence come to the verge of representing it. The last word of the book is, in fact, a sentence consisting only of her name: "Beloved."

What remains then, at the novel's end, are the subsequent arrivals of the ghost, the beginning of *Beloved* staged again. The repetition of her name traces over again the already told and remembered story, the story of an incomplete mourning that would again begin, because Beloved has been forgotten, and again end by preparing the space for its beginning. Concretely, no one can say that Beloved is remembered, her name known, or that the community lives with the memory of her, without also having to ask: Community—which community? Beloved—which beloved? One cannot really know her name, unless she is mistaken for Margaret Garner's baby. Of course, not even then would we have the knowledge of Beloved's name in the terms suggested by the epigraph.

What then? What then, I mean, when there is no after that has not in some sense already taken place? What option is there when the second, the subsequent, is a repetition of the first and when, in the meanwhile, between two repetitions as it were, all trace of Beloved disappears in the indomitable presence of the weather?

To the extent that the first coming of the ghost repeats itself but cannot exhaust itself, to the extent that the first reading opens the space of repetition and so the possibility of a second reading, we should also say that the end of *Beloved* is not an impasse. Between the beginning, which is the end, and the

---

16. *Beloved,* p. 275.

end, which is the beginning, we learn of Sethe, Baby Suggs, Denver, Paul D, and others living in 1873 on the outskirts of Cincinnati. They do not come back. Whatever the structure of the narrative that the strange ghost shapes and reshapes, *Beloved* also attaches a sense of finitude and of the impossibility of the repetition of human life. This is to suggest that there are two stories in *Beloved,* one of return and one of the impossibility of return, one of a crime committed in the past and one of human mortality and the forgetfulness into which human lives sink. One of the "disremembered and unaccounted for" and one of the limits of memory: "just weather." Not separate stories, but two stories that cannot be played out separately. Each needs and implies the other.

If one of the stories tends, through compulsion repetition, to suspend time, withdraw from the world, and regress to the immemorial, the other one is about the impossibility of escaping the discontinuities and breaks of worldliness. Judith Butler's understanding of what repetition performs is quite helpful here. "Perhaps," Butler suggests in a text on Freud's *BPP,* repetitions "serve in part to bind the past and future together, to provide ritualized and sensuous occasions for the invocation of the past and the convocation of the present. Indeed, what other route than repetition instates *the pleasure of temporal continuity* between the irrecoverable past and the unknowable future?"[17]

It is the devastated past, the impossibility of its repetition, the fragmentation of identity, the silence and forgetting that make possible the invocation of the ghost and the resulting "pleasure of temporal continuity." Hence, if the return of the ghost—the ritual, the novel—brings pleasure, it does so in the face of the past that cannot be brought back, and faced with a future that cannot be predicted. Which is also to say that haunting, not continuity as such, is a link through which a lineage and tradition are established. A haunting tradition speaking in the voice of the dead.

Along with the story of inevitable death, then, there is also, in the prosopopoeia, the story of endurance and continuation through haunting. *It* comes from the past as a ghost and will return (in the future) as a ghost. Which is also to say that when repetition, as Butler says, instates the pleasure of temporal continuity, other repetitions and repetitions of repetitions, ghosts and ghosts of ghosts, are unleashed. The conjuring of the ghost in *Beloved,* then, is both

---

17. Judith Butler, "The Pleasure of Repetition," in *Pleasure Beyond the Pleasure Principle,* Robert A. Glick and Stanley Bone, eds. (New Haven, CT: Yale University Press, 1990), pp. 259–276. (Butler's emphasis).

the condition of the possibility for the remembering of the past as well as a repetition (acting out) of the past which forces other repetitions. Not a community *of* ghosts, nor outright history, but a communion *with* ghosts.

Beloved does not recall the past as past and bring the past and the future into a continuous relation without always also repeating the past and instating unpleasure together with pleasure. Pleasure's unpleasure, if you will. Characters, however, repeatedly fail to recall a past event—the "real place," as it is called in the novel—as a fact. And it is because of the obstacles to reconstructing the experiences and interior lives of slaves, the obstacles, that is, to the story's being passed on that a novel about Sweet Home is possible in the first place.[18] As literature, *Beloved* then necessarily maintains the real place as "never going away . . . floating around out there outside my head," as, that is, a phantasm passing on and not passing on at the same time.[19] Sethe tells Denver: "Where I was before I came here, that place is real. It's never going away. Even if the whole farm—every tree and grass blade of it dies. The picture is still there and what's more, if you go there—you who never was there—if you go there and stand in the place where it was, it will happen again; it will be there for you, waiting for you."[20] What will happen when *you* go there is this "again." That which waits for you, the picture, the phantasm, or the history (of destruction) which will have endured the passage of time— *that* is "again." And it is through this repetition that you (Denver) become. Repetition takes place, to borrow Sethe's words, "when you bump into a rememory that belongs to somebody else,"[21] and it happens to *you*, whom this memory seeks. In some sense, then, it is *you* that is the memory and its ghost (phantasm). And the place of memory is real insofar as it awaits *you*, who is the

---

18. At the beginning of *Civilization and Its Discontents,* Freud represents mind processes as a "historical sequence in spatial terms" and calls the model a representation in "pictorial terms." Sigmund Freud, *Civilization and Its Discontents,* trans. James Strachey (New York: Norton, 1989), p. 19. The famous Rome example resonates quite closely with Sethe's description of "rememory" in the sense that the earlier buildings are somehow present, preserved in the new one erected in the same place. The new building in the place of the ruin does not substitute or cover over the ruin fully, they rather exist together.

19. *Beloved,* p. 36. The allusion here is to Morrison's four times repeated sentence in the last chapter of *Beloved:* "It was not a story to pass on." The third repetition reads: "This is not a story to pass on," and the fourth simply states "Beloved" (pp. 274–275).

20. *Beloved,* p. 36.

21. *Beloved,* p. 36.

witness to its endurance. Without *you,* this memory would not be, nor would there be a real place. But neither would *you* be if the place, the memory, were not there waiting. The question is open as to how, and as whom, *you* will emerge from "there."[22] For how does one distinguish between the repetition which instates temporal continuity (Denver's conscious acceptance of a heritage) and that which instates temporal discontinuity (Denver's unconscious acting out)? And so there is no sure way to disengage the *you* from the haunting, or, for that matter, the haunting from the conjuring of the ghost. What does seem certain, by the end of *Beloved,* is that there would not be literature if it were not for this confusion as to what the repetition of a traumatic event repeats, what identification identifies, and how this story and experience *pass on* or are passed on.

Thus far, I hope we have seen how *Beloved* duplicates, repeats on the level of its structure, both the haunting effect of the ghost's appearance and the *revenant's* trajectory. *Beloved*'s trauma and legacy are, if they are anywhere, in the very fact and effect of repetition—in the real place that endures as a picture—namely, in literature. And this is precisely what *Beloved* is, this trace of the past which passes and does not pass. Can the historical specificity or context of this narrative be located anywhere else or be anything else but the real which comes back and is there, in its return, for the first time? I will return to this question.

With the suggestion that a literary representation of an event does not stop with one repetition but calls for other repetitions, including unpleasurable ones, we have reached the convergence point of haunting in literature and of trauma as a historical experience. There is a convergence between the structures and the problematics of literature and trauma in the sense that both are

---

22. In a recent essay, Walter Benn Michaels criticizes the tendency in contemporary discourses on traumatic experience to idealize "cultural identities" and the past. A continuation of such an analysis would, however, have to take into account that, for example, in *Beloved,* ghostliness of identity points to an underlying, irreconcilable duality; the fact that slavery is, at least partially, a documented historical event which its memory does not necessarily either counter or deny; and that there are various kinds of memory (affective, cognitive, imaginative). What is at stake in "trauma narratives" is not so much an attitude toward history, as Benn Michaels seems to assume, but the nature of certain experiences which I call traumatic only because of the lack of a more precise term. Walter Benn Michaels, "'You who never was there': Slavery and the New Historicism, Deconstruction and the Holocaust," *Narrative* vol. 4, no. 1, (January 1996), pp. 1–16.

forms of repetition, although it may not be the same kind of repetition always and in each case. In order for us to understand more closely what it means that literature repeats and haunts, in the next part of this essay I will focus on the difference between literary representation and repetition compulsion, and will then give an outline of two tendencies in the thinking of trauma whose difference is especially instructive for the present discussion.

Repetition

The question now is, what is compulsion repetition and what is its relation to literary creation?

As I've mentioned, in *BPP* Freud draws a distinction between remembering, which he considers to be a kind of creation of a version of an event—"*remembering* [*erinnern*] it as something belonging to the past"—and on the other hand, repeating—"to *repeat* [*wiederholen*] the repressed material as a contemporary experience," that is, as an abreaction ranging from hallucinations, to nightmares, to more subtle forms of acting out: the *Fort! Da!* game his grandson plays with the spool, or the second slaying of Clorinda by Tancred.[23] The reproductions, Freud adds, "which emerge with such unwished-for exactitude, always have as their subject some portion of infantile sexual life."[24] The immediate context in which this distinction is drawn is a discussion about the beyond of the pleasure principle and so of the existence of what he terms, in advance, as it were, a death drive. Is there, Freud asks, such a primitive and domineering drive?

We are entering Freud's argument at a place (the second chapter) which is in many respects analogous to the beginning of *Beloved,* when the appearance of the ghost brings both pleasure and unpleasure. In *BPP,* Freud's grandson, Ernst, throws a spool into his curtained cot, beyond the veil hanging on its side, and reels it back out of the cot. As the spool disappears behind the veil, the boy gives "vent to a loud, long-drawn-out 'o-o-o-o,'" while its reappear-

---

23. *BBP,* p. 19. There is something to be said about the fact that for Freud this process of memory is *erinnern* and not *gedenken. Erinnern* and the noun *Erinnerung* imply an internalization or an introjection and, as such, is a certain form of a *da* move. *Gedenken* and *Gedächtnis,* on the other hand, designate retrieval of memories as a thinking process of recollection.

24. *BBP,* p. 19.

ance is accompanied by "a joyful 'da.'"[25] For Freud, this way of playing with the spool repeats the coming and going of his mother. Ernst is staging the game and in doing so, like the director of a play, is mastering what is most painful—his mother's going away. But the child is also merely repeating, not remembering, her absence, since he is unaware that the cause of his game is his mother's absence. If he were to remember this original point of trauma, we can surmise, Ernst would be most likely pulling the spool behind him as if it were a carriage. Freud notices that the game consists of two moments or movements, the *fort* and the *da,* and adds later that the game usually contains only the *fort* move, implying that the game can be considered "complete" in the *fort* movement only if this move somehow carries the other move within itself. It is hence a going-coming, end-beginning game regardless of which of its versions is staged.[26]

For Freud, trauma, child's play, and transference are all characterized by a compulsion to repeat "which overrides the pleasure principle."[27] In the *Fort! Da!,* the child who compulsively repeats is returned to an earlier stage of development. The hypothesis is that the game allows Freud's grandson to withhold himself from further advancement and to regress toward the "inanimate state." What is unpleasurable in the game is, Freud contends, the compulsion to repeat the initial event of injury, the mother's absence. But the

---

25. *BPP,* pp. 13–14.

26. For a longer discussion on the athesis of the death principle and the thesis of the pleasure principle, as well as on the status of the opposition more generally in *BPP,* see Jacques Derrida, "To Speculate—On 'Freud'" in *The Post Card: From Socrates to Freud and Beyond,* trans. Alan Bass (Chicago, IL: Chicago University Press, 1987), pp. 257–410. Derrida shows that what is doubled or divided once is doubled and divided again: that Freud himself plays a kind of *Fort! Da!* game with the death drive (and perhaps with the death of his daughter); that psychoanalysis as a science collapses into psychoanalysis as speculation; that this discourse folds back upon itself and haunts its own legacy; that the task of psychoanalysis (the advantage, advancement it offers) consists in thinking this fold, the impossibility of maintaining the binary and of continuing Freud's legacy without haunting. In the wider context of *BPP,* the game is neither that of life (pleasure principle) nor of death (unpleasure principle) but of, as Derrida puts it, "life death." Life in death, death in life, unpleasure in pleasure, pleasure in unpleasure are ways or forms of haunting which is itself one of the possible names for what Freud is trying to come to grips with in *BPP,* on both the autobiographical and the scientific-theoretical level.

27. *BPP,* p. 24.

game also allows Ernst to overcome the influence his mother's comings and goings have on him, that is, to renounce "instinctual satisfaction."[28]

Because the *Fort! Da!* game brings a substitutive satisfaction to Ernst, Freud rejects it as a manifestation of the death drive. Together with the game, Freud also dismisses tragedy from further consideration, adding at the end of the second chapter that an inquiry into its pleasure production "should be undertaken by some system of aesthetics." The pleasure principle, Freud reasons, can make "what is in itself unpleasurable [in tragedy, for example] into a subject to be recollected and worked over in the mind."[29] In spite of this rejection, Freud's text allows us to see that the boy's desire for the mother and his pleasure in her become complicated as another desire emerges in the very process of substitution. This is not a desire in the sense of a wish, but rather the other of desire, a desire that turns toward dissolution.[30] What I will inquire into further is the logic of the substitute that is operative both in the game and in tragedy. The play of presence and absence, their repetition in each other, will be pursued here not only as the *product* of a certain situation (an original trauma of separation) for which the game offers substitutive satisfaction, but also as the *condition* of the "original trauma," and as the condition of the analysis of the game that Freud offers. Thus, I shall be departing not from Freud's description of the *Fort! Da!*, nor from his judgment concerning tragedy, but from his implicit claim, made at the end of the second chapter, about the relation between the pleasure principle and the death drive. The death drive is not, as Freud seems to presume as he searches for examples beyond the game and tragedy, independent of the pleasure principle, but constitutive of it. As such, the death drive is at the core of both the game and tragedy, allowing a novel like *Beloved* to be both repetition and remembering, and more than that. The death drive, in this sense, does not *override* the pleasure principle, but rides with it even while negating it.

I would not pursue a reading of the *Fort! Da!* if the game had been played in its entirety; if it ended by allowing for mastery over loss and Ernst's taking

---

28. This, Freud adds, is "the child's great cultural achievement." *BPP*, p. 15.

29. *BPP*, p. 17.

30. A desire, as Derrida suggests, for that which cannot be shared, namely, death. See Jacques Derrida, *The Post Card,* especially "Couriers of Death" (pp. 353–368), where Derrida takes up Freud's conclusion that the organism wishes to die only in its own fashion and relates it to Heidegger's thinking of death. In *Beloved* the object of desire returns from the dead.

revenge on his mother "for her going away;"[31] if, also, *Beloved* were not a haunting novel. But, to put it simply, of what would one be a master if loss were entirely sublated in gain? In psychic life, or in reading, what would pure gain or pure pleasure be? More seriously, there is something in the dominance of the pleasure principle, in the completion and stasis it brings, that is itself other than mastery and pleasure, for these both come through, and we may add, pay the price of, compulsion repetition.

This is then to say that there are at least two things that the *Fort! Da!* repeats: the mother's absence and, as that absence is compulsively acted out, repetition itself. Now, because the throwing and reeling in of the spool offers the possibility of a substitutive satisfaction, we can say that this game is a more complex form of symbolic activity than is the compulsion to repeat. The loss of the mother is the beginning phase of the *Fort! Da!* and is represented *in* and *by* the *fort* move. (This is a phase of interpretation, not of the game itself and my claim is analytic, not ontological. In the game, all the stages defined here overlap, preventing one from separating representation from repetition compulsion.) Once the representation of the loss takes place and the attachment to the mother is mediated by the game, Ernst seems, on the one hand, indifferent to her comings and goings and, on the other, forced to repeat the game.

Why is the dominance of the pleasure gained through substitution so unstable as to need to be repeated? Perhaps "unstable" is not the most precise word since what takes place here is nothing *inconsistent,* but something which speaks to the nature of pleasure. What happens when the loss (of the mother) becomes a symbolic loss is that the game itself is played to lose. This is perhaps what is most difficult to see: that the *Fort! Da!* game is a losing game. An impossible game that can be played only insofar as it can never be finished. Or, at least, a game in which to play means to recognize that there is a loss. It is played as lost at both ends: in respect to the incomplete symbolization of the injury; and also in respect to the outcome of the game, which returns the game to its beginning.[32]

While yielding the pleasure of mastery, substitution also yields the unplea-

---

31. *BPP,* p. 16.

32. Since I am analyzing representation, it is worth noting that the loss in representation is what, historically, Plato's theory of ideas insists upon, referring to an economy that is not substantially different from the one discussed here. See, for example, Plato's *Phaedrus,* trans. R. Hackforth, in *The Collected Dialogues of Plato,* Edith Hamilton and Huntington Cairns, eds. (Princeton, NJ: Princeton University Press, 1973), pp. 475–525.

sure of subordination to symbolic activity, the discontent in becoming a subject, and the dissatisfaction in the loss of immediacy. In this sense, in the *Fort! Da!* there is no substitutive pleasure without displeasure. No gain or great cultural achievement without a repetition of the loss in the very gain. This is the gist of the argument Freud will make ten years after *BPP*, in *Civilization and Its Discontents*. In this later work Freud develops his understanding of unpleasure and presumes that the death drive is the reason why pleasure and happiness are not achieved in the work of civilization. While working to ensure pleasure, civilization finds itself, paradoxically, frustrating its goal and being compelled to repeat the attempt. Which is to say that the work of civilization is structured as repetition compulsion.

In the *Fort! Da!* game, the drive to repeat a representation betrays the unconscious function of gaming. Namely, its tendency toward dissolution and destruction. Having helped Ernst separate from the physical presence of the mother, the *Fort! Da!* game maintains another direct relation: that of the subject to himself. It is a direct relation even though or, rather, precisely because it is established in and as the game. Once there is substitution, however, the emergent subject is also undermined by that which—the compulsion to repeat, or the conjuring of the ghost I mentioned earlier—makes its emergence possible. In this instance a relation that leads to pleasure goes by way of the death drive. But, there is no such thing as a relation that the death drive would maintain. As an opposing tendency, as a drive toward dissolution, it negates precisely the possibility for a relation. In the *Fort! Da!* then, there is either absolute loss—a certain tendency toward nothing—or no loss at all but something quite different (if by loss we mean that Ernst, when he plays the game, has less than he had before). That which we might term loss but which is for Freud this tendency toward regression to an inanimate state, remains outside of the game, "beyond," as it were. The game unfolds toward it, touching it in its countless repetitions but never finally reaching it, never properly playing it. Yet in the game, there is a substitutive satisfaction, as if *it* were played. *It,* call it an object of representation, or the inanimate, real *thing,* is lost, missed, or lacking. Which is also to say that because *it* remains not played, there is, on the one hand, the game and, on the other, a beyond, an outside. An outside, I would add, that is at once an infinite possibility and a point of termination.

What is most important about the game for our purposes here is the extent to which the object coincides with the subject. Meaning that the subject who repeats, the author of the game, is simultaneously the subject resulting from the repetition. As far as artistic representations are concerned, we cannot say that they are outright traumatic, but that they are informed, driven by the same drive that instates the compulsion to repeat. Now, we should reformulate our question "how come literature repeats?" into a more significant one: how is it that literature does anything *but* repeat?[33] How is it that *Beloved* does anything but unleash the ghosts of the unburied past? Perhaps not all novels or games develop through this movement between *fort* and *da,* internalization and setting forth, absence and presence, but only those that have something to do with the death drive and trauma. It is, however, hard to imagine a game, an art work, or even a history which would not have at its core the principle of radical dissolution thematized by Freud as the death drive and located by Morrison in the figure of a *revenant.* What is a game or a novel if not an attempt to systematize, incorporate, remember a ghostly, haunting experience, doing so always incompletely, calling for a continuation? What would the alternative possibility be—a complete novel? What would the last play that ends the game be—a ghost that does not return?

Denver

When Sethe warns Denver of the past that is waiting for her, she says not only that there is such a troubled past which persists, but also that it is there *for Denver,* as if Denver is necessary for the horror to be "there." For Denver, who sees Sweet Home through her mother's eyes, the *there* where she "can't never go"[34] is inseparable from the relation she has with her mother. The image that persists and haunts her is, in this sense, linked to the mother Denver is afraid of. So that the source of haunting is the *relation.* Not just any relation, but one that is not fully established and that cannot be fully severed. It is a mother-

---

33. Gertrude Stein's, James Joyce's, Marcel Duchamp's, and Andy Warhol's artistic experiments with repetition come to mind. At this point we could make a link with another trend in the interpretation of repetition in the modern age, namely with technological reproduction. Of Walter Benjamin we could ask, does twentieth century art repeat compulsively or mechanically? What is the difference?, and what is the "aura" that is lost in compulsive repetition? See Walter Benjamin, "The Work of Art in the Age of Mechanical Reproduction," trans. Harry Zohn, in *Illuminations,* Hannah Arendt, ed. (New York: Schocken Books, 1969), pp. 217–252. It would also be interesting to ask whether minimalism in music—Steve Reich's, for example—has traumatic origins.

34. *Beloved,* p. 36.

daughter relation, and also, as we saw above, a relation between past and present or between representation and its object, between an individual and a collective, between the name of an individual and herself. There is haunting, we can then say, *because* the relationship within which an identity is produced cannot be either fully established or severed. In this sense Morrison speaks of the radical character of representation in her *The Nobel Lecture in Literature,* "Narrative is radical, creating us at the very moment it is being created."[35]

I hope that the above analysis of *Fort! Da!* has shown that the compulsion to repeat translates the wound into terms that are not entirely the wound's own and carries it (the wound) to the level of symbolization, allowing for the possibility of its identification and for the emergence of a subject (in/of trauma). In these terms, *Beloved* — its ghost — is neither a secondary copy of a "primary" traumatic event nor a repetition which allows us to trace another, prior trauma. *Beloved* is, to be sure, both, but it is so only by being more than either of these. The novel replicates (i.e., repeats) the original story — the Garner story — and traces back (i.e., represents) the traumatic event — of slavery, of a rape, of a motherhood, of an infanticide, and so forth. In representing the event, the novel in effect remembers the event as past, thus allowing the event to have a historical, and not solely an (unconscious) traumatic significance. But, if there is a trauma repeated in the novel, this is not a historical trauma but the one which can be more closely associated with a certain trauma of history. This is then a trauma of creation, a present trauma. "Anything dead coming back to life hurts,"[36] says Morrison through the mouth of the "*white*woman" whom Ella suspects of being a ghost.[37]

At any rate, *Beloved* is an aesthetic event, and it does not allow for an undisturbed articulation of the specter of meaning it brings about or conjures.[38] *Beloved*'s ghost makes way for what is other in interpretation and

---

35. Toni Morrison, *The Nobel Lecture in Literature, 1993* (New York: Knopf, 1994), p. 27.

36. *Beloved*, p. 35.

37. *Beloved*, p. 187.

38. In the introduction to his collection entitled *Toni Morrison,* Harold Bloom criticizes what he calls a "politicized response to narrative." Harold Bloom, ed., *Toni Morrison* (New York: Chelsea House, 1990), p. 1. While Bloom offers a valuable reminder about the importance of textual history for an understanding of the novel, I don't quite see that the two allegiances (to politics, or to aesthetics) can be separated. It is, however, an open question as to how one brings the two — the political intentions of the author and the text's aesthetics — to bear upon each other.

otherwise than interpretation: for a beloved that is not beloved, for a people that are not my people. Makes way for that which cannot be internalized or appropriated but gets somehow repeated, carried over, in repetition. It is precisely because the ghost's unnatural, strange, haunting presence cannot be reduced to one or another moral or historical claim, present trauma or a past trauma, that the novel brings ethical and historical relations to the fore. So that, in *Beloved,* the elements of a specific history depend upon the mode of relation that can be established with the past. Lacking a more precise word, I call that which is between present and past, between representation and its object, experience and a text, a relation. But this is also a nonrelation, precisely because we cannot say that *Beloved* brings the past back or that it represents slavery. What we have in the relation's stead is this novel: "Everybody knew what she was called, but nobody anywhere knew her name. Disremembered and unaccounted for, she cannot be lost because no one is looking for her, and even if they were, how can they call her if they don't know her name? Although she has claim, she is not claimed."[39]

Trauma: Structural and Historical

In the last twenty years there have been essentially two views of trauma, one that it is a structural disorder and one that it is a historical event. In what follows I will reconstruct the general understandings of trauma at the expense of the specificities of the particular authors addressed in my analysis. In spite of this reductiveness, I hope that some light will be cast on how we may approach trauma after Dominick LaCapra, Judith Butler, Jacques Derrida, Maurice Blanchot, Cathy Caruth, Shoshana Felman, Jacques Lacan, and Saul Friedländer, who will be mentioned here. My goal is not to dismiss the aporia between the structural and the historical (general/particular, textual/political), for, to say the least, it has brought about a necessary sensitivity and attentiveness to various exigencies in the study of trauma. I am rather interested in the logic of the development of a discourse on trauma which ends up offering this aporia. Additionally, we should try to see whether the aporia prevents us from looking more closely at the relationship between trauma and haunting.

In Dominick LaCapra's recent work, *History and Memory after Auschwitz,*

---

39. *Beloved,* p. 274.

the structural/historical distinction is at times presented as a distinction be-tween trauma in general and a particular trauma.[40] Trauma in general could be seen as a characteristic of literary or philosophical writing. Trauma in particular, on the other hand, is a consequence of a wound, an offense inflicted on a person by another person, as in a concentration camp, or by circum-stances, as in the case of the train accidents that Freud mentions in *BPP*. Perhaps there is then an abstract trauma *and* a concrete trauma? An abstract trauma which is due to a concrete offense, but two traumas—a haunting and an injury—nevertheless. The reason for this distinction is political and con-cerns the *(im)possibility* of a direct reference to an offense as a crime, and at the same time, the *obligation* to name the historical event which caused the injury, to call it by its proper name.[41]

The particular trauma is historical in the sense that it was caused at a certain time, at a certain place, and involved certain individuals. While historical trauma is also termed social, empirical, and factual, "abstract" trauma has an ahistorical or transhistorical status, and could just as well be called existential, transcendental, or textual. Once again Butler's reading of *BPP* can help us offer a closer look at what is here differentiated. One of the questions she asks is about the relation between the speculative construct, the death drive as informing the history of an organism as such, and the analytic construct, the potential the notion of the death drive may have for an under-standing of the effects of a particular offense as it shapes the life of an individual; for example, understanding the sadistic impulses of a survivor. At the end of her text, Butler brings the two together and concludes

> the unhappy repetitions of sadistic acts bear out a useless desire to repeat and repair a history of dissatisfaction. The effort to comprehend this pleasure that goes nowhere, that repeats itself endlessly as the infinite stutter of desire, requires a turn: not to instinct but to the particular history of injury which, internalized then externalized, becomes the focus of a sexual battle.[42]

---

40. Dominick LaCapra, *History and Memory after Auschwitz* (Ithaca, NY: Cornell University Press, 1997).

41. See, for example Saul Friedländer's "Trauma, Transference, and 'Working through,' in Writing the History of the *Shoah,"* *History and Memory* vol. 4, no. 1, (Spring/Summer 1992), pp. 39–59.

42. Butler, "The Pleasure of Repetition," p. 275.

So the distinction historical/structural can be also seen as a distinction between the speculative and analytic character of psychoanalytic theory, where the accent is on the way in which an analyst or a theorist can in a particular case determine whether repetition compulsion repeats instinctually *or* because of an injury. It is not necessary that one exclude either possibility, but the turning point in analysis happens when repetition is taken in respect to events an individual has gone through. In order to understand traumatic repetition, one thus needs to specify the event the survivor of an offense repeats. Analogously, it is important not only that *Beloved* repeats but that Sethe, in killing her daughter, acts out the rape and other humiliations she survived as a slave; Denver, afraid to leave the house at 124 Bluestone Road, acts out the violation of her mother.[43] It is hence slavery and the rape of Sethe that give (historical) specificity to their traumas.[44] After having identified the event, the analysis advances, for it names with a proper name the cause of trauma.

When LaCapra and Butler argue for the distinction between structural and historical traumas, repetition compulsion is not relegated entirely to a particular event which is repressed or disavowed and repeated. LaCapra and Butler would not disagree hence with Derrida and Blanchot, or Felman and Caruth, on the point that a trauma, a disaster, provokes a return to a previous

---

43. "Whatever it is, it comes from outside this house, outside the yard, and it can come right on in the yard if it wants to. So I never leave this house and I watch over the yard, so it can't happen again and my mother won't have to kill me too." *Beloved,* p. 205.

44. Much of *Beloved*'s criticism has indeed focused on this specificity. Let me here single out only a few paradigmatic essays. Besides the already cited Walter Benn Michaels's, "'You who never was there,'" see also Rebecca Ferguson, "History, Memory and Language in Toni Morrison's *Beloved,*" *Feminist Criticism: Theory and Practice,* Susan Sellars, ed. (Toronto: University of Toronto Press, 1991), pp. 109–127; Marilyn Sanders Mobley, "A Different Remembering: Memory, History and Meaning in Toni Morrison's *Beloved,*" in *Toni Morrison,* Harold Bloom, ed. (New York: Chelsea House, 1990), pp. 189–199; Mae G. Henderson, "Toni Morrison's *Beloved:* Remembering the Body as Historical Text," in *Comparative American Identities: Race, Sex and Nationality in the Modern Text,* Hortense J. Spillers, ed. (New York: Routledge, 1991), pp. 62–86; Helen Moglen, "Redeeming History: Toni Morrison's *Beloved,*" *Cultural Critique* 24 (1993): pp. 17–40; Naomi Morgenstern, "Mother's Milk and Sister's Blood: Trauma and the Neoslave Narrative," *Differences* vol. 8, no. 2, pp. 103–125; and Caroline Rody, "Toni Morrison's *Beloved:* History, 'Rememory,' and a 'Clamor for a Kiss,'" *American Literary History* vol. 7, no. 1, pp. 92–119.

trauma/disaster. They would not disagree, in other words, on the belated (*Nachträglich*) character of a traumatic event. But, they do regard differently the status of the (traumatic) event and, more specifically, the status of its occurrence. For Derrida, when he speaks of deferral, for Blanchot, when he mentions the happening-not-happening of the disaster, it is presumed that in the occurrence of a disaster there is something ontologically different from other events.[45] This is not to say that the disaster (Blanchot), or the conflagration of difference (Derrida), has not occurred. But: what has occurred?, what is this event?, how is it registered? ask both Blanchot and Derrida, each in his own way interrogating the ontological possibility that *there is* an event. How, indeed, would one think an utter annihilation? What is the thought that attempts to do this? What does such a thought make of the disaster? and so forth.

For Caruth, the cry "released *through the wound*" is an event that testifies to the otherness of the human voice.[46] A trauma narrative is thus seen as the story of the coming into being of the other. In Caruth's words, it is "the story of the way in which one's own trauma is tied up with the trauma of another, the way in which trauma may lead, therefore, to the encounter with another, through the very possibility and surprise of listening to another's wound."[47] Caruth further underscores that the writing she examines testifies, beyond an author's or a character's knowledge and intention, to "some forgotten wound."[48] This is not to say that a testimony to a historical event is necessarily imprecise, for its adequacy is not in question here. If a testimony is caught in traumatic repetition, this can only mean that there is something in history and in its writing which, as Blanchot suggests in *The Writing of the Disaster,* is other than history, something which has no temporal modality or destiny, and cannot be predicted.

When this un-said in the saying, or this un-experienced in experience, becomes itself as important—philosophically, politically, and historically— as the fact brought forth or begetted[49] in a testimony, then one faces that

---

45. Maurice Blanchot, *The Writing of the Disaster,* trans. Ann Smock (Lincoln, NE: Nebraska University Press, 1986). Jacques Derrida, *The Post Card.*

46. Cathy Caruth, *Unclaimed Experience,* p. 2. (Caruth's emphasis).

47. Ibid., p. 8.

48. Ibid., p. 5.

49. In *Three Case Histories,* Freud points to the etymology of the word "witness," noting: "A witness who testifies to something before a court of law is still called

aspectof testimony which for Shoshana Felman and Dori Laub is the testimony's most critical characteristic.[50] It is this inassimilable alterity, to which testimony also testifies, that marks the historical specificity of a certain event and period with an exigency to which the fact that such and such an act took place does not correspond. Crisis is, then, the crisis of a response to testimony. A crisis that concerns the continuation of witnessing rather than testimony as such, for how could we speak of witnessing "as such" outside of the chain reaction that testimony provokes? One should also bear in mind that Felman's analysis of witnessing is undertaken, as a rule, well after the historical occurrence in question and after the death of the participants in the event. In this respect, again, Felman's question concerns the response to the (re)emergence of the event in testimony, including the way a historical agent, a person, responds to what he or she says while saying it.[51] While one could here ask whether it is necessary that the historical event be witnessed by those who did not participate in it, perhaps the question that would yield a greater understanding of the trauma is, how does the catastrophe ever become absent?[52]

'*Zeuge*' [literally, "begetter"] in German, after the part played by the male in the act of procreation; so too in hieroglyphics a "witness" is represented pictorially by the male genitals." Sigmund Freud, *Three Case Histories,* trans. James Strachey (New York: Collier Books, 1963), p. 88. Given this etymology—testimony, testis—is it any wonder that today, especially considering contemporary feminist thought, there are calls for the examination of the concept of witnessing?

50. Shoshana Felman and Dori Laub, *Testimony: Crises of Witnessing in Literature, Psychoanalysis, and History* (New York: Routledge, 1992). Crisis is etymologically a turning point, not an overturning—*kata-strophe*—as it is usually treated.

51. See also Lawrence L. Langer's "Memory's Time: Chronology and Duration in Holocaust Testimonies," *The Yale Journal of Criticism* vol. 6, no. 2 (Fall 1993): pp. 263–274. And his *Holocaust Testimonies: The Ruins of Memory* (New Haven, CT: Yale University Press, 1991). See also William Wendell Haver, *The Body of This Death: Historicity and Sociality in the Time of AIDS* (Stanford, CA: Stanford University Press, 1996).

52. The turn I am making implies that there is a difference between two basic ontological possibilities for understanding the relationship between present and past: one, that their relation depends on the moment of presence. In this sense, the past is present in the present (through memory) only as absent. And another one, that the separation between past and present, presence and absence, can be drawn only arbitrarily, implying a certain imposition of measure that is not inherent in the relationship past-present. According to this line of thinking, past and present are always in a specific relation that can be neither established nor severed. For example,

Lacan's distinction between imaginary, symbolic, and real introduces a tripartite division into the thinking of the dualistic relationship between historical and structural trauma. For Lacan, the real does not have a structure, but neither is it independent of imaginary and symbolic structures. The real is both within and without structure. Hence, to equate the real with either the structural or the historical would be to reduce its function to the domain of symbolization, and to exclude that which remains unsymbolizable. In this sense, it is only in recognizing the limits of naming that discourses on either structural or historical trauma succeed in revealing something about the real. This is also to say that, for Lacan, historical and structural trauma necessarily collapse into each other because they are ontologically indistinguishable.

In respect to Butler's argument mentioned above, we could now ask whether witnessing and its continuation beyond the generation of survivors is possible if one turns away from the repetition she calls the stutter of desire? Is desire's repetition merely "useless," or is it that which, in its uselessness, makes the chain of witnessing possible? Is it not the case that the historical specificity of the event is manifested in and transmitted precisely through traumatic repetition? There are, then, historical periods and events where turning away from the stutter of desire is impossible, since it amounts to encountering another trauma. A subsequent, logical question would be, why use the same term for two politically and ethically disparate conditions—for the primary and the secondary witness, for primary (historical) and secondary (structural) trauma? This issue, undoubtedly, deserves close attention. Let me just note here that the authors I mention do differ in their use of the term trauma (and some don't even use it). To the extent that trauma marks an impossibility or at least a difficulty in naming that which is traumatizing, there is a plurality of names which circle around a wound. Instead of concentrating on two different terms for structural and historical trauma, I would like to suggest, then, that we define trauma studies as a discourse which both points to and interrogates certain constitutive limitations.

---

while Aristotle in his treatise on memory ("On Memory and Recollection") asked how it is that the past is present in the present, Plato's question was throughout his dialogues: how is it that past is ever absent from the present? The two possibilities lead to or come from quite different understandings of being, time, and history. The challenge for trauma studies lies in attempting to think beyond these two concepts of memory. Aristotle, "On Memory and Recollection," in *Aristotle in Twenty-three Volumes*, vol. VIII, trans. W. S. Hett (Cambridge, MA: Harvard University Press, 1986), pp. 289–313.

As for literature, what would it mean for it to turn away from the structural or instinctual stutter of desire? Would not such a turning away threaten to undercut the very possibility of literature? Moreover, isn't literature precisely a form of turning toward a catastrophe, an instinct, and a desire—an attempt to face them in the most radical and immediate way possible? In the case of *Beloved* the traumatic event is of historical proportions. Here trauma is not a specific event in an individual's history; rather, the singular trauma—trauma in *Beloved*—is that which gives specificity to one whole historical period. So that the "historical" and "structural" bear upon each other in *Beloved* in quite different ways than in the case of a patient in Butler's sense. Morrison attempts to represent the general in the particular—slavery in Sethe—but in presenting Sethe, *Beloved* falls short of representing either the general (the slavery) or the particular (Margaret Garner), and manifests only the singular, the unique (Sethe, Beloved, Denver, etc.). By which I mean that Sethe is a literary character that both substitutes and transforms the general condition of slavery and the particular experience of Margaret Garner. The aesthetic autonomy of *Beloved,* for example, its uniqueness, does not indicate its detachment from the historico-political context of slavery. It rather denotes the form in which *Beloved* can and does become a part of this context as it also reshapes it (in the here and now). In this sense, the aesthetic singularity of *Beloved* constitutes its historical specificity.

The difference between the discourses on trauma can be expressed also according to how the significance of *Fort! Da!* is interpreted. The question is whether Freud's analysis in *BPP* is also, as Derrida suggests, a *Fort! Da!* Whether a discourse on trauma/disaster is necessarily and essentially a *Fort! Da!*, that is, whether it in some way repeats the structure of deferral? If the answer is affirmative, the implication is that meaning—and not just the event's meaning, but the meaning of meaning—is deferred, and that trauma is present only through its repetitions. To pretend that the *fact* definitely names the *event* would, according to this line of thinking, be tantamount to foreclosing the possibility for a text; a definite delimitation between history and text, between trauma as an injury and trauma as a textual disorder, would erase any bearing that literature and memory have on the events or the lives of survivors; there would be only a present present to itself, a present that has obliterated the future and erased the possibility for a past.

Here we could say with Saul Friedländer that an approach to trauma worth pursuing lies not in attempting to name or delimit the crime "definitely," but rather in finding ways to negotiate between the historical (factual, actual) givens and its structural (underlying, unconscious) consequences. To historicize the Holocaust hence implies, in Friedländer's words, the "simultaneous acceptance of two contradictory moves: the search for ever-closer historical linkages and the avoidance of a naive historical positivism leading to simplistic and self-assured historical narrations and closures."[53] *But* remaining between these two moves may obscure the constitutional limitations to witnessing and historicization. By which I mean that that which allows us to distinguish between the two epistemological moves suggested by Friedländer may in some way be caught in trauma. I am not saying that constitutional factors are the cause of trauma, but that they cannot prevent it and that a set of givens (structure, constitution, *or* a history) is somehow dependent on trauma. A response to trauma needs therefore to take into account constitutional limitations on the level of the fundamental organization of an organism and of a society—to the extent that we can call it an organization and not a disorganization. As such, trauma discourse necessarily makes certain ontological and, of course, political claims.

What I want to argue here is not that the term structural is imprecise, although it is imprecise. Nor that the division structural/historical or experiential/textual is untenable, although it is untenable. My point is rather that a study of trauma is involved in reworking structures which only appear as either present or past, historical or structural, but which are neither. In effect, in describing trauma, one is reworking the possibility of the emergence of a structure, and is thus dealing with a becoming form. What, indeed, is the purpose of the study of trauma if one does not recognize that one is conjuring a certain kind of futurity, not something that has finished or that is past?

In this sense, one can get closer not to the Shoah, but to an understanding of what it means that meaning is absent. Not the meaning of a traumatic event, not its deep memory which remains, for Friedländer, opaque. Not the past moment when the event occurred. Instead, we are called to attend to absence of meaning in meaning—including the absent meaning of this pronoun "we." Is this what Friedländer has in mind at the end of his text when he cites Blanchot? "Working through," Friedländer writes, "may ultimately signify, in Maurice Blanchot's words, 'to keep watch over absent meaning.'"[54] Perhaps.

---

53. Friedländer, "Trauma, Transference, and 'Working through,'" p. 53.

54. Lawrence Langer's article "Memory's Time" ends with the same citation. Neither Langer nor Friedländer comment on how one would watch *over* absent meaning. Nor do they explain how they are borrowing this phrase from Blanchot. In Blanchot's text, these words, *"Veiller sur le sens absent,"* appear in italics in a separate

We have here reached another aspect of treating trauma (and its study). I should emphasize that by "constitution" above I am referencing not only the basic biological or psychological aspect/desire of an organism but also basic cultural or societal givens. By "organism," furthermore, I am referring not only to an individual but also to a group formed through a particular history that is/was shared. What I would like to propose, then, is that trauma, which leads to this absent meaning, has also changed what we mean by organism, culture, society, structure, history, and what we mean by meaning itself. To write on trauma, hence, implies dealing with singular, not general or particular, disruptions, including the disruption of the applicability of the terms and concepts we use to describe and understand trauma. Including, also, the disruption of the very possibility of making a claim or writing a text. This recognition of the radical disturbance (of constitutive elements) that is trauma seems to me to be a prerequisite for negotiating the relation between the structural and historical, literary and factual aspects of a trauma.

Accordingly, one cannot claim that in *Beloved* trauma is caused by historically specific events without also claiming that the literary event constitutes if not history as such, then what is most important about it—its specificity. In a literary work of art, this specificity, especially the specificity of naming, is hardly in the facts and dates. For the name, the claim, the fact, and the date are entrusted to the "unreliable," because imaginative, realm of memory. What is so specific about *Beloved,* then, is that it takes up facts, dates, and experiences and considers them as acts of naming, acts that are at once disastrous/ pleasurable, redeemable/unredeemable, speakable/unspeakable, creative/ destructive. In doing so, *Beloved* lays out a world as haunted by its own worldliness, by, that is, its historically specific here and now, which remains unspeakable, haunting. The stutter of its desire is its poetry as well as politics;

---

passage which stands alone and is preceded by a discussion on what it means to write ("To write is perhaps to bring to the surface something like absent meaning") and whether a commentary on writing can sustain an absent meaning. The French "veiller" or "veille" designates the ritual wake over a dead body, a vigil. *"La veille de Noël"* is Christmas Eve. In Blanchot "veiller" resonates with Levinasian insomnia. Thus, a whole spectrum of meaning from ceremonial wake through vigile (from *vigere,* to be vigorous or lively) to vigilance and vigilante, opens up complicating the notion of watching over. Is this complication, this chain of etymologies, writings, and translations, itself a form of "veiller"? If it is, where is and what is the absent meaning? Blanchot, *The Writing of the Disaster,* pp. 41–42. Blanchot, *L'Écriture du désastre* (Paris: Gallimard, 1980), pp. 71–72.

and the uselessness of its repetition, a characteristic of its aesthetic and political domain.

Also, the relation between matters of trauma and literary matters, between structure and history, is continually reestablished through transference. Transference may well be the key point in the study of trauma, since without it such study is inconceivable, and if its function remains obscured, quite probably irrelevant. Now it is a question of how transference and counter-transference take place in an analysis of either historical or literary events, and what one means by transference outside the psychoanalytic session.

Beloved

After this note on transference, I should mention that *Beloved* does not necessarily need to be treated as having the structure of traumatic neurosis, especially since Morrison, in speaking of racism, emphasizes the psychotic dimension of its effects. Apropos of Melville's *Moby-Dick,* she says: "The trauma of racism is, for the racist and the victim, the severe fragmentation of the self, and has always seemed to me a *cause* (not a symptom) of psychosis."[55] Although Morrison is most likely using "psychosis" in its colloquial sense, as a synonym for madness, we may want to raise the question of psychosis together with our question of trauma (traumatic neurosis). And so especially since *Beloved* may function differently for different American communities. What I am suggesting is that *Beloved* could at the same time be a marker of the materiality of the past which refuses to pass and an illusion, a hallucination. In this sense, *Beloved* would be acknowledging certain facts of American history, the fact, for example, that the traumatic past, and racism with it, are disavowed.

---

55. Toni Morrison, "Unspeakable Things Unspoken: The Afro-American Presence in American Literature," in *Toni Morrison,* Harold Bloom, ed. (New York: Chelsea House, 1990), p. 214, emphasis added. Here, as on previous occasions when I cite Morrison, I take it as my task not only to explicate but also to create a context (as if, from within *Beloved*) for the citation. At another place, discussing institutionalized racism, Morrison suggests: "Everybody remembers the first time they were taught that part of the human race was Other. That's a trauma." See Bonnie Angelo, "The Pain of Being Black: An Interview with Toni Morrison," in Danielle Taylor-Guthrie ed., *Conversations with Toni Morrison,* p. 258. Originally published in *Time* (22 May 1989), pp. 120–123.

While one cannot separate Beloved as a *revenant* from Beloved as a fantasy, and while the distinction I am making between trauma and psychosis is both problematic and tendentious, I would still like to mention that there is quite an important difference between two ways of entering into an analysis of *Beloved* as either a story of/in displacement (trauma), or as a story of/in foreclosure (psychosis). For in the case of displacement, one grapples with an obscured, opaque for Friedländer, relation. And in the case of foreclosure, one's task is to show the very obscurity and occlusion of ontological—but also sexual, political, historical, ethical, and racial—difference. In the case of foreclosure, we are dealing with the (im)possibility of admitting that there is trauma—an impossibility which, paradoxically, may be maintained by the very discourse on trauma. What I am driving at is that trauma studies, based on the assumption of the possibility of the transmission, repetition of trauma, may function as a strategy of prolonging compulsion repetition and of guaranteeing *jouissance* in disaster, and hence, of obscuring a foreclosure. Perhaps what I am describing here is an inevitable stage in coming to grips with trauma, a stage which would call for the realization of how difficult it is to remove resistance, to renounce the pleasure of one's suffering, and to acknowledge the impossibilities, the limits, that trauma imposes on thinking and working through it.

10

Obstinate Forgetting in Chile: Radical Injustice and the Possibility of Community

Brett Levinson

I begin not with an analysis, but with a parable derived from the recent Chilean film *Amnesia*. A middle-aged protagonist named Martínez, living more or less comfortably in Santiago in the early '90s, meets up with a former army general, Zúniga. During the Pinochet reign Zúniga had tormented this protagonist, then a soldier. The two men recognize one another; they go to a bar. Zúniga discusses the importance of forgetting the past, of moving on. He goes so far as to laugh at the fact that his ex-soldier had disobeyed an order. Martínez, on the other hand, openly discusses his desire for vengeance, even as his tone remains amiable enough for Zúniga to believe that this desire is not a serious one. In fact, however, the protagonist and another Zúniga victim, a former prisoner (who Martínez was supposed to kill, but did not), had previously mapped out a plan to assassinate Zúniga, and had been waiting for the opportunity to carry out their scheme, perhaps for some twenty years.

Taking advantage of the chance meeting with Zúniga, the two victims — the ex-prisoner, the ex-soldier — successfully execute the plot. They are about to hang their tormentor but, at the last instant, the protagonist refuses to perform the act. Instead, he brings Zúniga to his home, without removing the noose. In an astonishing final scene, the victims and the ex-soldier's wife consume a succulently prepared anniversary dinner while Zúniga sits on a chair, face in utter agony, rope still around his neck.

The incapacity to kill Zúniga is the protagonist's recognition of the immeasurability of what I will be calling radical injustice. In and of itself the wish to murder the tormentor points up nothing more than a desire for a payback. The ex-soldier wants to even the score, to balance the scales of justice. Yet what he eventually intuits is that nothing can compensate for the wrongs that he has endured (and witnessed, even perpetrated), since those wrongs lie beyond measure. The murder would not "even the score" but, on the contrary, would serve as final confirmation that no act, not even an act of vengeance, can counteract the grief suffered. This immeasurability is emphasized in *Amnesia* by the fact that the distress of the ex-soldier is not only tied to his victimization but also to his *victimizing*. Zúñiga had forced this soldier to kill two prisoners; and yet, because Martínez could have chosen his own death over the death of others, he is obviously responsible for his acts. Thus, and however much he may have been coerced, this timid, sensitive, decent protagonist is himself guilty of a heinous, perhaps irredeemable deed although, prior to the chance meeting, he clearly associated the liquidation of Zúñiga with an erasing of the past, and thus with the possibility of that very redemption.

We can now see why Zúñiga must be preserved, noose around his neck. For only as long as he is kept both in reach and alive is the potential for justice and redemption also kept in reach and alive. If Zúñiga is killed, on the other hand, the futility and dissatisfaction of the murder, and the impossibility of all restitution, will be verified. In other words, at the moment he is about to hang Zúñiga, the ex-soldier both obtains and disavows certain knowledge, namely, that the realization of the fantasy of justice would only eliminate that fantasy. The elimination of Zúñiga would leave the victim not "even" but without recourse to the *promise* of compensation that he possesses as long as vengeance/justice/redemption remain unrealized, of the future.

This parable, which touches upon the main thrust of a number of other films (e.g., *Death and the Maiden*) and narratives (Miguel Bonasso's *La memoria en donde ardía*), will serve as a point of departure for a tripartite discussion of postdictatorship in the Southern Cone. The first point I will consider concerns the link between the injustices perpetrated by the Southern Cone military regimes and the transition to democracy. The debate is by now familiar: Is the meting out of justice for military criminals the precondition for the advent of democracy or is it a demand which impedes this same advent? The question, as we know, hinges on the forgetting/vengeance dilemma which has become one of the commonplaces of postdictatorship cultural production and political controversies: Are amnesty (forgetting) and vengeance—neither of which can lead to any real justice, solution, or absolution—the only two ways of dealing with military crimes? In practice (rather than in theory) should

the lemma put forth during the transition period in Uruguay, "Neither forgetting nor vengeance—justice," be replaced by: "Either forgetting or
vengeance—no justice is possible"? Or can we track down more optimistic
prospects?

The second issue I will consider concerns history. The fact that *Amnesia*
revolves around an anniversary scene is not superfluous. Anniversaries usually signal the passage of time. Yet it is clear, in the film, that the characters
remain stuck in the past: for them, time cannot proceed since the past is never
overcome, never relinquished. Anniversary, rather than passage, emerges as
eternal presence of the same, an endless circle. In fact, we will see that both
forgetting (where the past is ignored) and vengeance (where the past becomes
an obsession) block the flow of history, and hence the possibility of transition.
But how can nations move beyond this stagnation? Given the difficult issue of
military crimes, how can time, thus the transition process, be (re)started after
the dictatorship's fall?

The last theme I will address is that of identity. It is apparent from the
various discussions of the so-called "new Latin American social movements"
(many of which are linked to postdictatorship concerns)[1] that current political theories developing in Latin America are both skeptical of identity and
identity politics, and somehow unable to think the political beyond the subject
of self-representation, that is, beyond identity. Yet is the postdictatorship,
postdisaster predicament perhaps a demand that theory inaugurate a postdictatorship politics beyond—or, better said, at the limit of—the self, the I,
identity politics, and perhaps politics itself?

I

I would like, first, to carve out a theory of radical injustice. Radical injustice,
as I am attempting to formulate it, is related to the immeasurability of certain
wrongs. Of course, one could say that all wrongs, all crimes, are essentially
immeasurable. In fact, compensation for any wrong is grounded on an arbitrary, thus problematic "scale" of equivalence and/or exchange; no necessary
equivalence between crime and punishment exists. X punishment balances Y

---

1. See Arturo Escobar's fine summary of this matter in *The Making of Social
Movements in Latin America: Identity, Strategy, and Democracy,* ed. Arturo Escobar and
Sonia E. Alvarez (Boulder, CO: Westview Press, 1992), pp. 78–83.

crime, thus bringing the perpetrator "to justice" not because X and Y are *essentially* (or even relatively) equal, but because conventions have formed and tables have been set up so as to equate two very different phenomena (the suffering of an individual or of society as a whole, on the one hand; and the punishment received or dispensed, on the other). In this sense, the law is structured like a language. Saussurean linguistics teaches us that a signifier is linked to a signified arbitrarily, not necessarily: the signifier refers to the given signified through difference (bat is not cat) and repetition (a signifier must be matched to a signified more than once for it to become part of a language system), in other words, through habit, through mere convention. A punishment "equals" a crime similarly: through difference (e.g., punishment A is "more" than punishment B) and repetition (Y crime has traditionally received X punishment). With radical injustice, however, no conventions exist or can exist, no table of measurement has been or can be forged. Radical injustice, that is, emerges not when a crime is committed, and not when the law appears as insufficient and/or erroneous, but when every convention surfaces as obsolete—as pertaining to another time and place—and, therefore, every act of restitution as impossible.

Here, however, it is necessary to put out a pair of warning signs. First, my notion of radical injustice does not presuppose or part from a given philosophical concept of justice. I am interested not in justice per se (in a phenomenology or in the "being" of justice) but in the *sense of justice* that victims of political violence might experience (my understanding of the "victim," I should add, is derived from portrayals put forth in the films and narratives mentioned in this study, as well as from many other documents such as the Argentine *Nunca Más,* Osvaldo Soriano's two collections of "testimonios,"[2] and Adolfo Aristarain's film *Time for Revenge*). This "sense" may or may not be related to "true justice," or to justice as it has been so rigorously discussed by philosophers and political theorists since at least Aristotle. But it is not my purpose to respond to the question: Can "justice" actually be served in the postdictatorship context? My question is: Can those who have survived the wrongs (either wrongs these people themselves endured, or wrongs endured by others who are the survivors' concern—loved ones, for example) of various military regimes feel *as if* justice has been served? If with "typical" wrongs the victim, awaiting the meting out of the "correct" or "conventional" punish-

---

2. I am referring to Soriano's *Artistas, Locos y criminales* (Buenos Aires: Bruguera, 1983) and *Rebeldes, Soñadores y fugitivos* (Buenos Aires: Editora/12, 1987).

ment, feels *as if* some kind of restitution might be impending, in radical injustice wronged individuals (such as those portrayed in *Amnesia*) are exposed to an inequity for which they *feel* no "adequate," "correct" or "conventional" punishment—indeed, no convention at all, and thus no punishment at all—exists or even can exist.

Radical injustice, therefore, is not the result of a crime so heinous and radical that it cannot be measured. Indeed, to make such a claim is to have already measured—by referring to the "so" in "so heinous"—the radical injustice, and thus to have eliminated its definitive feature: immeasurability. Rather, the injustice is heinous and radical *because* it cannot be measured, because a specific victim (whether an individual or a group), within a particular judicial, social, and/or political situation, cannot perceive any potential compensation for his/her (their) suffering, whatever the actual crime may have been, and whatever the actual pain may be.

The second warning, already hinted at, is the following: the faltering of justice should not be confused with the failure to prosecute fully or even partially, with the weakness of the law. It is not simply that victims of Southern Cone military regimes are unable to perceive equivalency between the distress that they have suffered and a given punishment or lack of punishment. They cannot perceive equivalency—in the absence of an arbitrary equivalency—between the distress and *any* punishment, even and especially an *ideal, utopian,* or *imaginary* one. They face radical injustice, in other words, because they are unable to avow the conventions, habits, and rituals which allow for the accepting of the crime/punishment exchange: not of a specific exchange, but of the possibility of the exchange itself. And without even the potential for such a "transaction," these victims understand their victimization as forever beyond restitution.

II

Radical injustice is connected to the problem of melancholy as analyzed by Julia Kristeva in the book *Black Sun:* as an issue of poetics.[3] The melancholic is a person who is unable to depict a traumatic experience. She cannot turn this experience into an image, a re-presentation or, most importantly, into a

---

3. Julia Kristeva, *Black Sun: Depression and Melancholia,* trans. Leon S. Roudiez (New York: Columbia University Press, 1989).

memory: one which, as a memory, would attest to the fact that the event occurred in the past. The melancholic, that is, fails to mourn, to get over the pain, to accept the past as past and the dead as dead. Without access to re-presentation or memory he/she confronts not the absence of the trauma but its interminable, living presence. Above I suggested that radical injustice is not an injustice that is first overly severe, and then cannot be measured; it is not radical and severe until it cannot be gauged. Something similar can be said of melancholy. In melancholy, representation fails not because an event is too traumatic; rather, an event becomes too traumatic because, for a particular person in a given situation, representation and remembrance (memory) fail.

One might wonder, however, what "failure to represent" could possibly mean here. In fact, the women upon which Kristeva bases her analyses are, for the most part, capable of speaking, often quite competently; they merely are unable to speak about their pain. Yet all pain, it could be argued, is beyond representation.[4] In attempting to represent painful *events* and, indeed, in attempting to represent any event qua event, one is forced to submit a unique happening or experience to universal paradigms and arbitrary conventions; and as universals, these paradigms a priori evade or erase the specificity of that experience. If representations (narratives) sometimes stand in for pain, they always mark in some way or another the avoiding or voiding of that pain. What then is so special about the melancholic's avoidance?

Luisa Valenzuela's short story "Cambio de armas," one of the finest tales about dictatorship in Argentina, supplies an answer.[5] Laura, the protagonist, has been physically tortured and captured. She then undergoes another form of torture: she is locked away in a house, drugged, and sexually abused by a military figure. Her trauma as the story opens, however, is above all related to her incapacity to remember her own history. Laura is the classic melancholic; she has not yet turned the past into the past, into a memory or re-presence, and hence lives with the impossible, stagnating presence of that past.

Valenzuela understands, however, that this non-representation has little to do with voice, with the mere act of speaking. Laura can speak, however

---

4. In fact, as Elaine Scary has shown in *The Body in Pain: The Making and Unmaking of the World* (New York: Oxford University Press, 1985), pain is never an object for representation, for it is never an object at all. Rather, it is the very limit of objectification and representation.

5. Luisa Valenzuela, *Cambio de armas* (Hanover, NH: Ediciones del Norte, 1988), pp. 113–146.

difficult speaking may be for her. Non-representation here is instead linked to the arbitrariness of the signifier. This is made clear in the story's opening passages, where Laura meditates on certain proper names, many of which she cannot recall. For Laura, in fact, all nouns, all language, are structured like proper names: words are signs *arbitrarily* placed on bodies (referents) which come to designate those bodies through sheer repetition or habit. Laura has not forgotten language, but meaning, or at least the habits which make meaning possible. That is, she has forgotten the social conventions which induce speakers to forget the arbitrariness of signs, and therefore to "remember" the signifier/signified relation: signification, representation. In essence, Laura is prevented from reconstructing the truth of the past because she confronts the truth of language. Instead of remembering her history through language, she remembers language itself—language is structured like a proper name, via the arbitrary relationship, imposed by convention, of words and things—and she cannot disavow this arbitrariness, a disavowal necessary if she is to conceive language as a system of re-presentations capable of re-membering the past: language as a vehicle for marking the distinction between past and present, represence and presence, for mourning.

Postdictatorship victims often become involved with problems not unlike Laura's. Their trauma, however, is not the inability to disavow the arbitrary relationship of signifier and signified but of punishment and wrong. The dilemma is not one of representation but of restitution; terrors remain present not because events cannot be recalled but because they cannot be absolved. The victim has been wronged; he/she desires compensation. Yet when he or she discovers that no object or act can potentially equal the wrong, the debt ceases to be a debt: a debt, after all, is a debt only if there exists some promise, however remote, of payment. Otherwise the debt converts from a debt into pure loss, loss without a possible return. A victim expects payment or retribution, but his or her damage falls beyond redemption, into the abyss of total deprivation. Yet the violation, as absolute damage, does not disappear. On the contrary, it remains eternally present as "the thing" which possesses no account (nobody is being held accountable: thus the injustice).

Here, though, a series of questions arise. At exactly what moment is the *possibility* of equivalence (however arbitrary) between crime and punishment, hence the possibility of feeling a "sense of justice," lost? At what point in the justice process does justice not merely fail but fail absolutely? Is there not always space for another "appeal" to justice? These questions are answered in *Amnesia*: radical injustice is unveiled when the last judgment, the most exaggerated, most extreme form of compensation imaginable—in this case, vengeance—proves to be unrelated (not adequate or inadequate but unrelated) to the wrong that was endured.

III

This answer, of course, only alters the question. If radical injustice emerges when the most drastic form of compensation fails to compensate, why would a victim feel that any given "extreme" form (such as vengeance) was in fact the most radical, the very limit of punishment? To respond, it is necessary to push further the ideas presented thus far. Because the particular disasters we are discussing are not simply about the impossibility of justice. They concern the limits or impossibilities that are at work in any political impetus. Postdictatorship, in this vein, is the sign of the finitude of the political itself, a finitude which does not impede politics but which, as I will argue, makes a new politics possible.

Perhaps no text points to these matters in a more profound manner than Lawrence Weschler's *A Miracle, A Universe: Settling Accounts with Torturers*. I am thinking here particularly of the beautiful and terribly painful description of the postdictatorship situation in Uruguay, found in the second half of this brilliant study.[6] Here, Weschler discusses a 1989 Uruguayan referendum to repeal an amnesty law. Following the Uruguayan dictatorship, military criminals were granted immunity; later, the referendum, a proposal to lift this decree and to begin the process of bringing military criminals to justice, was put to vote. In a narrow decision, apparently not altogether on the "up and up," the "people" determined that the decree should not be repealed. The military criminals were not and could not be prosecuted.

The question is: why were the criminals granted impunity by the new democratic government in the first place? The answer, ironically, was related to democracy itself. What the events in Uruguay reveal is not, as even Weschler would want us to believe, a perversion of democracy, but the democratic process as itself caught up in a dreadful perversity. To see this, we need only consider the "equation" which made the original amnesty decree possible: the transitional government traded off the "crimes" of the so-called subversives for the crimes of the military. This government argued that in a

---

6. See Lawrence Weschler, *A Miracle, A Universe: Settling Accounts with Torturers* (New York: Penguin, 1990), pp. 173–236.

democracy, in a political system whose ground is fairness and equality, one could not prosecute certain criminals and not others. If the government was to put the military on trial, it should do the same for the subversives. The gesture was, needless to say, absurd, perplexing, and disturbing: the two sets of "crimes" bear little relation to one another. But we must ask ourselves, given precisely this non-relation, whether the trade-off was an abuse of proper justice, or a mirror of that same justice: justice's uncanny double, the aberration which reveals the rule. At the very least, the exchange unveils that if the equivalence of wrong X and punishment Y is arbitrary, then any Y, *including another wrong or injustice,* can potentially balance that wrong. The very fact that the Uruguayan government opted to measure not injustice with punishment, but non-punishment (impunity for the military) with non-punishment (impunity for the subversives) reveals the arbitrariness of "equality" itself. In fact, "equality" here is nothing more than an empty, violent tautology (A equals A, the signifier "non-justice" equals another signifier "non-justice") in which injustice is no longer measured at all. Instead, all infractions against the law are deemed the same, not because they are determined to be equal but because they go unmeasured. In this "balancing act," everything is even because nothing counts and, again, nothing is accounted for: the past clings to the present.

Here, however, we are touching upon another issue. Transition is not a revolution or a coup. A transitional government, by its very definition, does not break from its past but inherits it. Unlike a "revolutionary" government, this regime cannot rightfully liquidate the former enemies but must deal with them democratically. The Southern Cone postdictatorship administrations inherited their pasts in the form of a debt or obligation (and not just an economic debt)[7]: an obligation to right wrongs, to bring perpetrators to justice, and justice to victims. Yet this debt, for the various reasons detailed by texts such as Weschler's, eventually emerged as unpayable.[8] This is perhaps

---

7. It would be interesting to examine the relationship between the national debt and the debt owed to victims. On the one hand, they are very similar, since they both point toward the difficulty transitional governments encounter as they attempt to deal with their "inheritance" or their past. But the two debts might also be seen as mutually exclusive, since payment of the national debt invariably involves the embracing of capitalism and right-wing policies which impede the payment of the "other" debt.

8. The most obvious reason for this non-payment is that the military never relinquished its stronghold; the army was more powerful than the transitional governments that were considering prosecuting the military officials.

how we should think through one of the government's arguments for amnesty, outlined by Weschler: prosecution of military criminals, the government claimed, would result in endless trials. The democratic process, the
future well-being of the people, would be put on hold until these trials—the
past itself—was resolved and absolved. Time and movement would stagnate;
any future democracy wherein citizens might enjoy a "level playing field"
would have to wait until the past fields were evened out, balanced. In essence,
democracy would have to precede the transition toward democracy—thus
the impossibility. To be sure, these sorts of claims represent political strategies,
schemes to maintain the right in power, and to promote the new neoliberalism; yet they also point up a painful truth. In fact, for Southern Cone
transitional governments, the debts of the past overflow and overwhelm the
regime, whose situation impedes measurement of the past, even as democracy
hinges on that judgment. Postdictatorship democracy is evaluated on how it
judges the injustices of the dictatorship when these injustices show themselves
to be—politically, economically, ethically—beyond measure.

I do not want to underestimate the Uruguayan government's postdictatorship corruptions, amply documented by Weschler, which blocked the prosecution of army criminals and the general process of justice. And yet these
corrupt acts must be understood as effects, not causes, of the radical injustice.
As awful as this corruption may have been, it was not responsible for the
nonmeasurement and nonjudgment of the dictatorship's crimes. Rather, corruption was the way the government attempted to avoid this immeasurability,
and thus the unfathomable abyss located at the foundation of the democratic
process. A close reading of *A Miracle, A Universe* reveals this: by granting
amnesty to criminals the Uruguayan government was not asking victims
to overlook past crimes, but to overlook the immeasurability of those
crimes—to overlook, that is, the government's incapacity to deal with its own
inheritance/debt, its own history.

Only now can we grasp why vengeance, in postdictatorship films such as
Amnesia, plays such an important role. Revenge, for the victims of military
governments, is posited as the only measure of justice after all "political" or
"democratic" measures have failed. Revenge is the attempt to disavow radical
injustice via the claim that some justice—a divine justice—*beyond the law*
(revenge is illegal) and beyond government exists.[9] Yet vengeance, as trans-

---

9. My ideas here are informed by Peter Fenves's comments on Jacques Derrida's
theory of a justice beyond the law or "right," put forth in *Specters of Marx: The State of*

gression, ultimately reveals not the limits of the law and of government—
typically, transgression surpasses the limits of the law, thus reifying or calling
attention to those limits—which fail to measure injustice, but the limits of
human measurement itself. Or to put this another way, vengeance emerges
here as the limit not of the law but of the "free, unrestricted" imagination,
of the "free" subject. The victim, no longer obeying the rules of society or
the restrictions of the unjust law, imagines vengeance as the most extreme
method of restitution/absolution but, as happens in *Amnesia,* the injustice far
outweighs the imagined measure or "scheme," the imagination itself. Revenge does not offer to these figures a glimpse of justice but of the final,
irrevocable irrecuperability of the damages suffered: of the complete inadequacy of both the legal and the illegal, the possible and the impossible, the
real and the imaginary, the practical and the ideal, the actual and the utopian,
obedience and transgression. In this sense, one can argue that military regimes, horrible as they are, are not disastrous for the national psyche as a
whole (although they are obviously disastrous for certain individuals), since
they also invariably hold the promise of better times: the times-supposed-to-
be-better that citizens often come to believe will emerge when the dictatorship
falls. The national disaster materializes only *after* the dictatorship (see, for
example, novels such as *Una sombra ya pronto serás* by Osvaldo Soriano),[10]
when that promise is rescinded, when the time of utopian *justice* and equality
is no longer put off but materializes: not as utopia but as ceaseless dystopia, as
a disaster which snatches every hope for justice, every utopian future, indeed
the future itself, into its abyss in advance.

It is no wonder then that victims ultimately accept truth, not justice, as
compensation for the wrongs committed. Weschler emphasizes this point
repeatedly, noting how today's Brazilian and Uruguayan victims would
ultimately take solace not in bringing criminals to justice—a possibility that,
in any case, is no longer viable—but in obtaining the truth about the past. But
this "truth" is not truth in its traditional sense: adequation of representation to
actuality, of language to real events. Truth, indeed, here has little to do with

---

Debt, the Work of Mourning, and the New International, trans. Peggy Kamuf (New
York: Routledge, 1994). Fenves pointed out at a roundtable discussion with Derrida at
the University of Chicago that vengeance is also a justice beyond the law. He seemed
to want to call into question Derrida's notion of justice for its failure to address the
closeness of vengeance and justice.

10. Osvaldo Soriano, *Una sombra ya pronto serás* (Buenos Aires: Editorial Su-
damericana, 1990).

what one might expect: the disclosure of criminals or of unknown information, a disclosure which might embarrass and ostracize the torturers, hence
giving victims a sense of justice. In fact, as Weschler indicates, these kinds of
truths—who were the torturers, who they tortured, where they did so, and so
forth—are pretty much public knowledge. Truth, rather, is the *acknowledgment* by criminals or by the government itself of their acts: confession.[11] Thus,
we must ask ourselves: given this emphasis on self-acknowledgment or confession, is not the last measure, the final "yardstick" by means of which victims
strive to overcome the injustice of the law, not vengeance at all, but forgiveness? Is it not true that wronged individuals want the criminals to acknowledge their crimes so that these victims can then forgive, thus both relieving
themselves of the past's burden, and beginning anew? And on another level is
it not possible that the survivors of disaster (such as the protagonist of *Amnesia*)
feel guilty precisely for having survived (they are therefore not the "true"
victims, since they did not suffer the most radical injustice: death), and are
actually seeking *self-forgiveness* as they strive to forgive those who are "truly"
guilty?

Weschler addresses these inquiries through a reading of a section of Hannah Arendt's *The Human Condition*. He begins by focusing on Arendt's
statement that vengeance, as a response to political injustice, only perpetuates
the violence. Forgiveness, on the other hand, is the precise opposite of vengeance; it allows human beings to release themselves from the past, and to
open up toward the future.[12] But as Weschler notes, Arendt also believes that
acts which cannot be punished cannot be forgiven. This is why the pardoning
of past crimes can never be confused with forgiveness. Victims can only
forgive by giving up the option to punish; and when immunity is granted, they
are denied this option.

In her deliberations upon forgiveness, in fact, Arendt brackets out crimes
such as those committed by military regimes.[13] She holds that this sort of
terrorist activity, which she (after Kant) labels *radical evil,* can only be judged,
possibly forgiven, by the gods. Only divine, infinite judgment can pardon or

---

11. See *A Miracle, A Universe,* pp. 3–4.

12. Hannah Arendt, *The Human Condition* (Chicago: University of Chicago
Press, 1958), pp. 236–243.

13. Weschler's reading of forgiveness in Arendt is in fact somewhat erroenous.
Arendt's discussion of forgiveness concerns people guilty of the crimes, but who did
not and could not have known what they were doing. In connection to forgiveness,
she never addresses crimes such as those of a military regime.

condemn radical evil. In other words, for Arendt, there exists no mortal or finite judgment of radical evil; not even forgiveness presents itself as an option. Mortals, it would seem, are capable of infinite wickedness; yet they possess only finite means (such as vengeance) to measure or weigh that wickedness. Human justice, human forgiveness, human *anything,* not only fall short of radical evil; they fall infinitely short. This is what the aborted act of revenge exposes to the ex-soldier in *Amnesia*: not only the finitude of mortal judgment, but finitude and mortality themselves—the experience of limits, or the limit-experience.

IV

Is it possible that this limit-experience might point to a politics of postdictatorship? To answer, I would like to look at two books which, in different ways, contemplate this question. The first is Philippe Lacoue-Labarthe's *Heidegger, Art, and Politics,* where the crisis of modern politics is examined in terms of the *end* or limit of politics itself. The other work, Alain Touraine's *Return of the Actor,* takes an opposite approach. For Touraine, the crisis of the political does not hinge on politics per se (politics as a general concept) but on certain contemporary political operations. Touraine believes that, while democratic practices and revolutionary social movements are today much less feasible than they were 25 (or so) years ago, these sorts of political possibilities can and must be redeemed.

Lacoue-Labarthe tackles the difficult issue of the Heidegger Affair, and of Nazi Germany in general.[14] His main thesis parts from a discussion of Hölderlin's notion of tragedy; here I will offer only a cursory, reductive summary of this portion of the argument.[15] For Lacoue-Labarthe, Hölderlinian tragedy is, finally, man's recognition of his mortality, his finitude. The finitude is realized when the tragic hero, touched by the gods, is separated from these immortals, irreparably reduced to his/her finite being. This "consciousness (resulting from the impossiblity of "remembering" or representing

---

14. I am not directly touching upon the more famous, more obvious parts of Lacoue-Labarthe's argument: his theory of a "National Aestheticism" and his notion of fiction.

15. See Philippe Lacoue-Labarthe, *Heidegger, Art, and Politics,* trans. Chris Turner (Oxford: Basil Blackwell, 1990), pp. 41–45.

the lost, divine, infinite moment: that linguistic impossibility is precisely what marks the limit of the self) of finitude, of the withdrawal of the gods, is the punishment the hero must bear for hubris: for the desire to be god-like. In tragedy, then, the hero is less sentenced to die than he/she is condemned to the irrevocable acknowledgment of his/her essential mortality, of his/her temporal, finite existence—to the confrontation with the possibility that nothing of the self is limitless, eternal, infinite, transcendent, necessary, universal.

Key to the present deliberations of postdictatorship is Lacoue-Labarthe's "translation" of this discussion into an explanation of Nazism. Lacoue-Labarthe first emphasizes that Nazi Germany, while certainly not some version of a collective tragic figure, bears an uncanny resemblance to such a tragic being. Like tragic figures, Nazi Germany struggled to become eternal, transcendental, infinite, and universal: god-like. Yet unlike the typical tragic character, Germany never paid for this hubris with the terrible recognition of its unalterable mortality. On the contrary, the nation disavowed this knowledge by displacing its finitude onto the Jew. That is, instead of confronting their essential mortality, the Germans assumed that this "finitude" was not essential at all—it could be overcome—but was the fault of the Jew, who "limited" the Germans, preventing them from being who they really were: infinite, universal.[16] The attempt to annihilate the Jew, therefore, was Germany's attempt to surmount its own spacial/temporal finitude and mortality—now embodied by the Jew—in the name of the eternal German spirit. If in typical tragedy the tragic figure pays for his or her hubris with the recognition of mortality—complemented by his incapacity to know precisely why he is punished for his transgressions—in the aberrant tragedy of Nazi Germany the character guilty of hubris relieves himself of this recognition by making another pay: the Jew.

Lacoue-Labarthe's reading of Nazism can only be understood if we examine his critique of the modern subject: the subject of self-representation. This modern subject (as traditionally understood), Lacoue-Labarthe shows us, is a transcendental, eternal, or infinite principle that comes into view by means of

---

16. Of course, it was by means of the Jew that the Nazis sustained their fantasy of wholeness in the first place: the "limit" that the Jew "imposed" on the Nazi generated the fantasy of a nation without limits. One could here draw a parallel between the Jew and "the subversives" of the Southern Cone military regimes. For the subversives were both the people the governments perceived as limiting the movement into universal or "limitless" culture—capitalism—and the illusion that made this fantasy possible.

its historical representations. The subject, in fact, pre-exists these representations; yet because it is transcendental, it remains invisible to the limited, sensual, human eye (the human eye is not all-seeing; it perceives only finite objects). Enter representation or *mimesis*: representation is the finite appearance of this infinite idea (the subject); it permits the transcendental concept to be perceived and intuited by historical beings. Or to put this in other terms, representation is a mirror which, possessing a frame, reduces the infinite subject to finite proportions; these reflections then bring the subject into the range of "human" vision.

However, in the same way a mirror image is by definition not the actual thing that is reflected in the mirror, the historical representation of the subject is not itself the subject. This statement holds not only because a reflection is not "the thing itself" but also because, as we said, a reflection (like a mirror or picture) is finite. And as a finite object, an object with limits, an image or a representation is a being that comes to its end; as historical entities within time and space, objects/reflections "die." Yet in the West true Being is linked to permanence. The Being of an entity by definition transcends all the passing, temporal, mortal, contingent manifestations or "mere images" of this Being.

Lacoue-Labarthe uses this logic against itself, demonstrating that if the subject can only appear through its historical representations, then these mirror reflections or representations—as false, unreal, limited, mortal, contingent—do not come on the scene after the transcendental subject is born, but pertain to that birth: there is no presence of the subject before representation. The limit or death of the subject (representation) always already belongs to that subject. The subject, that is, is a priori marked by the finitude which its representations ultimately *represent*.

The subject of self-representation, then, is for Lacoue-Labarthe defined by a refusal to recognize not its connection but its essential connection to finitude/representation. In fact, the transcendental subject uses representation as a means to draw the line between itself and its own historicity. Historicity, finitude, and representation are deployed so that the subject can disavow its link to this same finitude. In other words, representation ultimately shows the "I" only by revealing the difference between this "I" and the representation itself—between the infinite and the finite, the eternal and the mortal, the ideal and the historical—much in the way a mirror image (insofar as it is recognized as such) always unveils the distinction between a reflection and the real, and thus *the real itself as that which is not a reflection.*

The Nazi subject, as the foundational principle of the Nazi nation, merely acts out the drama of the subject itself. Yet the representation or finite object that the Nazi fought to disavow, the mortal being from which this subject had to separate, was not any representation but the representation of representation: the Jew was not simply a finite object, but the very embodiment of finitude. In attempting to eradicate finitude, the Nazi deployed the Jew as the scapegoat, as the stand-in for finitude itself: as the object that needed to be overcome. Lacoue-Labarthe demonstrates how this could happen through an analysis of one of the stereotypical depictions of the Jew: the Jew, it was said, possesses no representations or culture of his/her own, but merely imitates or steals from other people's cultural representations. Jewish representations represent not the true Jewish Being, but other representations. The Jew, that is, represents representation itself; and, if this is true, then he represents the limit that representation represents. The prejudice—this idea that the Jew possesses nothing of his own, but steals or appropriates from others—therefore leads to a liquidation as the Jew is the substitute for the very limits that the Nazis needed to erase so as to become universal or eternal subjects: *Geist*.

For Lacoue-Labarthe there is no existing politics, not even democracy, that is not caught in these structures of self-representation. Every current political system, according to Lacoue-Labarthe, is essentially an identity politics (a term Lacoue-Labarthe never uses, of course), a politics striving to overcome the limits which determine the subject. This is not to say that systems such as democracy are forms of Nazism, or even that they are like Nazism. It is to say, rather, that Nazism is the culmination, the final terrifying realization of a modern Western epistemology grounded on the transcendental subject of self-representation: the subject which believes it can divorce itself from the limits or representations—*mimesis*—which make it a subject in the first place.

Let us, with these ideas in mind, turn to Touraine's *Return of the Actor*. Touraine has emerged as one of the most important theorists for Latin American political theory today.[17] Concerned above all with social movements, he defines these movements as specific struggles which, as they produce new organizations and coalitions, directly influence the political sphere at large, as well as the course of history. A social movement therefore cannot be reduced to a mere situation. For example, a rebellion in which the government (or a factory, a school, a hospital, and so forth) concedes something to the "rebels" is not, in and of itself, a social movement. This rebellion could only be

---

17. See Escobar's discussion of Touraine in *The Making of Social Movements in Latin America*, pp. 71–72.

considered a social movement if it helped shape present and future policy, rules, laws, and history itself, beyond the specific situation.

The key word for Touraine here is representativity: "Democracy must be identified with the notion of representativity, above all."[18] He believes that democracy is a true or strong democracy only insofar as it opens a space for social movements or for new coalitions. These coalitions, while they must grow out of specific conflicts and must form independently of state control (so as not to reflect already existing policy), must also attain "representativity" within the State. A genuine democracy would allow these "non-State" social movements eventually to intervene in the State apparatus. This tells us why Touraine can praise "minority movements"—what we, in the United States, might call identity politics—only with great trepidation. Such movements, according to Touraine, defend either a private space, or a public but nonpolitical space; they struggle in opposition to, but in isolation from the State. Touraine, as we said, is seeking something else: coalitions which effect change at the State level, at the level of policy making and history.

Rather than dwell on the possible problems within Touraine's theories, I want now to examine his final remarks. Touraine concludes by calling for a return to the subject, dubbing the subject the only possible political actor of our time. By subject, of course, he means the subject who is represented by State policies. Yet he is not referring to any State; he is alluding to a democratic State whose practices and laws would be the result of the coalitions we have just now been discussing. Within Touraine's democratic program, that is, State policy would reflect its political subjects because those subjects would make the policy. The State, ideally, would become the sum total of these various subjects of self-representation.

What Touraine fails to acknowledge, however, is the very issue we have been discussing: "representativity" hinges on the problem of limits. This is not only true for the ontological and epistemological reasons outlined above: a representation is always a reflection; and reflection, like a mirror, must recur to frames, borders, and boundaries. It is also true for practical reasons, reasons of praxis. After all, no State, however ideal or utopian, can represent the interests of *every* subject (this is not only impossible; it is undesirable since it would mean that the democratic State would have to make room for every

---

18. Alain Touraine, *Return of the Actor: Social Theory in a Postindustrial Society*, trans. Myrna Godzich (Minneapolis, MN: University of Minnesota Press), p. 151.

reactionary or totalitarian interest). Certainly, within an ideal democracy *anybody* should be allowed to be represented; but not *everybody*. Political representation, even from a utopian standpoint, represents a majority of the people, meaning it must determine who and what pertains to that majority. Indeed any politics, like any act of representation, is about such difficult, perhaps impossible decisions, about the need to draw these kinds of limits.[19]

This is true not only of state politics but also of Touraine's coalitions or social movements which, as we said, emerge from particular conflicts, ideally leading to an alteration of governmental/institutional positions. In fact, these non-State struggles necessarily harbor within themselves other, even smaller struggles, which will not necessarily be represented by the new public (State or institutional) policies that the social movements hypothetically generate. For example, a given worker's movement may favorably modify factory policy. Yet this new policy may fail to address women's issues within the workplace, issues that, deemed as overly specific or as a "private" problem by the workers themselves, may have been left out of the original workers' demands. Touraine's social movements, in other words, could well alter the lives of the majority of the people involved in the movements themselves, and they could well alter policy; but *insofar as representativity is the issue,* they only do so through the marginalization of certain sectors and certain interests within that very struggle. These marginal sectors then become the State's new, *unrepresented,* excluded, violated minority. For Touraine, then, State policy is altered less through the representation of new social actors than through a shift in the make-up of the actors who are not represented.

My intention, then, is not to critique Touraine for reducing political activism to "representativity"; I am critiquing his refusal precisely to think through the relationship of politics and this representativity, of politics and the domain of finitude—his refusal, in other words, to consider the limits of the political (and hence the political itself, which is in large part the setting of limits). This refusal, of course, is most visible in Touraine's distinction be-tween the "private and non-political" and the "public and political." In fact, as Chantal Mouffe points out, politics today cannot part from or assume (as does Touraine) these kinds of separations; instead, politics concerns the way power relations determine such separations in the first place and, by extension, the

---

19. See Chantal Mouffe, "Democratic Politics and the Question of Identity" in *The Identity in Question* (New York: Routledge, 1995), p. 42.

way power decides the *limits* of the political—what does and does not belong to that political realm—a determination which *is* itself the political.[20]

Our concern, however, is the relationship of this issue of limits—or of their disavowal—to the experience of radical injustice. The victims of this injustice, as we have seen, confront a situation for which no policies or procedures, no laws and no justice beyond the law, no precedents and no chance of setting a precedent, exist. The predicament, in other words, is one that representation cannot address since the predicament, for the victim, is utterly singular, unique, without antecedent or model. The subject of radical injustice comes into being not beyond or outside the politics of representation, but at its limit: precisely at the historical time and place of the absolute failure of convention and repetition—conventions and repetitions that (as demonstrated above) make re-presentations possible. Yet this fact, far from resolving the issues at hand, only brings us to a final question: Does radical injustice in the postdictatorship situation point to the limit of politics or to a politics of the limit, to the limit of the actor-subject (as defined by Touraine) or to an actor-subject of the limit?

V

My contention is that both a "politics of the limit-self" and a "self of the limit of politics" represent key responses to the postdictatorship predicament. I will first attempt to explain why I believe this; I will then address the "theoretical" nature of my speculations. Yet we might begin by asking: Why should the "limit-self" even merit consideration? Simply because it is unavoidable: a politics of disaster or radical injustice must, ultimately, be a politics of Otherness, and the "limit-self" is the condition of such a politics. In fact, within any politics based upon the subject of self-representation (such as the one articulated by Touraine) no Other can appear. This is due to the two-step process, already described, by means of which such a subject assembles itself: the subject gives itself to reflection, and then distinguishes itself from that image. This mirror image, in philosophical parlance, is an object. If I have described the subject as the being which posits, and then sets itself off from its representations (its limits), thinkers of modern subjectivity usually depict this same

---

20. Chantal Mouffe, "Democratic Politics and the Question of Identity," pp. 42–45.

structure as follows: the subject is a being which posits, and then sets itself off from an object. Like a mirror image, which possesses no being of its own but reflects Being, this object itself is without Being; it is merely the territory which opens a space for the appearance of the subject. Thus, not even another person, for the subject of self-representation, is actually an "Other." He or she is merely an object which allows the subject to see itself in the "other's" space, and hence to extend its territory.

In truth, only exposure to the limit can lead to an engagement with an Other: to an ethics, and to a politics of alterity. On a surface level, this should be obvious: a limit or border can only exist when an Other appears beyond the self, pointing up the simple fact that the self is not all, and that this self therefore possesses limits. This, it should be emphasized, is a frightening proposition: if the self is finite, hence mortal and contingent, its being is not guaranteed, given in advance as is an essence, but is always already shaky, under the threat of annihilation. A finite self is not exposed simply to the other but to the-other-who-could-take-its-place. In the engagement with this limit, therefore, life and death is at stake. However, it is important to recognize that this Other is not out there, is not a given. It emerges only when the self exhausts itself, goes to the limit, *but finds that there is still more,* something or someone beyond its appropriations and objectifications: something *Other* that is this self's concern, but outside its domain (dominance).

What is actually at issue here, however, is the self's concern for and, even beyond this concern, *demand for* the Other. For why should a self engage an Other, and thus the problem of ethics, at all? What would motivate a victim *not* to appropriate this "Other," convert him or her into an object which, as an object, would attest to the limitless space, immortal nature, in short, precisely the *subjectivity,* the *representativity,* that radical injustice denies this victim? No doubt, one calls to an Other only when there is a demand for that Other. The subject engages the Other, and engages the Other as Other (not as an object to be appropriated, an object of the self)—engages its own death: the Other who could take its place—the moment an Other space, a space beyond the self, appears as the Self's matter, a matter of urgency, of existence, of moving past disaster and melancholy, even of life and death: *I have exhausted every resource, I have gone to my limit and I have been taken to the limit, but a task (justice) beyond me, though of my total concern, remains—I need another's aid.* This is why the experiences of radical injustice and of disaster, as exposure to the finitude of all that is human—precisely the finitude that Latin American totalitarian projects (such as dictatorship), in striving to stand for the All, and in trying to enter "universal" culture or culture without limits (Western capitalism), want to eradicate—might also represent the ontological "foundation" of important postdictatorship communal or political activity.

At the very least, the recognition of this limit-experience points to an alternative to vengeance and amnesty, both of which, as demonstrated above, impede transition, obstruct any break from the past. For if the limit-experience in fact pushes the self toward the Other, commitment to the Other represents a gesture that neither "forgets" (as does impunity) nor avenges devastation, loss, and radical injustice. Rather, this commitment stands as an active response to the disaster, a means for building coalitions which are the result, even the "illegitimate child" of the disaster, but move beyond it, initiating possible future generations. The limit-self, turning toward the Other via a third party—the limit itself: radical injustice, disaster, death—opens toward the future as it "remembers" or mourns the past; in essence, this self "actively forgets" the unaccountable vis-à-vis the production of the novel organizations. Hence, the limit-experience, not subjectivity (as Touraine would have it), stands as the condition of possibility for a (not *the* but *a*) new political actor, for novel political organizations after dictatorship, for forgiveness (not the victims' forgiveness of the military but their forgiveness of themselves) and, finally, for the "ungluing" of the present from the past, a restarting of time: the beginnings of the transition process. My claim, then, is not merely that the limit-experience, for those trapped in the postdictatorship predicament (such as the characters of *Amnesia*), is the prerequisite for a better history; for these people, it is the prerequisite for any history whatsoever.

No doubt, a reader could complain that this theory of the limit-experience remains just that: a theory. The criticism is completely valid; but it is also points to the need to address precisely the questions that are raised in this study. I fully agree that my study might be improved via an analysis of actual postdictatorship organizations (such as the Mothers of the Plaza de Mayo), ones made up of individuals who have actually gone through the "limit-experience." Have the kinds of coalitions I am discussing formed? Can they? If they have formed, are they effective? If they have not, why not? I also might have examined the specific nature of the various sorts of experiences or traumas which expose the postdictatorship self to his or her limit: the experience of torture, of exile, of hunger, of poverty, of mistreatment by the courts, of artistic or literary repression, and so forth. Do these different "limit-experiences" (indeed, taking place in different nations), if they give way to community, give way to distinct kinds of communities? Perhaps, too, I should have offered a "demonstration" of my theory: How exactly might the politics of the limit-experience be put into practice?

These possible improvements, however, ignore the fact that neither empirical observation, nor practical programs, nor theory—nor any other response, including activism—can resolve the question of community and/or politics after devastation. In fact, these various approaches, in addition to all of the disciplines (history, political science, literature, cultural studies, philosophy) by means of which one might take up these approaches, come up against the unresolvable limit of radical injustice. Theory is no more or less adequate than any other response to the matters discussed in this essay because every response misses the mark, and it does so unconditionally. The study of postdictatorship, of community after disaster, or of radical injustice, is the exposure of every discipline to its limit, and thus to the need of other disciplines: *as a theorist (or an empiricist, an activist, an historian, a political scientist, etc.) I have gone as far as I can go, which is why I must call to another sort of scholar and/or to another tactic.* This is not to imply that the joining together of various "replies" will solve the problem of postdictatorship, fill in all the gaps. It is to say, rather, that the limit-experience represents not only the ontological (if anarchical) "foundation" of a new postdictatorship politics; it also represents the possibility of a communal, interdisciplinary, Latin Americanist project which, recognizing the limits of each of its many disciplines and approaches, *performs* the finitude—hence the ethics and politics—that it analyzes.[21]

---

21. The ideas put forth in my final few paragraphs represent nothing more than an adaptation of the brilliant thesis put forth by Christopher Fynsk in his essay, "And Suppose We Were to Take the Rectorial Address Seriously . . . Gérard Granel's *De l'université*," *The Graduate Faculty Philosophy Journal for the New School of Social Research,* vol. 15, no. 1, 1991: 334–362.

11

Representation, History, and Trauma: Abstract Art after 1945

Herman Rapaport

In recent years there has been increasing sensitivity on the part of academics to the experience of psychological trauma suffered by victims of war. Increasingly we are beginning to ask why it is that so little has been done about the experience of trauma for those who have undergone extreme hardship and unspeakable suffering. Why has the historical acknowledgment of the traumatic sufferings of victims of persecution and war sometimes been so difficult to achieve, even in societies that are not in historical denial? Although cultural works can never take the place of legal justice, psychoanalytical therapy, and material restitution, they have nevertheless been enlisted as substitutes. Works of art, in particular, are traditionally given the cultural privilege of addressing what much of the rest of society cannot: the fact that historical trauma exists and that we must remember what has happened to victims, if not literally, then metaphorically. This was especially evident in German expressionist art immediately following the First World War, though instances could be found elsewhere, as in Picasso's *Guernica*, which responded to the traumas inflicted by the Spanish Civil War.

Immediately after the end of World War II, the extent and extremity of crimes against humanity became public knowledge as descriptions and photographs of the Holocaust were disseminated in the popular press and war criminals prosecuted at Nuremberg. The dropping of atomic bombs on Japan, while not deemed a war crime, registered in the popular imagination as an unspeakable act of destruction that resulted in unimaginable suffering on

the part of those who survived instant vaporization. Here, too, history had
been characterized by traumatic events never before known. Oddly, in the
years immediately following the war, much art seemed to respond to the past
by way of a flight into abstractionism. At the very least, one could infer that we
had now entered an age when the unspeakability of history could only be
addressed by the unspeakability of art. Whereas prewar expressionism, surrealism, and cubism were stylistically suitable for the depiction of historical
trauma, much abstract art after the war negated the possibility of any content
that might be used to depict trauma along the lines of, say, Georg Grosz,
Ludwig Kirchner, Pablo Picasso, Max Ernst, Salvador Dali, and numerous
others. However, far from being a simple refusal or inability to engage
historical trauma, the flight into abstractionism responded to a break with the
past that was representational, historical, and traumatic. In the three accounts
that will follow, I want to show that the convergence and nonconvergence of
breaks deemed to be representational, historical, and traumatic is significant
not only for an understanding of postwar abstractionism, but for an understanding of how representation, history, and trauma interrelate.

I

We know that immediately after the end of the Second World War, the Allied
focus on war crimes helped to enable the imposition of a period of normal-
ization that assumed a firm historical break with the past. The physical
destruction of the war was no doubt sufficient enough to clarify for Japan and
Germany that defeat signified a major historical rupture of this kind. Yet, the
victors hurried to establish new social, political, and economic realities that
would encourage a strategic forgetting of the immediate past in order that
history not rewrite itself. In Europe, Heinrich Böll's *The Clown* is among
the strongest literary responses to this immediate postwar period in that it
chronicles the sudden lack of acknowledgment in Germany among Hitler's
willing accomplices of their lack of ethical responsibility toward even their
own family members during the war years. Max Frisch's *Diaries* and Rainer
Werner Fassbinder's *The Marriage of Maria Braun* are other artistic examples
of representing a period when life was ambiguously situated in the aftermath
of a historical break that was difficult to accept despite the physical devastation that instantiated it and the new political and economic regimes that were
determining Europe's future. Of course, the reestablishment of high culture

was itself central to the maintenance of the historical break after the physical clean up of Europe. That is, art was encouraged to show a representational break with the past that indicated the permanent presence of a historical caesura marking the so-called "postwar period."

Recognition of a historical break should not overlook the fact that populations ravaged by war had experienced what one could also call a traumatic break. This concerns what Cathy Caruth puts in the form of a question: "is the trauma the encounter with death, or the ongoing experience of having survived it?" In considering the historical interval that separates the end of World War II from the beginning of the postwar period, one is necessarily considering such a traumatic break in which the difference between what Caruth calls a "crisis of death" and a "crisis of life" or survival is not an entirely decidable interval. Indeed, the time that separated the war from the period that followed was largely a formal historical break that was contradicted by the traumatic break that accompanied it. That is to say, if the historical break can be said to absolutely demarcate a time that is decidedly different—the time of a decided change of affairs if not of social, cultural, and political reality—the traumatic break failed this test of time, given that the traumatic break was a narrative of belated experience, a compromised moment that lived in suspension between what Caruth calls "the story of the unbearable nature of an event and the story of the unbearable nature of its survival."[1]

What I am calling the traumatic break is a temporality in which the subject is condemned to remember and imaginatively relive a past that is sealed off by a historical break whose new political world order insists upon a radical forgetting of the past and a privileging of the present and future. That the historical break was intended to suppress acknowledgment of there being a traumatic break was, of course, part of a realpolitik that had decided society should not look back at the past but move on *as if* the past were unimportant and dispensable, *as if* it were a past that was, in essence, incapable of determining anything that might happen after the historical defeat of Japan and Germany. Helpful in the fabrication of this historical illusion was the flight of art into radical abstractionism, since this stylistic move was in and of itself a representational break with not only fascism but with many of the avant gardist movements that had been in effect during the prewar period, among them, expressionism, fauvism, surrealism, and cubism.

---

1. Cathy Caruth, *Unclaimed Experience* (Baltimore, MD: Johns Hopkins University Press, 1996), p. 7.

Paradoxically, the postwar representational break also had the advantage of restoring the broken teleology of modern art by continuing some of its imperatives, albeit in ways that represented a break with those aspects of prewar abstractionism that were deemed to contain residual elements from art of an earlier time (expressionism, figuralism, psychologism, etc.). The same situation characterizes the field of musical composing. It was convenient that Anton von Webern (decried as a degenerate composer by the Nazis) had been killed in the last days of the war, because this enabled young European composers to both claim and surpass Webernian serialism under the rubric "post-Webernianism." Karlheinz Stockhausen, Pierre Boulez, and Luigi Nono represented flights into abstractionism that meant composing music which was structurally indecipherable to even the trained ear. Indeed, the ideological point of this new music was to demonstrate an absolute aesthetic or representational break with past tradition.

Given the retrograde ideological uses of figuration and historical representationism during the 1930s and early 1940s, it is hardly surprising that European artists also tried to push abstract painting so far that by the late 1950s Yves Klein and others would start thinking in terms of the death of painting. As in the case of music, there was a deliberate attempt to push the medium of painting to such abstract lengths that art would simply reach an ultimate limit beyond which it could no longer go, hence achieving the limit of its extinction. Some historians, Clement Greenberg among them, have viewed this teleology as one of progressive negativity wherein by a process of incremental reductions, painting is stripped bare in stages to its absolute moment of appearance *as* art, all the inessentials having been bracketed or set aside. Just as contemporary composers could orient their flight into abstraction upon a historical break with the work of a famous precursor of musical abstractionism like Webern, abstract painters could orient their postwar development in relation to a historical break with their precursor Piet Mondrian, whose principles were directly relevant and whose oeuvre stops around 1945. As in politics, the aesthetic historical break of abstract composers and artists did not greatly emphasize what I have been calling a traumatic break.

Still, it is not as if trauma had been entirely forgotten. In *How New York Stole the Idea of Modern Art*, Serge Guilbaut argued that American abstract expressionism was ideologically influential immediately after the war and that its ideology of individualism and free will was rather significant for the determination of abstract painting in Europe. According to Guilbaut, American abstract expressionism was an ideological construction advanced by the American government in its bid to prop up an ailing European culture on

American values. Although this view is controversial, there certainly was an attempt by Americans to provide the visual arts in Europe with a "new start." As if to endorse a total historical break, American abstract expressionists argued that the horrors of World War II should not be depicted. They argued that showing such scenes of carnage would merely trivialize the past and turn it into kitsch. As Guilbaut puts it, for American artists in the immediate postwar period, "it had become impossible to represent the diffuse anxiety and fear that defined modernity without falling into the grotesque or the facile, without, in a word, making kitsch. Dwight Macdonald said it well: to describe was to accept the unacceptable. It was to incorporate an object into an expressive system by means of a code that sapped all critical force and revolutionary significance."[2] Behind this phobia of kitsch, of course, lay the communist legacy of the 1930s in which leftist artists like Diego Rivera were in danger of becoming nothing more than the illustrators of propaganda. Indeed, abstract expressionism was, if anything, tied to the deep resentments leftist artists had in being relegated to the role of describing oppression for the sake of some very obvious communist orthodoxies. So that when the end of the war came, American expressionists took pains to avoid what Guilbaut calls "the trap of illustration."

Abstract expressionism's resistance to turning art into a visual commentary on the ills of society and history is commensurate with Theodor Adorno's remarks in *Negative Dialectics* that historical trauma can no longer be responsibly depicted. "After Auschwitz, our feelings resist any claim of the positivity of existence as sanctimonious, as wronging the victims; they [the feelings] balk at squeezing any kind of sense, however bleached, out of the victims' fate."[3] These two propositions are nonsequiturs, even if the second statement is the reverse of the first: just as it is problematic to feel any positivity of existence, it is problematic to suppose there is anything good to be extrapolated from the negativity of inexistence, that is, the deaths of the victims. What is to be had from our feelings about the Holocaust is, nevertheless, something that Adorno calls "absolute negativity," a negativity that "shatters the basis on which speculative metaphysical thought could be reconciled with experience"

---

2. Serge Guilbaut, *How New York Stole the Idea of Modern Art,* trans. Arthur Goldhammer (Chicago, IL: University of Chicago Press, 1983), p. 197. Further references will appear in the text.

3. Theodor Adorno, *Negative Dialectics* (New York: Contiuum, 1973), p. 361. Further references will appear in the text.

(362). It is on this basis that Adorno equates a representational break with a traumatic break that coincides with a historical break.

Adorno's suspicion is that in the past—that is, before Auschwitz—cultural works were still capable of reconciling experience, however traumatic, with speculative metaphysical thought. As long as death was understandable as an individual experience—as the experience marked by contingency, say, that of a soldier being hit by a bullet—this reconciliation could be brought about. However, "in the concentration camps it was no longer an individual who died, but a specimen—this is a fact bound to affect the dying of those who escaped the administrative measure." In other words, the killing itself was abstracted in such a way that it would not make sense to represent the victims, anymore, as individual subjects, since this would miss the point of the horror as "administrative measure." "Auschwitz confirmed the philosopheme of pure identity as death" (362). It is this pure identity that cannot be accessed by an art that acknowledges the specificity of individual suffering and trauma, since to get at absolute negativity and pure identity one has to be prepared to deal with what Adorno calls "total indifference," the *un*differentiatedness of victims as translated into the feeling or subjectivity of the perpetrator as *in*different. One conclusion that is hovering in the margins of Adorno's speculations is that the Nazis had perpetrated a crime that falls outside of any possible cultural response and that, as such, this crime cannot be grasped by history, sociology, philosophy, or art as we know it. Hence the crime institutes a representational break with tradition that concerns the convergence of what I have been calling a traumatic and historical break.

Like those who had questioned the possibility of an artistic representation of the horrors of World War II, American abstract expressionists had come to a similar conclusion about the artistic representation of history and trauma. That is, even while the war was taking place, they were looking for a means to address the recent historical past by means of an aesthetic that would not fall into the trap of trying to reconcile experience with speculative metaphysical thought in the form of painting. Problematic, however, is that this nonrepresentational respect for the victims of traumatic historical events had the consequence of encouraging a turning away from and forgetting of the literal historical horrors that caused people to perish. It also discouraged recognition of what it meant to have survived what Adorno called "total indifference." As Guilbaut puts it, "avant-garde art became an art of obliteration, an art of erasure" (181). If one considers that, like Adorno, the abstract expressionists linked a traumatic break with a historical break, it may not be too surprising that they sought a mode of representation that avoided traditional painterly responses to human suffering and historical calamity, a mode of representation that effaces the content of both history and trauma.

This observation is relevant to the abstractionist practice of naming a painting "Untitled." After the war, many abstract works appeared under this rubric. While one cannot generalize about all paintings entitled "Untitled," I think there is an argument to be made that in some cases the untitling of art approaches Maurice Blanchot's conception of the *neutre*. It is a notion summarized quite well by Leslie Hill in *Maurice Blanchot*. The *neutre* is

> . . . a name for the namelessness of the name, a concept whose purpose is to conceptualize that which precedes all concepts. Neither immanent nor transcendent with regard to language, it is both a word and not a word, a modest trace that in its very discretion bears witness to the discretely nameless character of that to which it refers . . . the *neutre* is perhaps best understood as a movement of perpetual effacement and re-inscription that is logically prior to all conceptual distinctions.[4]

In painting, the word "Untitled" can have affinities with the *neutre* in that the "untitled" may have the effect of a perpetual effacement and re-inscription as it reiterates itself in the oeuvres of many abstractionists. Furthermore, "untitled" is not only a name for the namelessness of the painting's name, the placelessness of the painting's name, or the conceptlessness of the painting's name, but it is also a word that could stand for something that precedes all concepts and that therefore comes *before* the positing or stating of the work as a representation of the already conceived or conceivable. This relates to Leon Golub's remark in 1955 that the abstract expressionists sought "an action that is pre-logical, pre-cognitive, and amoral." Moving toward what Golub called the primitive, abstract expressionism was to be considered unconscious. "There are no uniform or iconographic means . . . through which the supra-formal aspects of such paintings could be defined."[5] Speaking of the abstract paintings of Barnett Newman, Harold Rosenberg has argued that "the commonsense response to Newman's paintings that there is 'nothing' in them ought not to be dismissed—Newman's meaning lies in how this noth-

---

4. Leslie Hill, *Maurice Blanchot* (London: Routledge, 1997), p. 132.

5. Leon Golub, "A Critique of Abstract Expressionism," in David and Cecile Shapiro, *Abstract Expressionism: A Critical Record* (Cambridge, UK: Cambridge University Press, 1990), pp. 90–91.

ing is received . . . he worked with emptiness as if it were a substance."[6]
Just as Newman's art is prerepresentational, Jackson Pollock's paintings were,
in Pollock's own view, destroyed by commentary. The *neutre* should not just
be predisclosive, but indifferent in its singularity and absoluteness to naming,
knowing, identifying. The *neutre* is an expectant indifference that stands
alone before what Blanchot calls the "unknown." "To think the unknown is
in no way to propose it as 'the not yet known,' the object of a knowledge still
to come, any more than it would be to go beyond it as 'the absolutely
unknowable,' a subject of pure transcendence, refusing itself to all manner of
knowledge and expression." For Blanchot, "the unknown will not be revealed, but indicated." As *neutre,* the "Untitled" condition of the work indicates without revealing the unknown, communicates its presence without
disturbing its mysteriousness. "The neutral supposes a *relation* that is foreign
to every exigency of identity, of unity, even of presence."[7] This suggests that
the relationship of the "untitled" to the "unknown" is alien to exigencies of
intuition, imagination, or empathy that are predicated upon a relation based
on mutual understanding. The "untitled," then, is precisely that which disen-
gages itself from an understanding of others, a nameless state of expectancy
or apprehension that indifferently awaits the arrival of what is unknown.
In Barnett Newman, Jackson Pollock, and Clyfford Still, painting is less
an image than an "event," a nameless state of expectation in which myth,
figure, and concept are withheld. Pollock's drip paintings, therefore, might be
thought of as marks that exist as nameless entities indicating the unknown
without revealing it. Such marks are absolute and indifferent insofar as once
they have appeared, they must not be changed.

The *neutre* is therefore one way of imagining abstract expressionism's
representational break, given that such a moment does not contain or figure
the content of the historical or traumatic breaks noted above, since this
representational break precedes and withdraws from such specifically formu-
lated notions of collective and individual experience. Yet, this same representational break does correspond to these other breaks insofar as American
abstract expressionism was taken up as a postwar art form that set itself apart
from past European tradition. In short, the representational break exists
independently of anything historical or traumatic even though it has the

---

6. Harold Rosenberg, *Barnett Newman* (New York: Abrams, 1971), p. 61.

7. Maurice Blanchot, *The Infinite Conversation,* trans. Susan Hanson (Minneapolis, MN: University of Minnesota Press, 1993), p. 300.

capacity of taking place *as if* it were the very historical and traumatic breaks of which it is not, strictly speaking, a part. In the work of figures like Pollock, Mark Rothko, or Franz Kline, the act of painting is often considered the discharge of an unconscious acting out that is, in essence, the repetition of something prior, namely, a break in the history of visual representation which also happens to be a break in artistic consciousness that is, at the very least, analogous with trauma. And yet the representational break that is abstract expressionism always remains something other than and remote from trauma. For the representational break is what Adorno above called an "absolute negativity," the shattering of any common ground upon which experience can be reconciled with speculative metaphysics, or, in our present context, aesthetics. Trauma, as Caruth addresses it, would be the psychological analogue to speculative metaphysics, a psychological analogue that the representational break of American abstract expressionism of the 1940s and 1950s avoids or even subverts.

II

That there was a cultural break in the history of modern art that registers the shock of a traumatic break of historical consciousness was not only reflected in American abstract expressionism but in a somewhat closely related international abstractionist movement which included artists like Hans Hartung, Pierre Soulages, Antoni Tapies, Maria Helena Viera da Silva, Wols (Alfred Otto Wolfgang Schulze), Mark Toby, and Cy Twombly. In *The Anxious Object* Harold Rosenberg argued that this group of abstract painters had replaced nationalism and regionalism by means of "mythology, manner, metaphysics, or formal concepts." Rosenberg observed that "for their art, the earlier requirements of actual or imaginative presence in a given environment had become meaningless. [. . .] Their works fulfilled themselves in becoming universal." Just as serial music had become an anonymous international style that made it impossible to recognize one composer from another (compare, for example, Roger Sessions's later atonal symphonies to those of Karl Amadeus Hartman), abstract art had succumbed to formalist devices that reduced all art to composition:

> Released from place, and the traditional, sensual and political ties imposed by place, art tends to derive increasingly from experiences of art. Repro-

ductions, slides, art publications and, to a lesser degree, the worldwide circulation of actual works, draw the artist situated anywhere into an immediacy of response to the global gallery. The tempo of art becomes a world tempo.

In other words, Rosenberg had noticed another kind of neutrality into which abstractionism had fled. Rather than responding to the world of lived experience, art was turned into a business that recursively and neutrally responded to itself as art about art. This followed from the fact that "extremist forms in art" had become acceptable in the 1950s "as a reflex to incomprehensibles in science and technology and to the bafflement of philosophy."[8]

Perhaps most typical of the new internationalist school of abstractionism was the French painter, Pierre Soulages, who in recent years has been enjoying a revival in interest. An artist who refused to paint during the Second World War, Soulages started painting immediately after the Nazis were defeated. Significant is that Soulages's oeuvre consists of more or less untitled paintings—he refers to them in the generic, "Painting," plus size, plus date—that blend the sinister with the sublime. As such, they obliquely suggest trauma in contemporary society. Viewers familiar with Soulages's early work can agree that it reflects a cubist orientation stripped bare of vitalism. Whereas Picasso invoked sex and violence in many of his paintings, Soulages stripped his work of transgressive figuration and chromatic affect. Indeed, Soulages focused on compositional problems in a way that could be accused of academicism. And while none of Soulages's paintings could be called masterpieces, it has to be said that the masterpiece or tour de force was never a part of Soulages's aesthetic vision and that in contrast to the wildly fluctuating quality of Picasso's or Chagall's oeuvre, the voluminous oeuvre of Soulages maintains a level of aesthetic quality that as a whole easily surpasses that of most modernist masters. What separates international abstractionists such as Soulages from innovators like Picasso, Kandinsky, and Klee is a level of steady serial production that tries to work through a restricted number of compositional problems rather than invent entirely new compositional vocabularies. Whereas high-modernist abstractionism had a biographical and regional semiotics (consider, for example, Matisse or Chagall), painters like Soulages, Wols, Toby, and da Silva precluded such cultural signs from enter-

---

8. Harold Rosenberg, *The Anxious Object* (Chicago, IL: University of Chicago Press, 1990), p. 211.

ing their works. Yet, even in this highly neutral professionalized world of art production where nothing from the life world intruded onto the purity of abstract composition, one senses that a humanist-existentialist ideology was nevertheless at work. In other words, there is recognition of a certain traumatic and historical break in not only the avoidance of biographical, historical, and regional content, but in the very stylistic flight into abstractionism as an alien space.

In a review of Mark Toby's 1961 show at the Musée des Arts Décoratifs in Lyon, France, the poet John Ashbery wrote that "these lines somehow give an impression of the trajectories traced by the millions of lives in a great metropolis."[9] Whereas Toby's finely meshed abstract structures were not in and of themselves metaphors for the modern cityscape, they were taken by Ashbery and, no doubt, other viewers as architectural landscapes. This was also true for the paintings of da Silva, whose designs suggested cities of glass in which perpendicular structures symbolized architectural principles of angularity and transparency endemic to the office-building aesthetic of the metropolis. Like Toby's, her abstractions emphasized the detailed delicacy and angularity of a construction that is as anonymous as it is enigmatic and visually inviting. Typical of both Toby and da Silva is the relation between architectural alienation (what in the 1950s was seen as the grid work of "organization man") and its aesthetic compensation (translucent artifice, the sublimity of glass and metal, the openness of closed forms, etc.). Such instantiations of the international style of abstraction called attention to a humanist understanding of the social subject as part of the very society whose architecture dwarfs and overwhelms him. Whereas these abstract designs do not go so far as to suggest trauma per se, they do articulate the place where trauma is inscribed into the alienation of the social landscape into which moderns are thrown. That there is aesthetic compensation for such alienation makes this kind of abstract art ambiguous in its indictment, an ambiguity attractive to corporations who have put such art on display in their lobbies and mezzanines.

Soulages fits more or less directly into this architectural/environmental context. His work evokes the ambiguity of the abstract construction as a metaphor for the cogito's situatedness in man-made space. For all their massiveness and obscurity, the large black forms in Soulages radiate a light and umbra that are aesthetically comforting, a sublime aftereffect that mitigates the oppressiveness of the massive girder-like structures that block our

---

9. John Ashbery, *Reported Sightings*, p. 189.

vision and deprive us of entering the space that is the canvas. In a description of *Painting 14 March 1955*, Paul Vogt writes that "the vehement action of the painter's brush has made way for a powerful system of buttresses composed of heavy black beams. A large and solemn construction binds color and form into a solid framework of paint laid on with various color and form into a solid framework of paint laid on with various sizes of palette knives rather than brushes." Vogt's description presumes that Soulages's forms approximate architectural structures that would characterize the sorts of massive steel structures that are typically found in cityscapes. "The balanced composition of sweeping black beams stands like an ominous symbol before an open ground lost in indefinable depths." Speaking of Soulages's use of light, Vogt says that it illuminates the ominous shapes from behind "to arouse strong spatial tensions and a visionary feeling."[10] This speaks to the existential significance that Vogt imputes to the painting: the modernist tectonic world is ominous and yet sublime. We are surrounded with gigantic and ominous forms that are in tectonic tension—their forces thus being out of our control—and that are also counterpointed against indefinable depths, abysses of space that are themselves dark, mysterious, and threatening. Indeed, this aesthetic is precisely that of the architects of the deconstructive school—Daniel Libeskind, Bernard Tschumi, Zaha Hadid—who delight in the proliferation of extremely complex architectural patterns whose indefinite and polymorphous cascades of serialized structures resemble the kind of anonymous and yet sublime space that characterizes the tectonics of Soulages. Taken at its most reductive extreme, perhaps, both the kind of constructivist panoply advanced by "deconstructionist" architects and tectonic compositional practices advanced by painters such as Soulages suggest beauty is all we have as compensation for an architecture of inhumanity. In Soulages's work, dark abysses of alienation reflect a traumatic break with the social, sometimes marked by a calligraphic style that suggests the loss of *Gemeinschaft* and advent of *Gesellschaft*. It is a loss that is part and parcel of international abstractionism as *Geschäft*. And it is here that trauma has been ideologically recuperated and normalized by the very forces of its production. This is the place in the arts where the corporate world extends its consolation that we're all victims of trauma and that trauma is the price we pay for civilization. A traumatic break, then, is supposedly being repaired by the commonality of a historical break

---

10. Paul Vogt, *Contemporary Painting* (New York: Henry Abrams, 1981), p. 62.

which is, in fact, not that of 1945 but of a prior moment that concerns the crisis of modernity, namely, the loss of *Gemeinschaft* and the advent of *Gesellschaft*.

This representational break with the past is most ambivalent in Soulages because it both relies on and breaks with the historical abandonment of *Gemeinschaft*. Soulages's representations are, after all, highly commercial in their ideological content and production/distribution. If his flight into abstraction recalls *Gemeinschaft* by way of negativity—say, his hectoring tectonic bars that cancel out fields of luminous light—it is a break from communal rural life whose trauma is nevertheless collective: the trauma of "modern man." Indeed, it is an inevitable historical trauma—that of progress—whose historical break has to be accepted and whose trauma will be compensated with the advent of new human-made forms, among them, Soulages's abstract paintings. Of note is (1) that the historical break of 1945 has been displaced and pushed back into an indefinite past commensurate with the onset of modernism; (2) that the representational break known as "post-war abstractionism" universalizes trauma and denies its immediate historical specificity in terms of social and political antagonisms marked by events that are themselves unrepresentable or unspeakable; and (3) that Soulages's representational break is, in fact, a positive affirmation of and identification with capitalism that is itself most interested in a forgetting of the past in every sense except the story of capitalism's transformation of economy from that of *Gemeinschaft* to that of *Gesellschaft*. It is here that the self-reflexivity of international abstractionism is directly reinforced by the self-reflexivity of capitalism.

III

In the early 1980s, a number of exhibitions in Germany introduced viewers to the New German Expressionism which was the heir to not only German expressionism of the 1920s—Ludwig Kirchner, Emile Nolde, Otto Müller, and so forth—but also to American abstract expressionism and postwar international abstractionism. A. R. Pencke's neoprimitivism and its swastika symbolism, Georg Baselitz's upside-down figures (reminiscent of Mussolini's upside-down corpse), and Georg Immendorf's *Café Deutschland* series in which East meets West with symbolic ferocity were just a few examples of the return of the historically repressed. Among the most controversial of these painters has been Anselm Kiefer, whose early work consisted of a series of self-portraits in which he gives the Nazi salute, a gesture banned in West Germany. Indeed, much has been written about Kiefer whose reinscription of Nazi mythology and history has struck some viewers as objectionably ambiguous, as if Kiefer were in some kind of love-hate relationship with the past that was National Socialism. Whereas American expressionism avoided the direct translation of trauma into representation, and internationalist abstractionism denied or at the very least made trauma palatable as a social concession, German expressionism visually acted out historical trauma by reusing images associated with National Socialism in inflammatory ways. Suddenly nothing was in suspense and everything was determined by traumatic Promethian analogues.

Central to the work of Kiefer and some of the other New German Expressionists has been the attempt to undo the consciousness of the historical break of 1945 that, in both West and East Germany, served to enable a collective disavowal and forgetting of the Third Reich. What makes Kiefer disturbing is the fact that by undoing this historical break he permits an identification with Nazism that then becomes foundational to contemporary German cultural identity. Hence specters of trauma materialize in Kiefer's paintings in terms of a fixation on the traumatic historical desecration of Fatherland.

Unlike Soulages, who downplays trauma by universalizing it as the general malaise of our time, Kiefer focuses on the politicization of trauma as an identitarian issue whose history has never been allowed to play itself out due to the intervention of an historical break imposed by the Allies after the defeat of Germany. In Kiefer's work, the Fatherland as nation-state has suffered unspeakable pollution or spoliation, an unspeakability that Kiefer attempts to represent by mixing straw, sand, lead, tar, and other substances into his paint. The result is the production of landscape paintings with a worked-over quality that creates the illusion of barren tainted lands where traumatic events had once occurred. Unlike the New York School or the international abstractionists, Kiefer brought abstractionism into historical relation with figuration for the sake of commemorating a past that has always existed in the popular European imagination as both attractive and repulsive.

In claiming center stage as a history painter who works on a grandiose scale, Kiefer has used the ready-made vocabulary of the Holocaust, as in his symbolic appropriation of Paul Celan's poem, "Todesfuge," which in a striking series of paintings is marked by reference to Shulamith (Celan's figure from the *Song of Songs*) and Margarete (a figure Célan took from Goethe's *Faust*). Far from untitling his paintings, Kiefer has given them captions that have a mythological force. "Dein aschenes Haar, Sulamit" and "Dein goldenes

Haar, Margarethe" are refrains from Celan's famous poem that entitle a number of paintings and, in many cases, serve as inscriptions painted on the surface of the canvases. Hence in opposition to postwar international abstractionism, Kiefer supplies historically loaded phrases that reference the traumatic ground upon which representation rests. For Kiefer trauma is not only the ground or support for art, but it is the undoing of the historical quarantine of the Third Reich. By acknowledging the trumatic break, Kiefer undoes the historical break. Moreover, *his* representational break is itself a break with postwar abstractionism that nevertheless maintains strong ties to figures like Clyfford Still whose black surfaces have very much the same aesthetic effect as Kiefer's. In *"Dein goldenes Haar, Margarethe,"* Kiefer uses oil, emulsion, and straw on canvas to depict a landscape of fleeing parallel lines that cut diagonally across the canvas in order to suggest not just furrows in a field but train tracks, if not fences or barriers. The braid of golden straw and their black ashen counterparts painted on the canvas are echoed by an arc of writing whose words read *"Dein goldenes Haar, Magarethe."* Whether the landscape is supposed to invoke the site of a former death camp is left to the viewer's imagination, though in the context of Kiefer's many other paintings (which reference the Fatherland as a wasteland of unspeakable evil and death) the historical allusions are obvious enough. In commenting on Kiefer's *Sulamith-Margarethe* paintings, Mark Rosenthal says that "In Kiefer's view, Germany maimed itself and its civilization by destroying its Jewish members and so, by frequently referring to both figures, he attempts to make Germany whole again. His action is certainly provocative, for some would contend that until very recently there was a virtual taboo in Germany against even mentioning the past existence of its Jews."[11] What Rosenthal could also have mentioned is the fact that when Kiefer, a German painter, transforms the history of the Holocaust into paintings with an aesthetic impact that allows for the transformation of the abject into the sublime and the sublime into the abject— Shulamith into Margarethe; Margarethe into Shulamith—he is, in fact, using the ground of trauma as a means to convert political and historical catastrophe into an aesthetic representation that plays with the reversibility of the terrible and the beautiful. This is what the American abstract expressionists and international abstractionists tried to avoid. In fact, abstractionism in general has assumed untranslatability to be central to the notion of "composition" which, like the new critical understanding of literature, was not supposed to

---

11. Mark Rosenthal, *Anselm Kiefer* (New York: Abrams, 1986), p. 96.

"mean," but simply "be." Kiefer, whose canvases are in their own way as aesthetically powerful and compositionally pathbreaking as anything ever attempted by the American abstract expressionists, nevertheless risks the introduction of allegorical references that might well banalize if not otherwise overpower the expressionist surfaces that are key to his work.

Here Kiefer runs the risk that what Adorno has said about Wagner may be applicable to Kiefer himself. "What predominates is already the totalitarian and the seigneurial aspect of atomization; that devaluation of the individual vis-à-vis the totality, which excludes all authentic dialectical interaction." Striking for Adorno is not just the "nullity of the individual"—its extermination—but the requirement to represent this nullity or neutrality by way of a "descriptive motiv."

> However, it is not just the nullity of the individual that has such dire implications for the Wagnerian totality, but rather that the atom, the descriptive motiv, must always put in an appearance for the sake of characterization, as if it were something, a claim it cannot always satisfy. In this way the themes and motivs join forces in a sort of pseudo-history.[12]

That Kiefer's paintings depict a pseudo-history of this sort could be argued once one understands Adorno's point that Wagnerian art "extirpates the qualitatively individual" for the sake of a unified totality that is mythological in scope and hence ahistorical or, in Adorno's terms, absolute. Adorno considers such art uncritical because it traffics in the "already known" by way of mobilizing an array of clichés that pretend to be profound existential symbols. The Wagernian aesthetic, according to Adorno, knows nothing of formal development; instead, development is replaced by repetition and transposition. Wagnerian art therefore reflects a state of immutability and timelessness. "The eternity of Wagnerian music, like that of the poem of the Ring, is one which proclaims that nothing has happened; it is a state of immutability that refutes all history by confronting it with the silence of nature."[13] When Kiefer replaces the figure with natural elements like a braid of straw he is, in effect, practicing a Wagnernian aesthetic in which the extermination of the individual is marked by the presence of a motiv that embodies the silence of nature, if not the immutability of vegetative life. In Kiefer, as in Wagner, it

---

12. Theodor Adorno, *In Search of Wagner* (London: New Left Books, 1981), p. 50.
13. Ibid., p. 40.

would appear that time is abolished. Kiefer's tendency toward what some have called an operatic tendency—many of his large canvases could work as backdrops for an opera on the fall of the Third Reich—is reinforced by his serial or cyclical form of composition. In this, Kiefer is not unlike his contemporaries Immendorf, Baselitz, Lüpertz, and even Beuys, who all seem to be stuck in a political-historical aporia whose symbolism fixates everyone at a certain time that is nothing other than the traumatic break which both American abstract expressionism and international abstractionism attempted to address by way of avoidance. What distinguishes Kiefer, of course, is that whereas most postwar abstract art is rooted in an acceptance of *Gesellschaft* (recall Soulages), Kiefer regresses to *Gemeinschaft*. Not the individual person but the Land as ground-tone of traumatic existence is Kiefer's principal subject.

Yet, in defense of Kiefer, it could be said that in taking distance from both American abstract expressionism and the international school of abstraction, Kiefer demonstrates how the depiction of a traumatic break not only invalidates the imposition of an historical break, but destabilizes the understanding of there being a representational break that can be legitimized in terms of a postwar politics of the arts. Whereas Soulages displaces the historical break by moving it back in time, Kiefer wants to entirely destroy this break in order to restore a historical consciousness that the Allies purposely attempted to suppress in the fear that for a state like Germany, history is barbarous knowledge. That the reactivation of a traumatic break might well restore historical consciousness as opposed to merely introducing an endless suspension or hiatus of what Adorno dismisses as "Wagnerianism" and Caruth calls "unclaimed experience" is precisely what Kiefer seems to have had in mind. In short, for Kiefer there may be the possibility that a reimplementation of a traumatic break is a form of historical demystification, a means of recovering the historically repressed for the sake of giving back to Germany a temporality with a memory. It is here that the traumatic break invalidates both the representational and historical breaks that are supposedly at one with it. Here, of course, we can see how mystified Adorno may have been in assuming that the traumatic, historical, and representational breaks are all to be unified. Kiefer's critique does not come from philosophical speculation so much as it does from the attempt to bring abstract expressionism and history painting into relation.

If we look back over the three moments of postwar abstractionism discussed above, it should now become clear that in each instance one of the three caesuras—representational, historical, traumatic—was emphasized over and above the others. In the case of American abstract expressionism, the *neutre* characterized an emphasis upon a representational break to which both history and trauma were subordinated. While the representational break could be used as a metaphor for both a historical and traumatic break, the fact is that the abstract expressionists were anti-conceptual and reluctant to engage in traditional mimetic gestures. In the case of international abstractionism— and particularly in the case of painters like Soulages—it is the historical break that received most emphasis. Not only was abstractionism viewed as a new postwar phenomenon that had divested itself of representational or figural elements—compare Yves Klein with the early Kandinsky, Pierre Soulages with Pablo Picasso, Mark Toby with Paul Klee, Ellsworth Kelley with Jean Arp—but it distinguished itself as "modern" in the sense of having made a radical break with *Gemeinschaft* and a pact with *Gesellschaft*. It is this histori-cal break with the past that, in turn, subordinates and normalizes questions of trauma and representation. Just as trauma becomes the universal trait of "modern man's" alienation (and the gender here is male), abstractionism becomes the normal condition of the alienated social subject's awareness of himself as "organization man." In the case of New German Expressionism, as we have seen, it is the traumatic break which is highlighted and which serves to undermine both the representational and historical breaks emphasized by abstract expressionism and international abstractionism. In particular, Kief-er's attention to history as traumatic break calls into question the construction of Germany as a nation that has been condemned to carry on as a postwar phenomenon whose terms are every bit as abstract as the art favored by those cultures that had defeated Hitler in 1945. That the turn to trauma has political and historical implications that transcend the art world, if not the sociology and psychology of victimage, is one of the issues that has been quite over-looked in what we call "trauma studies."

12

Transcryptum

Bracha Lichtenberg Ettinger

I

Trauma and repetition, the feminine and art, revolve around the impossibility of annulling an originary repression (Freud's *Urverdrängung*) and accessing a psychic Thing encapsulated and hiding behind it in an outside captured inside—in an "extimate" unconscious space, to use Lacan's expression. The Thing is traumatic and aching; we do not know where it hurts and that *it* hurts. It struggles unsuccessfully to re-approach psychic awareness, but only finds momentary relief in symptomatic repetitions or, by subterfuge, in artwork, where its painful encapsulation partly blows up. In psychoanalytic thinking, the Thing behind originary repression is a "woman"—it is related to the feminine "dark continent" and is entirely foreclosed. Lacan's gaze as *objet a*,[1] like Lyotard's *figure-matrice* (matrix-figure),[2] deals with the figurality of this archaic Thing in the visual-psychic zone, by recurrences of present/absent conjunctions and pulsational scansions correlating to phantasmatic alternations, articulated via the impossibility of encounters of impulse, drive, and *jouissance* with desire, and the impossibility to find the lost archaic mental

---

1. Jacques Lacan, *The Four Fundamental Concepts of Psychoanalysis,* trans. A. Sheridan (London: Norton, 1981).
2. Jean-François Lyotard, *Discours, Figure* (Paris: Klincksieck, 1971).

object, separated by a castrative schizm. The Freudian/Lacanian Thing is the unseen object of originary repression. Invisible in principle, it is for Lyotard, as matrix-figure, the original absence as an absence of origin. Its locus is a non-place of donation where the unexpected event—the work of art—may be born.

The symbolic organization of psychic experience is fatally linked, in Lacan's theory, to the concept of lack. The *objet a* is a trace of the loss of part-objects, a trace of the subject's schize from its own bodily orifices and from its mother's body; it indexes the libidinal loss in the creation of primary meaning in terms of the disappearance and appearance of the primary object I call *archaic m/Other*.[3] The rhythm of repetition created by absence/presence alternations stands for the disappearance/return of the archaic m/Other, notched and burnt onto the kernel of the Thing. The emergence of meaning contracts the *rhythms of the interval* that trace the repetition of her pain-ful withdrawal, and these rhythms suggest, for Fédida,[4] repetition *as* the mother; therefore, primary meaning-creation is this repetition itself of in/out, presence/absence pulsational and phantasmatic scansion. The enactment of the invisible matrix-figure channels eruptions of on/off beats from body to visuality to disturb it from a libidinal within.[5] Hidden behind the screen of phantasmatic vision, rendered inaccessible by originary repression, the Thing with its affective tones thus finds incarnation in the aesthetic art object and induces both the coming into subjective existence and the emergence of de-signified meaning. However, we are here in the intrapsychic unconscious field, where trauma, its amnesia (forgetting) and repetition, the Thing and originary repression are to be understood as intrapsychic phenomena. Differ-ence in recurrences is created here, like in Duchamp's "infra-thin," for a celibate, individual psyche, a subject split from the m/Other and mourning its losses and separations, a subject subjugated to the only-One sexual differ-ence—the phallic difference leaning on the mechanism of castration—for gaining any symbolic signification.

Torok and Abraham describe the creation of an intrapsychic crypt ("hid-den place" in Greek) as a result of a traumatic loss, both libidinal and

---

3. See the presentation of the child's play in Sigmund Freud, *Beyond the Pleasure Principle, Standard Edition* 18, pp. 7–64 (London: Hogarth, 1955). Hereafter *SE*.

4. Pierre Fédida, *L'absence* (Paris: Nrf/Gallimard, 1978).

5. See the analysis of Lyotard's matrix-figure in Rosaline Krauss, "The Im/pulse to See," in *Vision and Visuality,* ed. Hal Foster (Seattle, WA: Bay, 1988).

narcissistic. Inside an inaccessible crypt, the lost object of love and of narcissistic gratification secretly dwells like a phantom. The crypt is a result of a special process of unconscious inclusion—"conservator" repression—that is neither a phantasm of incorporation, whose function would be to keep an illusionary pre-traumatic psychic equilibrium, nor a process of introjection that would have recognized the loss to allow both mourning and growth. As long as the crypt doesn't collapse, there will be neither melancholy nor a process of mourning. The self has no access to its secretly crypted phantom that does, however, haunt the transference and countertransference psychoanalytic relationships and all other relationships of love.[6]

Following this conceptualization of the crypt, Green describes a narcissistic traumatic wound that is not a result of loss of a real object, and a depression that is not connected to mourning of the object of love. The subject's wound arises, and its depression stems from a brutal change in the maternal imago, who from an object that narcissistically gratified the child becomes an object that is emotionally invested elsewhere—by her own bereavement. The mother suddenly becomes mentally absent for the child, psychologically "dead;" she is absorbed elsewhere by her own trauma. This sudden emotional detachment is for the subject a catastrophe without meaning. From now on the subject is unknowingly nostalgic and grieving for a lost relationship that gets encapsulated within its psyche without introjection. Instead, affected with signals of anticipated catastrophe, the subject is from now on united by identification with the "dead mother," in recathecting (libidinally investing) the traces of *her* trauma within himself. Via the subject, it is now the desire of its object (its other's desire, its mother's desire) that would, like by procuration, be satisfied.[7]

What mechanisms would account for the reappearance, rather than the secretive burial, of traces of the trauma of the other—for eruptions of its crypt and its phantom in the psyche of the child, a phenomenon attested by Dina Wardi, who treated the second generation of the *Shoah*'s survivors?[8] Clearly the "conservator repression" doesn't account for this phenomenon because no

---

6. Nicolas Abraham and Maria Torok, *L'écorce et le noyau* (Paris: Flammarion, 1987).

7. André Green, "La Mère morte," in *Narcissisme de vie—Narcissisme de mort* (Paris: Minuit, 1983).

8. Dina Wardi, *Memorial Candles: Children of the Holocaust* (London: Routledge, 1992). I would like to thank Griselda Pollock who has drawn my attention to this book and to the connection between its ideas and my work as an artist. The question

firsthand traumatic event is at its basis, and yet, neither the Lacanian mechanism of psychotic foreclosure in its strict definition is at work. Traces of repression from "before" articulation become evident while there was yet no repression of signifiers that would have elevated the event onto a neurotic level. This phenomenon calls for rethinking the enigma of both originary repression and phylogenetic memory. "The buried speech of a parent becomes in the child a death without sepulcher. This unknown phantom comes back then from the unconscious. . . . Its effect can go to the point of traversing the generations."[9] The survivor (first generation) lives in a chronic traumatic state, where only the denial of suffering and the perseverance of amnesia and oblivion allow the continuity of psychic life. The survivor's child (second generation) carries the weight of the buried unknown knowledge of and for the survivor while being recathected by the survivor as a carrier ("memorial candle") of the survivor's lost objects and crypted phantoms. The question for such a second-generation subject is: how to come into contact and get rid of the weight of a trauma inside itself, a trauma that was not directly experienced, whose story was untold, and which was neither incorporated nor introjected by the survivor itself, and was not directly included and isolated either. Here we realize the necessity for the subject who carries its others' (parents') crypt for/in place of them—in their place yet inside herself and for them—to bridge to an originary trauma in the form of a Thing that the other unknowingly "expresses" through me and with me, but that is not a part of my individual history as a separate whole subject, and not even, strictly speaking, a product of an inter-subjective relationships.

The phantom as the mental working, now inside *my* crypt, of the traumatic secret of someone else, makes me think of the Freudian uncanny aesthetic affect.[10] Processing the phantom is processing what for Freud would be an

---

of the transmission of trauma in art and the relations between trauma and the feminine is one of her major issues. See, for example, Griselda Pollock in the following essays: "Gleaning in History or Coming After/Behind the Reapers," in *Generations and Geographies in the Visual Arts,* ed. G. Pollock (London: Routledge, 1996), and "Abandoned at the Mouth of Hell," in *Doctor and Patient* (Finland: Pori Art Museum, 1997); reprinted in G. Pollock and Penny Florence, eds., *Looking Back to the Future: Essays from the 1990's* (Newark, NJ: B&G Press, 2000).

9. Abraham and Torok, *L'écorce,* p. 297. Compare with Freud, "Moses and Monotheism," *SE* 23, pp. 7–137.

10. Ibid., p. 391. Freud develops the idea of the *Unheimliche* aesthetic affect in "The Uncanny," *SE* 17, pp. 217–252.

impossible mission (outside of artworking) because it presumes the capacity for bypassing an originary repression without lifting it, and what for Lacan would be impossible (outside of artworking) for a supplementary reason as well: because materials that have never been repressed by the subject can't be returned from its "unconscious structured as a language."

I am proposing that the crypt—with its buried unknown knowledge, with what couldn't be admitted and signified by the mother as loss and was buried alive in an isolated nonconscious intrapsychic cavity together with the traumatism that has caused it, the signifiers that could have told the story but remain detached and isolated, the images that could have held together the scene and the affect that had accompanied it—this crypt, transmitted from the m/Other to the subject can be further transmitted from the subject to yet another subject. A crypt, transmissible in a psychic sphere we call matrixial, can become in a subject a lacuna that corresponds to an unsymbolized ancestral event—an event not of its parent, but of its parent's parent. Thus, we can conceive of a chain of transmission, where a subject "crypts" an object/other/m/Other, who in turn had crypted her own object/other/m/Other, so that *the traumatic Thing inside my other's other is aching in me*. We are going to propose that in similar veins the traumatic Thing of the world is aching in artworking.

Like a phantom, the object of the ancestor's desire and loss is buried alive in its crypt together with the traumatism that its loss has caused her, and now I carry in my internal crypt the crypt of the crypt of my m/Other, like a crypt within a crypt. Thus we are conceiving of a Thing that, although it is treated by my own originary repression, it was never "mine" in any direct experiencing. The phantom that is coming alive through me is already the object of desire of its own object, and the Thing that is now incarnated by me was originarily already included and foreclosed by/for someone else who is linked to me—by my *non-I*. Here, when it is the object who "wears the subject like a mask" while the crypt constructs the internal boundaries of the subject like a castle—is the subject's psychotic-like position not in strange proximity to that of the contemporary artist who, according to Lyotard, is inhabited by the Thing as if the Thing still dwells outside, and who is "de-habitated" out from her own habitat, from her own body and history, by the Thing?[11] In their relations to emerging possible significance of/for such a Thing, certain

---

11. Jean-François Lyotard, "L'anamnèse," in *Doctor and Patient* (Finland: Pori Art Museum, 1997).

contemporary artworks are what I am naming *transcryptum*. Transcryptum is the art object, operation, or procedure that incarnates trans-cryption of trauma and cross-inscriptions of its traces, where the artwork's working-through of traumatic amnesia is a trans-cryptomnesia: the lifting of the world's cryptomnesia ("hidden memory" in Latin) from an outside with-in.

The creation of intrapsychic crypt and the identification with it (endocryptic identification) are considered psychotic phenomena.[12] I propose that they are such only in what can be looked at as a pretraumatic era, but in our era, which I consider posttraumatic, where there is no pretraumatic psychic reality and where no "innocence" can be presumed,[13] such psychic reality can't remain *only* psychotic. It is contemporary art as transcryptum that gives body to this "knowledge of the Real" and generates symbols for what would otherwise remain foreclosed from the transmitted trauma of the world. Such a posttraumatic era becomes, then, trans-traumatic. But to understand all the transgressions that such a reality entails as, precisely, non-psychotic anymore, we need to shift the psychoanalytic phallic paradigm and add to the intrapsychic dynamics, the object-relations and the inter-subjective perspectives, *a trans-subjective perspective*.[14] Thus, we are stepping further and aside from both the "dead mother" (analyzed in the field of narcissism), the crypt and the phantom (analyzed in terms of the object's introjection versus incorporation versus inclusion), when we assume the trauma as wandering in what I have named a matrixial borderspace.

The Thing participates in an always-already transgression, with-in-to the

---

12. For Abraham and Torok, the creation of a crypt is precipitated by a shameful incestual secret shared with the object before its traumatic loss, so that both its phantasmatic incorporation and its healthy process of growth-leading introjection are impossible. The analytic work consists of opening the crypt and encountering the phantom, liberating the inclusion into a process of introjection and mourning by recognizing the libidinal and narcissistic value of the object hidden behind the secret of its shameful transgression. In the trans-subjective perspective that is offered hereby, the crypt can't be considered psychotic, and it is not based on any shameful incestual secret. Here, a different kind of transgression, not Oedipal and forbidden but a prebirth/feminine transgression, is always already assumed.

13. Abraham and Torok presume this innocence. See *L'écorce,* p. 307.

14. On the shift of psychoanalytic perspective for thinking trans-subjective subjectivity in psychoanalysis, see Adrienne Harris, "Beyond/Outside Gender Dichotomies: New Forms of Constituting Subjectivity and Difference: Introduction," *Psychoanalytic Dialogues* 7:3 (1997): 363–366.

feminine inasmuch as it is processed by way of a "supplementary" non-phallic difference, though it can, in parallel, be processed by castration as well—be schized by a phallic mechanism.[15] In a world where the trauma is already in the relationships from before any "origin" of subjective or inter-subjective chronological time, the trauma of the other of the m/Other and her crypted transmissible phantoms are a part of my non-conscious scope, because her *cryptograms* (encoded matters) are *already* shared and shareable. Trans-cryption is a transgression of the individual psyche. It transgresses the boundaries between death-drive and life-drive in a way that allows us to continue Lacan's analysis of the tragedy of Antigone while it transgresses also the boundaries between *I* and *non-I*.[16]

What in a pretraumatic era would have been a psychotic potentiality—the subject's urge and failure to revive the phantom of the other and to open up its isolated crypt—enables in the posttraumatic era both individual psychic survival and trans-generational continuity against a total disintegration of both the individual psyche and the generational filiation. However, for claiming such transmissibility we must conceive of an a priori shared psychic space of trans-subjectivity. This requires rethinking the archaic period in terms of a trans-subjective stratum where the Thing, the thing-Event and the thing-Encounter were inseparable-yet-differentiated from one another and from their witnessing, inscription and meaning, where trauma was inseparable-yet-differentiated from phantasm, and where *I* was separated-in-jointness from *non-I*. I have called such a sphere the matrixial stratum of subjectivization, and based it on a feminine originary difference.[17] This psychic sphere will be presented in the following section.

---

15. I am using Lacan's famous formula that a feminine difference is "supplementary," but the scope of this article wouldn't allow the analysis of its meaning. See Jacques Lacan, *Le Séminaire de Jacques Lacan, 1972–73, Livre XX: Encore* (Paris: Seuil, 1975). I have interpreted this in a matrixial perspective in Bracha Lichtenberg Ettinger, "Supplementary Jouissance," *The Almanac of Psychoanalysis* n. 1 (Tel Aviv: GIEP, 1998).

16. See Jacques Lacan, *Seminar VII, The Ethics of Psycho-Analysis, 1959–60*, trans. D. Porter (London: Norton, 1992). I have clarified elsewhere the difference in the reading of this tragedy when a transgression of *I/non-I* is added to the transgression of death/life, in a passage with-in-to the feminine in "Transgressing With-In-To the Feminine," in *Leonardo's Glimlach* (Gent: Gent University, 1998).

17. See Bracha Lichtenberg Ettinger, "Matrix and Metramorphosis," *Differences* 4:3 (1992): 176–208, and "The Becoming Threshold of Matrixial Borderlines," in *Travelers' Tales,* ed. Robertson et al. (London: Routledge, 1994).

In summarizing the development of the concept of trauma in psychoanalysis, Masud Khan develops the concept of *cumulative trauma* as a supplement to the paradigmatic traumatic situations of castration anxiety, separation anxiety, primal scene, and Oedipus complex (in terms of intrapsychic dynamics of loss), as well as birth, loss of object, and loss of the object's love (in more object-relations terms).[18] Cumulative trauma is a silent and invisible result in the subject of the breaches over the course of time from infancy to adolescence in the mother's role as a protective shield. The failures in this maternal emphatic role appear as a regressive shifting of the mother–child relationships into either symbiosis or rejective withdrawal. We may, in a posttraumatic era, view the continuity of the mother–infant relationship itself as already producing a *multiple and diffracted originary relational matrixial trauma,* where traces of the trauma of the m/Other are encrypted in the child, and traces of the trauma of the child are inscripted in the mother, not as a result of any catastrophic event or exchange, but because the wandering of the trauma and its traces between partial-subjects participates in the matrixial sphere, in the kernel of the Thing and in any originary repression. The term originary matrixial trauma doesn't intend the archaic-as-earliest, but any traumatic Thing interwoven in trans-subjective and sub-subjective web before or beyond the time and space of the "whole" subject. A trans-crypted trauma of the other might become to me originary and open a lane of unconscious cross-scription if it becomes the secretly bleeding kernel around which other experiences, earlier or later in time, get reorganized so as to offer and sacrifice this Thing, again and again, as their haunting and fascinating non-conscious center, origin of compulsive phantasmatic repetitions or repetitive actings-out in transferential relations, but also of creative differentiating in recurrences and co-in/habit(u)ating via artwork, as we shall see later on. Relational matrixial traumas are veiled by originary repression, but the Thing here is considered shareable in a trans-subjective psychic space, such that what is veiled for one partial-subject can be exposed by an-other, and what is crypted in an *I* is inscripted in a *non-I*.

II

Already before birth, in the late prenatal period, the subject-to-be aspires in phantasm and contacts traumatically a woman—in whose trauma, phan-

---

18. M. Masud R. Khan, *The Privacy of the Self* (London: Hogarth, 1981), pp. 42–58.

tasm, and desire s/he already participates. The *jouissance* that spurts on the level of feminine/prebirth encounter, and the links between the trauma and phantasm of the becoming subject-to-be (*I*), male or female, and the trauma, phantasm, and desire of the woman who will become its archaic-m/Other (*non-I*), both of them in their status of partial-subjects and partial-objects for each other, constitute a matrixial cluster of desire meeting with reality and trauma meeting with phantasm. Archaic traces of contact with the female body as *jouissance* are engraved; they are remembered without recollecting and revealed in a phantasm saturated with imprints of trauma of/for partial and shared subjectivity.

Female subjects have a double access to the matrixial sphere in the Real, because they experience the womb both as an archaic out-side and past-site, out of chronological time, as "anterior"—which is true for male subjects as well—*and* as an in-side and future site, actual, future and "posterior" time. Whether they are mothers or not, this time out-of-time is a potentiality for repetition which might get actualized. Where the out-side and past-site are both female's and male's on a corpo-real scale, this in-side and-future-site are female's, in the corpo-real dimension and as bodily potentiality. Female subjects have a privileged access to this matrixial time where the future traumatically meets the past, and to this matrixial site where outside meets inside. This privilege is far from being a source of pleasure. Rather, this is an access to a surplus of fragility. Aside of art's time-space, male subjects are more radically split from this archaic site of potentiality, since their link with it stays in the archaic *outside* and *too early* that is forever *too late* to accessing in the Real of the separate body of the whole subject. Men however enter in contact with matrixial time and site, affected, like women, by jointing-in-difference with others, in transference relations and via art.[19] As an aesthetic-artistic filter, the matrixial apparatus serves whoever can yield and tolerate this fragile, fragmented, and dispersed mode of becoming. Various non-conscious lanes, which are opened toward and from originary matrixial difference that is linked to femaleness, are not limited, then, to women only, though they do carry a special resonance for women when they treasure and filter their bodily vibrations.

Thus, the matrixial sphere and its processes (that I have named: *metramor-phosis*) is a non-phallic difference, feminine in the sense just presented and also because it is beyond the phallic difference. A matrixial erotic antennae of the

---

19. See my "Trans-Subjective."

psyche, always joining-in-separating with/from the Other, is modeled upon this difference that operates like a special kind of swerve[20] with-in border-linking, which leaves traces. Swerve and borderlinking compose a differentiating potentiality and operations in the field of emotive sensibility or affection, which participate in traumatic differentiating-in-jointness of the *I* with the archaic m/Other. The matrixial sphere is a borderspace for channeling waves, trans-scripting imprints, tracing, and exchanging traces from traumatic and enjoying encounters of *I(s)* with *non-I(s)*. These are mounted on unconscious lanes opened by the following archaic events: by originary Thing-encounter with my m/Other, where imprints of Thing-event—imprints of traumatic encounters not of me, but of my *non-I*(s) which are transmitted to me, are cross-scribed as well and repressed. These traces and imprints are experienced by *I* and *non-I* that are fragmented and assembled partial-subjects. These cross-scriptions are uncognized by "me" as an entire subject in separated self-identity. The matrixial sphere is a borderspace of encounter of the unconscious of several individuals, where a nonsymbolic movement of linking between the unconscious of several subjects on the partial (sub-subjectivity) and the transitive (trans-subjectivity) dimensions takes place. The matrixial non-conscious stratum is processing diffracted and assembled trans-subjective and sub-subjective waves, imprints and traces. In a matrixial borderlinking, traces of trauma in me are not "purely" mine. Not only am I concerned by my own wound, and not only is the encounter with the Other traumatic for me, but I am also concerned by the trauma of the Other. Not only is the trauma of the other also my wound, but I am also concerned by the trauma that the other must ignore in order to survive, by the Other's crypted trauma, which in itself can already be transmitted to my m/Other and to me from yet an-other. Traces belonging to others that were connected to my own *non-I* continue their diffraction and assemblage through me.

The matrixial unconscious sphere is a borderspace of simultaneous co-emergence and co-fading of the *I* with the uncognized *non-I*, in neither fusion nor rejection. Composite partial subjectivity produces, shares and transmits assembled, im-pure and diffracted objects/*objet a* via conductible border-

---

20. I have named "swerve" a differentiating potentiality which is a borderlinking operation in the field of affection. It can be compared to *"écart"* in the field of perception. See Bracha Lichtenberg Ettinger, "The With-In-Visible Screen," in *Inside the Visible,* ed. C. de Zegher (Boston, MA: MIT, 1996), and Maurice Merleau-Ponty, *Le visible et l'invisible* (Paris: Gallimard, 1964).

links. Even though the matrixial is modeled upon a certain conception of feminine/prebirth intimate sharing, the womb is conceived of here not primarily as an organ of receptivity or "origin" but as a *psychic capacity for shareability,* primarily linked to borderlinking to a female body—a capacity for differentiation-in-co-emergence and separation-in-jointness, where distance-in-proximity is continuously reattuned. *I*(s) and *non-I*(s) interlace their borderlinks in metramorphosis, created by, and further creating—together with and by matrixial affects—relations-without-relating on the borders of presence and absence, a movement of borderlinking between subject and object, among subjects and partial-subjects, between me and the stranger, and between some partial-subjects and trans-subjective-objects.[21]

Traces circulate in a trans-subjective non-conscious zone by matrixial affects and by waves—which I have named erotic antennae of the psyche—that disperse different aspects of traumatic events between me and several others (to begin with, between *I* and m/Other). Thus, as I cannot fully handle events that concern me profoundly, they are fading-in-transformation—a mode of repressing with-in the matrixial other—while my *non-I* becomes wit(h)ness to them. If, then, because of a highly traumatic value of events, I can't psychically contain "my" wounds at all, in the matrixial psychic sphere, "my" imprints will be trans-scribed as traces in the other. Thus my others will process traumatic events for me, like my archaic m/Other had metabolized archaic events for my premature and fragile partial subjectivity.[22] "Woman"—or the matrixial-feminine difference—emerges here not as an "essential" difference nor as a social construct. A trans-subjective figure is interlaced, whose psyche is not confined to one-body but is a weaving of links between several partial-subjects and partial-objects, and its difference conceived as affective swerve and borderlinking, doesn't obey the oedipal-phallic principle of castrative difference. Metramorphosis is the originary human potentiality for such reciprocal yet asymmetrical crossing of borderlines between phantasm and trauma and between *I* and *non-I*. It induces instances of co-emergence and co-fading *as* meaning of trans-subjectivity, and trans-

---

21. To Winnicott's notion of subjective-objects I add the trans-subjective potentiality, and I suggest to conceive of primary trans-subjective-objects as the infant's internal objects felt and metabolized by the m/Other where both infant and mother originate and assume a movement of linking between object and subject.

22. On the mechanism by which the mother processes events for the infant, see Wilfred R. Bion, *Learning from Experience* (London: Karnac, 1984).

scription as the potentiality for an inoubliable memory of oblivion,[23] a trea-
suring and redistributing of events one can't recollect because they have been
treated by one's own originary repression and are also trans-scribed in, and
trans-crypted from the other who thus is turning into a m/Other.

The idea of trans-scription which is pluri- (of several) and cross-scription,
fits for trans-crypted traumatic Thing, fading-in-transformation with the
other, that produces traces of/for trans-subjective originary repression. It is a
means for thinking the enigma of the imprints of the world of the artist, of the
artist's potentiality to transform the world's hieroglyphs, and of the viewer's
capacity to join in this process. When in art a sense emerges, it offers meaning
for what has just been born into trans-subjectivity and would otherwise be
foreclosed, beyond significance.

Metramorphosis is a poietic process of affective swerve and borderlinking,
of inscriptive exchange, between/with-in several matrixial entities. It dissolves borderlines to become thresholds for a trans-subjective passage to a
surplus of fragility. Its *co-naissance* — knowledge of being-born-together — is
a crossed transcription of trans-cryption. It is a subknowledge of which we
receive sense in visual arts by inventing or joining a screen where originary
matrixial repression is partially lifted or bypassed to allow the originary
matrixial trauma some veiled visibility. A matrixial *impossibility of not-sharing*
with the other is profoundly fragilizing; it demands its price and originates its
beauty.

In art, engravings of affected events of the Other and of the world are
unknowingly inscribed in me, and mine are inscribed in others, known or
anonymous, in an asymmetrical metramorphic exchange that creates and
then transforms the junction and assemblage of the partial subjects and partial
objects who participate in it actively or passively. Matrixial memory of an
event, paradoxically both in/of oblivion and inoubliable, a memory charged
with a freight that a linear story can't tell, is transmitted and cross-inscribed.
The memory of the transcryptum affects our erotic antennae, our com-
passioning and languishing "eyes" — or scopic desire. It carries dispersed
signifiers to be elaborated in further borderlinking with others or with the
artwork. Fragmented traces of the event's complexity, from inside and outside and out of time, compose fractured and diffracted unforgettable memory

---

23. On memory, oblivion, and "memory of oblivion," see Lyotard, *Doctor and
Patient* and Bracha Lichtenberg Ettinger, *Matrix: Halal(a) — Lapsus: Notes on Painting, 1885–1992* (Oxford: The Museum of Modern Art, 1993).

of oblivion that can't be entirely inscribed in either me or others but only trans-scribed and transmitted when diffracted and transformed in transference and via artwork. The transcryptum produces an image, sign, or symbol where the Thing that enveloped the amatrixial trauma—and was enveloped by originary repression—can be coming into symbolic meaning for the first time.

Such a trans-scription of intimate yet anonymous encounter-Thing and event-Thing concerns artists and viewers facing the artwork in different ways, times, and sites. On the artistic matrixial plane, I know *in* the world by my erotic tunings, and others affectively know in my oeuvre where the world's traces are transformed and engraved. Such knowing of and in the Other is a transgression which transforms the frontiers between *I* and *non-I*. The gaze becomes an erotic antennae embedded with-in co-affection, whose waves make sense as transformation on the level of this borderspace. Apparitions from traumatic cross-inscription are known in the transcryptum, even though what is "told" is not a story and what is "seen" illustrates nothing. Matrixial awareness channels the subject's desire toward the trauma of another who by definition is never a total stranger-Other if affectively border-linked to me. In the same way that my awareness can't master you via your traces in my psyche, there is no joining in the matrixial gaze which would be without separation. The desire to join-in-differentiating with the artwork like with the Other doesn't promise any harmony, because joining is first of all with-in the other's crypted trauma in its relation to my wound that echoes backwards to my archaic trauma and archaic encounter with my own m/Other, and therefore provokes a risk of fragmentation and dispersal. A matrixial gaze[24] upsurges a desire for dangerous encounters. On the ethical plane the matrixial accessibility implies becoming vulnerable in Levinas' sense: in the matrixial shareability I am being exposed to the Other to a point where the Other becomes traumatizing to me. Metramorphic borderlinking is an *erotic co-response-ability*: a Eurydician tuning of the erotic antennae of the psyche, always in dangerous proximity to Thanatos.[25]

24. For a detailed analysis of this gaze see Bracha Lichtenberg Ettinger, *The Matrixial Gaze* (Feminist Art and Histories Network—Fine Arts, University of Leeds, 1995).

25. See Emmanuel Levinas in conversation with Bracha Lichtenberg Ettinger, *"Que dirait Eurydice?" Barca!* n. 8, 1997; trans. C. Dicker and J. Simas, *What Would Eurydice Say?* (Paris: BLE Atelier, 1997).

When in a transgression with-in-to the feminine we add to the notions of intrapsychic crypt and endocryptic identification the idea of a matrixial trans-cryption and metramorphic cross-scription, we can understand how the crypted trauma of my other's others can become an open, not secretive and isolated, wound in me. Thus, words and affects said and lived in/by the *I* for and in place of the other escape psychotic destiny and become a psychic reality par excellence of our trans-traumatic era. I am working through the unsymbolized phantom of the others, not in phantasmatic emphatic identification and not even as witness that is excluded from the libidinal event[26] but as a wit(h)ness[27] that closes its petals on a secret heart-wound of the other that continues to unknowingly bleed from the trauma of the other. Coming from "another world"—it receives meaning with-in me. Thus, such another world, which for Abraham and Torok is the "non-symbolizable" par excellence,[28] is given meaning for the first time by the artwork as a transcryptum and is symbolized in the transcrypt's *transtextuality*. The artist is interweaving a transtext of the otherwise non-symbolizable world. Likewise, trans-crypted material can open up in the transference-countertransference psychoanalytic experience, only in transtextuality—and not in inter-textuality—where *I* bring into the text the others of (and for) the other, like when, as shown by Dina Wardi, a child re-lives and works-through the trauma of the mother's loss of her own mother.

III

We shall go back now to the elusive intrapsychic remnant of the Real— matrix-figure, *objet a*, or gaze—that in artworking bypasses the originary repression and is still saturated with the Thing's trauma and *jouissance*, to try to further analyze what happens when it operates in a trans-subjective unconscious field stretched between several individuals unknown to each other, or between several uncognized partial-subjects. Such a transgression in art of the celibate boundaries discloses the *matrixial aesthetic borderspace*, where rhythms of the interval capture and trace co-engendering with/by the

---

26. See Abraham and Torok, *L'écorce,* p. 305.

27. Wit(h)nessing is becoming a participatory witnesses to an event one didn't directly experience.

28. Abraham and Torok, *L'écorce,* p. 306.

stranger and the world. Art then grooves the routes of enactment of erotic aerials of the psyche, conducting and transmitting, dispersing and assembling joint gazes, lost figures, and crypted traumatic elements between different subjects rendered furtherly partial and fragilized through their very participation in this metramorphosis. A borderlink that transgresses the opposition between inside and outside, original and ready-made emerges, where a gaze wanders, scattered and sprayed among several floating eyes in a nomadic place, and it is impossible to re-gather the matrixial gaze's traces without coemerging or cofading with a stranger. Gazes may be joined in a labyrinth, woven in the course of creating the matrixial aesthetic borderspace itself. A possibility to access via artwork one's own trauma hidden behind the gaze by originary repressions is opened if an unexpected encounter with an-other occurs, an other who is partially affected by the gaze, thus establishing a borderlinking-without-relations to the *I*'s archaic m/Other. Several *I*(s) and uncognized *non-I*(s) are interlaced in matrixial time and space, opening together the wounds of nomadic traumas repeatedly, working-through to re-in/di-fuse celibate and encapsulated places.

Anamnesis works in psychoanalysis through infinite recurrences of an immemorial, yet always present, originary scene, and artwork, says Lyotard, emerges by working-through via anamnesis to give traces to the invisible in the visible. In art, repetitions in anamnesic working-through do not reestablish the lost object but make present the unpresentable Thing, crypted in the artwork's unconscious. The Thing keeps returning because its debt can't ever be liquidated. This Thing inhabits the artist as if it dwelled outside, or rather, it is the artist who is de-habitated out from its own habitat by it, from its own body and history.[29] The artist's body is invoked by Lyotard as a monster inhabited by, and concealing the non-place of, a "thing without face."[30] If the subject is founded by what Lyotard calls a *recurrent intermittence* of its losses and returns, to enlighten the Freudian *Fort Da* that establishes an object by two distinct movements—constitutive of the earlier matrix-figure and the on/off beats—a *spasm* is now brought forward where an appearance is bound up with disappearance in one and the same movement. Where artwork testifies to such an event, an artist pays for it in her own body conceived as affection.

In anamnesis that takes place in the artwork, the return of the "same" via a

29. See Lyotard, *"L'anamnèse,"* p. 108.
30. On the non-face, see my *Matrix Halal(a)—Lapsus.*

spasm is never the same according to Lyotard, for it carries the marks of the peril of disappearance in the appearance. Spasm thus gives birth to the artwork's apparition amidst recurrences as a threshold. The artist's gesture Lyotard refers to is that which creates a space of suspension inside recurrences and contracts recurrences as alternations in a spasm, where an event is repeatedly processed but in difference, and artwork affects space-time-body to create a "minimal" soul—an *anima-minima*.[31] Artworking is tracing a spasm in suspension, delineating recurrent intermittence of disappearance in appearance.

But what if art triggered potentiality for *co-spasming?* And what if the spasm that is still a celibate "state of birth" (Merleau-Ponty) was shared by/via the artwork as a matrixial borderspace of co-birth? Subjectivity would then be suspended to allow archaic trans-subjectivity with the m/Other to operate anew its borderlinking, transmitting, and dispersal. When an intrapsychic rhythm of interval transmits its effects with-in co-spasming, it operates a rhythm of a swerve with-in a borderlinking between several partial subjects, and the concealment of a non-place of a Thing without face makes a side-place for a potential shared production/revelation of a *heimliche-affect*[32] at the heart of wandering. The crypt is transformed into a slightly known space in such a wandering between *I* and *non-I*. A *heimliche-effect* operates via such compiled *co/in-habit(u)ating*, where a gradual passage from intrapsychic amnesia into trans-subjective cryptomnesia takes place via the transcryptum. Now recurrences do not produce the same, not because they carry the marks of risks of disappearance in appearance for the artist as a separate individual. Rather, recurrences implicate matrixial co-affecting and events of encounter and wit(h)nessing. These events take place alongside different connective points in a transferential borderspace beyond different times and places, where what could have been a *no-place* of a phantomic existence is transformed into a wandering no-One-man's-land, which is a potential homeplace by virtue of recycling-in-transformation grains of shared trauma of partial-subjects and partial objects, and of reiterating co-affecting. With each recycling and co-affecting, an ephemeral, composite, unexpected place is successively crystallized. The product—unconscious *heimliche-affect*—is inseparable from the process that creates it—the metramorphic

---

31. Jean-Francois Lyotard, "Diffracted Traces," in *Halala—Autistwork* (Jerusalem: Israel Museum, Aix en Provence: Arfiac, Paris: BLE Atelier, 1995).

32. This is a reference to Freud's aesthetic concept of *Unheimliche—*Uncanny.

co/in-habit(u)ation—with-in each singular *severality*. Me and stranger(s) matrixially co/in-habit(u)ate with-in/by working art. Swerving and border-linking as a transgression of affect participate in the coming into being of the artwork as transcryptum.

The move into the realm of trauma that I observe in certain contemporary artworks is a move toward a matrixial sphere, where the Thing as "woman" gives/receives new meanings. The world carries in this second half of the twentieth century enormous traumatic weight, and we are unknowingly living it through its massive transitive effects on us. Transtextual writing and transcrypted visual art bring the transmissive posttraumatic effect into the surface of culture and produce images and words that might absorb and diffract it. The beautiful accessed via art today and redefined by it proposes new possibilities for affective apprehension of this transitivity while producing new effects of the impossibility of not-sharing. In metramorphosing with a transtext or a transcryptum that exposes these effects while veiling them, you find yourself swerving in dangerous proximity to a traumatic event or encounter, as if you have always been potentially sliding on its margins. You are threatened by this swerve and borderlinking, yet also attracted by a mysterious hope to re-find, for further absorption and working-through, what had faded away for you or for the other and got dispersed, on condition of fragilizing yourself, since this beauty is the effect of borderlinking by a wound and co-emerging with a traumatized other. In a post-, trans-traumatic era, the psychic trauma is no more entirely personal, and it can only partially be cicatricized, and only in borderlinking to others, in further trans-subjective and sub-subjective trans-cryption and cross-scription.

The matrixial gaze conducts imprints from one paradox: "events without witnesses,"[33] and passes them on to another paradox: *witnesses who were not there*. It is this paradoxical conjunction of the "impossible" witnessing via withnessing that I have named "wit(h)nessing." Wit(h)nesses are both the artist and the viewer, in different ways, in their contact with a transcryptum. The viewer will embrace traces of the almost-missing event while transforming it—and itself—by weaving via the artwork a transferential thread to others, present and archaic, cognized and uncognized, future and past, dead and alive. The viewer is challenged by the transcryptum to join a specific

---

33. An expression by D. Laub in Shoshana Felman and Dori Laub, *Testimony, Crises of Witnessing in Literature, Psychoanalysis and History* (London: Routledge, 1992).

anonymous intimate encounter with several—not one, not endlessly multiple—others. Its gaze is carried by an event s/he did not experience, and through the matrixial web an unexpected affective reaction to it arises. New artistic effects emerge, where Aesthetics approaches Ethics beyond the artist's intentions or conscious control. Not as an intended message and not by any particular theme, wit(h)nessing is an artistic effect that transgresses the domain of aesthetics. I therefore suggest that certain art today, from different fields and unclassified by formal or technical means, is leading the transformation of the scope of the artistic-aesthetic itself, in a bending toward an in-between borderspace: between aesthetics and ethics (ethics in the Levinasian sense).[34]

The transcryptum is an offering of a possibility to capture in/via art vibrations of a matrixial originary Thing folded in gazes and screens. The effect of beauty becomes then the access via metramorphosis, by art-object or art-event, art-process or art-operation, to the trauma of the Other. What affects you in/by art is what offers reaffectation-as-redistribution of traces and absorbency of traumatic imprints of Thing-event, Thing-encounter, and wit(h)ness-Thing, diffracted and in splinters.[35] A matrixial trail, skirting on the borderline between perception, sensation, and emotive affect is vibrating at the edges of visibility when a passion based on marks of shareability becomes affectively transgressive *again* and labors anew in com-passion, to perforate the screen of Vision. When a world, internal and external, from which the artist transfers and to which s/he transmits, is shared with-indifference via the artwork, this world is only born the instant the artwork awakes its strange beauty, pain, and languishing—languishing as both yearning and ebbing—while swerving and joining-in-differentiating. A potentiality to permeate and interfuse a borderspace with-in others becomes beauty articulated in the bending of aesthetics toward ethics, when the artwork vibrates, and the spectator attracts to itself and transmits back to the work and onwards to others and to the world, such an emotive openness for borderlinking and such a surplus of vulnerability.

The scopic antennae register imprints that return from the world and

---

34. I would like hereby to challenge Adorno's remark that had problematized the sense of creating poetic art after the *Shoah*.

35. R. Huhn reflects on the question of resorbation of residues in/by art. See Rosi Huhn, "Das Problem der Entsorgung in Kunst und Kulture als Passage zum Positiven Barbarentum," Passages [d'après] Walter Benjamin (Mainz: Schmidt, 1992).

transmit a centerless gaze on the transcryptum's screen. The gaze is channeled from outside and inside to meet the eroticized antennae of the sharing-viewer. When rhythms of swerving with-in borderlinking are co-affected, recurrence stands for the fading and transformation in returning of the archaic "woman"-m/Other-*encounter,* notched and burnt onto the kernel of the Thing. Meaning does not dwell in the whole and separate subject but is created by gradual changes in borderlinks and by further linking. The biography of recurrences-in-difference is recorded in its metramorphosis: in the successive changes in the borderlinks suspending between different rhythms of recurrent intermittence. Each co/in-habit(u)ation captures/reveals a *specific impossibility of not-sharing,* a specific impossibility of not encountering, via specific wit(h)nessing with-in a fragile extimate trans-crypted zone. Co/in-habit(u)ating is inseparable from the subjects' affecting one another and being thus transformed while creating a joint transgressive subjectivity-as-encounter, at the price of their being dispersed into partial-subjects—not split by a castrative cut—and assembled into amalgamated temporary assemblage, but not fused.

I feel pains in the traces of the other when the other knows with-in me. The trauma of others crypted in my *non-I*(s) and unconsciously known by my *non-I*(s) is incarnated by me in our trans-subjective psychic matrixial border-space that is shared by several partial-subjects, dead or alive, known or uncognized. Partial-subjects and partial-objects can be subtracted from a shared metramorphosis in halts, pauses, lags in the process of co-emergence and co-fading, when the rhythm of co-spasming suddenly freezes or isolates a difference in swerving, positing subject and object in certain relations. Subtracted and isolated out of subjectivity-as-encounter, withdrawn from wit(h)nessing-without-event, subjects and objects arise then at a certain distance, upon the arrest in the fluctuating distance-in-proximity between the grains. Renewing the borderlinking would then call for fragilizing oneself even at the risk of anticipatory identity catastrophe, even at the risk of the collapse of the fragile matrixial gaze and of the disintegration of the screen. Via art, erotic antennae weave together partial-subjects and im-pure objects that unknowingly, and without being cognized by each other, negotiate trauma in the process of co-in/habit(u)ating. In this process, a trembling meaning emerges.

A rhythm of swerving in borderlinking by transmission and transference conducts toward an unforeseen space while creating it out of a crypt while transgressing the individual off/on beats. A rhythm never reaches total "on" or total "off" states, because it is attuned by several co-spasmings. The artist as a partial-subject takes part with-in and testifies to/for a non-symbolized world that effects and affects while anguishing and soothing, tearing and stitching hollowed spaces, opening in them a rhythm of interval for an exiled phantom—a rhythm suspended like a rotating sea-wave between its fading and its next birth. The painful movement of fading of this wave is already the transient return-in-transformation of the archaic "woman"-m/Other-*encounter-Thing,* trans-crypting and co/in-habit(u)ating.

The transcryptum has consequences for the theory and practice of psychoanalysis. Apprehending trans-cryption allows for weaving transtexts in the transferential relationship, for giving meaning to the experience of cross-scription, and for bringing into the analysis the relief of symbolic significance supplied by new signs, images, and symbols offered by contemporary art. Art makes almost-impossible new borderlinking possible, out of elements and links already partially available in splinters, which are going to be transformed in ways that can't be thought of prior to artworking itself, prior to their shifting with-in-to the screen of vision and to their appearance as a transcryptum, where transgressive and repressed encounter-Thing and event-Thing find new forms, where trans-subjective-objects find new bodies. The transcryptum has the potentiality to transform the amnesia of lone traumatic events, crypted in me or in the other, into a cryptomnesia—a hidden memory that can only emerge in affective joining-in-separating with-in a surplus of fragility shared with-in difference.

Post-Scriptum

My work negotiates a fragile borderspace between painting and psychoanalysis. From the invisible and the indicible I try to attain a with-in-visible screen, accessed only if shared-in-difference with several others, and a with-in-dicible scriptum that can only be written as transtextuality.

For the last seven years I have been working on two series of paintings: the "Autistworks" and the "Eurydices." There, the idea of transcryptum received its trembling first nonverbal articulations. But painting does not surrender to theory, and theory does not collapse into painting.

I do not wish to abolish the borderlines between practices and theories and between painting and psychoanalysis, but rather, to complexify their links. If I cross some borderlines, it is in-side painting to begin with that the transgression arises—and I try from with-in the effects and affects of artworking's transgressions to cross some phallic borderlines of the psychoanalytic theory, and to allow these effects and affects to enlarge the understanding of the transferential web and to slightly transform psychoanalytic practice.

Thus, by continually negotiating the limits of the visual in and by the visual which is never "purely" such, the spiritual and symbologenic potentiality of artworking infiltrates other boundaries that are unconsciously, synaesthetically, affectively, and symbolically linked to it. Infiltered and thus opened up, they can now allow for further apprehending, making sense, thinking, healing, and becoming vulnerable.

Index